EU Labour Law

ELGAR EUROPEAN LAW

Founding editor: John Usher, *formerly Professor of European Law and Head, School of Law, University of Exeter, UK*

European integration is the driving force behind constant evolution and change in the laws of the member states and the institutions of the European Union. This important series will offer short, state-of-the-art overviews of many specific areas of EU law, from competition law to consumer law and from environmental law to labour law. Whilst most books will take a thematic, vertical approach, others will offer a more horizontal approach and consider the overarching themes of EU law.

Distilled from rigorous substantive analysis, and written by some of the best names in the field, as well as the new generation of scholars, these books are designed both to guide the reader through the changing legislation itself, and to provide a firm theoretical foundation for advanced study. They will be an invaluable source of reference for scholars and postgraduate students in the fields of EU law and European integration, as well as lawyers from the respective individual fields and policymakers within the EU.

Titles in the series include:

EU Consumer Law and Policy
Stephen Weatherill

EU Private International Law
Harmonization of Laws
Peter Stone

EU Public Procurement Law
Christopher H. Bovis

EU Criminal Law and Justice
Maria Fletcher and Robin Lööf with Bill Gilmore

Judicial Review in EU Law
Alexander H. Türk

EU Intellectual Property Law and Policy
Catherine Seville

EU Private International Law
Second Edition
Peter Stone

EU Labour Law
A.C.L. Davies

EU Labour Law

A.C.L. Davies

Professor of Law and Public Policy and a Fellow of Brasenose College, University of Oxford, UK

ELGAR EUROPEAN LAW

Edward Elgar

Cheltenham, UK • Northampton, MA, USA

Published by
Edward Elgar Publishing Limited
The Lypiatts
15 Lansdown Road
Cheltenham
Glos GL50 2JA
UK

Edward Elgar Publishing, Inc.
William Pratt House
9 Dewey Court
Northampton
Massachusetts 01060
USA

A catalogue record for this book
is available from the British Library

Library of Congress Control Number: 2012930568

ISBN 978 1 84844 998 5 (cased)

Typeset by Servis Filmsetting Ltd, Stockport, Cheshire
Printed on FSC approved paper
Printed and bound in Great Britain by Marston Book Services Ltd, Oxfordshire

Contents

Preface

My aim in writing this book was to provide an intelligent and thought-provoking introduction to EU labour law. The book has three main objectives. First, and most obviously, I want to introduce you to the main provisions of EU labour law. This is not a textbook and it is not possible to do this at a high level of detail: the aim instead is to give an overview of the most important and interesting points. Second, we will examine some of the history of EU labour law. Again, the book cannot offer a detailed historical account, but we will consider how EU labour law emerged when it is helpful to do so. For example, disagreements among the Member States when a new directive is proposed often explain the compromises to be found in the directive itself. Third, I want to explore the major policy issues in EU labour law today. These are both substantive – related to the content of EU labour law – and procedural – relating to the way it is created and enforced. Some of the substantive policy issues we will examine include the so-called 'constitutionalisation' of EU labour law (in which greater emphasis is placed on workers' rights as human rights) and the policy of 'flexicurity' currently advocated by the European Commission (which is about combining flexibility with security, to enable the EU to be competitive on a global stage). Some of the procedural issues to be considered include the role of the social partners (trade unions and employers' associations) in formulating EU labour law, and the role of the Court of Justice in interpreting the provisions of EU labour law and giving guidance to national courts.

The book is organised as follows. In Part 1, I will introduce the main policy themes that I want to explore in the rest of the book. Chapter 1 will focus on substantive themes: on the reasons why labour law might be dealt with at EU level and on the factors influencing its content today. Chapter 2 will analyse the procedural themes, identifying the main actors in EU labour law and examining their roles. In Part 2, the larger part of the book, I will consider a selection of the main topics in EU labour law in the light of the themes identified in Part 1. I will not attempt to consider every theme in every chapter: instead, each chapter will consider two or three themes that are most relevant to the topic under consideration. It is best to regard the themes as strands to be woven in and out of the Part 2 chapters, with a different group of strands coming to prominence in each chapter. Since part of my purpose is to whet your appetite for the study of EU labour law, each chapter will conclude with some suggestions for further reading among the vast literature on the subject.

A couple of caveats are in order. First, I have assumed some very basic knowledge of EU law: of the Treaties and institutions, the legislative process and major doctrines such as supremacy and direct effect. If you need clarification (or a refresher course) on these matters, it is best to look them up in one of the well-known textbooks on EU law. Second, I have written the book from a UK perspective. Although my focus is on labour law at the EU level and not on its implementation in the 27 Member States (at the time of writing), it is sometimes interesting to consider how EU labour law fits with national traditions. Most of my examples are drawn from the UK just because it is the system I know best.

This book states the law as it stood in September 2011, though I am grateful to the publishers for allowing me to incorporate a few minor updates during the production process.

Acknowledgements

I am very fortunate to work in Oxford with a wonderful set of colleagues in labour law and related areas, who help to create a stimulating environment for teaching and research. Whilst they bear no responsibility for errors in this book I would like to thank Alan Bogg, Cathryn Costello, Sandy Fredman, Mark Freedland, Chris McCrudden and Wanjiru Njoya. I would also like to thank the Dean, Timothy Endicott, for his support.

Brasenose College provided two terms' sabbatical leave, which was a great help in bringing this project to completion, and I owe a debt of gratitude to my colleagues there, particularly Bill Swadling and Tom Krebs, for shouldering additional administrative burdens and for keeping my spirits up during the writing process. Lots of other people helped with the latter, but special thanks are due to Peter, Beatrice, Michael and Edward Groves.

Finally, my biggest thanks go, as always, to my parents, to whom this book is dedicated, for their interest in the progress of the book, and for their love and support.

A.C.L. Davies
Oxford, October 2011

Abbreviations

ARD	Acquired Rights Directive, Directive 2001/23/EC
BEPG	broad economic policy guidelines
BUSINESSEUROPE	Confederation of European Business, formerly UNICE
CEC	European Confederation of Executives and Managerial Staff
CEEP	European Centre of Employers and Enterprises Providing Public Services
CFI	(European) Court of First Instance
CRD	Citizens' Rights Directive, Directive 2004/38/EC
EC	Treaty of Rome, as amended; European Community; European Commission
ECHR	European Convention on Human Rights
ECJ	European Court of Justice
ECtHR	European Court of Human Rights
EES	European Employment Strategy
EGF	European Globalisation Adjustment Fund
ESF	European Social Fund
ESM	European Social Model
ETOR	(dismissals for) economic, technical or organisational reasons
ETUC	European Trade Union Confederation
ETUI	European Trade Union Institute
EU	European Union
EWC	European Works Councils
I&C	information and consultation of employees
ILO	International Labour Organization
NGO	non-government organisation
NRP	National Reform Programmes (previously National Action Plans – NAP)
nyr	[case] not yet reported
OMC	open method of co-ordination

PWD	Posted Workers Directive, Directive 96/71/EC
PrWD	Pregnant Workers Directive, Directive 92/85/EEC
SE	*Societas Europaea*
SNB	Special Negotiating Body (for negotiating EWC)
TCA	transnational company agreement
TCN	third-country national
TEU	Treaty on European Union
TFEU	Treaty on the Functioning of the European Union
UEAPME	European Association of Craft, Small and Medium Sized Enterprises

For my parents

Table of treaty provisions

Table of regulations

Table of directives

Table of cases

PART 1

Introduction

1. Themes in EU labour law

EU labour law can be complex and confusing, and just occasionally down-right annoying, but it is always fascinating and sometimes even inspiring. This chapter tries to set the stage for the rest of the book by explaining what EU labour law is and the techniques we will be using to get an understanding of the legal materials. We will then turn to an exploration of some of the explanations or justifications for the existence of EU labour law in one form or another. The chapter concludes by discussing some current themes and controversies in the subject.

WHAT IS EU LABOUR LAW?

There is less agreement than you might suppose about what exactly EU labour law includes. We need to think carefully about the significance of 'EU', 'labour' and 'law', and about the place of EU labour law within EU law more generally.

The obvious difference between EU labour law and national labour law is that EU labour law forms part of a supranational legal system. Of course, as any student of EU law knows, EU law has some key features which make it a special kind of supranational legal system with deep penetration into national legal systems. One such feature is the doctrine of supremacy, which means that EU law wins when there is a conflict between EU law and national law,[1] and another is the doctrine of direct effect, which means that (under certain circumstances) EU legislation can be applied by the national courts without any need for the national government to transpose it into the legal system.[2] The supranational character of EU law matters for the purposes of a discussion of EU labour law because EU labour law and national labour law do not necessarily seek to regulate exactly the same things.

National systems of labour law regulate the relationships between workers, employers and trade unions. Of course, this may be done using

---

[1] Case 6/64 *Costa v ENEL* [1964] ECR 585.
[2] Case 26/62 *van Gend en Loos* [1963] ECR 3.

a variety of different techniques: by laying down detailed rules of labour law, or by creating the conditions in which employers' associations and trade unions can bargain and reach collective agreements, for example. EU labour law sometimes works in this way.[3] For example, by supporting the 'social dialogue' (to be discussed further in Chapter 2), the EU seeks to encourage EU-level trade unions and employers' associations to reach agreements which may eventually filter down into national-level collective bargaining.[4] But most of the time, EU labour law is about regulating the way in which the *Member States* regulate their labour markets.[5] So it takes place at one remove from the employers and working people whose lives it will affect. For example, most EU legislation in the field of labour law takes the form of directives. These require the Member State to take steps to ensure that provisions they outline are given effect in national law.[6]

A consequence of the EU's role in regulating the Member States' activities is that, in order to gain a complete overview of EU labour law in action, we would need to consider how it has been transposed in each of the 27 Member States and how effectively it is applied. But this would be a mammoth task, given the need to understand and analyse materials from 27 different legal systems. It is certainly too much for one person. Sometimes, we can gain some insight into these matters by looking at studies conducted by the Commission into the implementation of particular EU measures in the Member States, or by academics who are experts on their own legal system. Sometimes we will draw on the UK as an example. But we will not try to be comprehensive.

Having looked at the 'EU' element of EU labour law, we can now turn to the 'labour' element. National labour law has been around for much longer than EU labour law. So should we take the chapter headings we would normally find in books on national labour law and use them to organise the EU materials?[7] For some topics, this would work perfectly well: discrimination or working time, for example. However, this strategy might lead us to ignore the way labour is treated in the context of the internal market created by the EU. For example, what happens when a firm

---

[3] It may be worth noting that the EU institutions are, themselves, employers. Employment relationships with EU officials are governed by the Staff Regulations of Officials of the European Union (Regulation 259/1968). These are an interesting subject of study in their own right but we will not attempt to cover them here.

[4] Articles 152 and 154–5 Treaty on the Functioning of the European Union (TFEU).

[5] The complexity of this is nicely captured by W. Streeck, 'Neo-Voluntarism: A New European Social Policy Regime?' (1995) 1 ELJ 31.

[6] Article 288 TFEU.

[7] For a fascinating analysis of the ways in which EU labour law has been conceptualised, see B. Bercusson (2009), *European Labour Law* (2nd edn, Cambridge University Press), Chapter 3.

wins a contract in another Member State and wants to take workers from its own Member State to perform the contract? Which state's law governs those workers' terms and conditions?[8] EU labour law might therefore include some topics that we do not usually find in national labour law. Another reason for not just translating our national chapter headings into the context of EU labour law is that the EU does not have competence (the power to legislate) on some very important topics in national labour law.[9] These are pay, freedom of association and the right to strike. As we shall see, the fact that the EU cannot legislate on these topics does not necessarily stop it from getting involved, but we need to think carefully about how to structure our analysis of the EU's involvement in these areas. Relying on 'national' chapter headings might lead us to over-emphasise the EU's role.

What about 'law'? This book is obviously not the place for a jurisprudential inquiry. But EU labour law takes a variety of different forms. Directives are a form of 'hard' law: the Member States must transpose them into their national legal systems by the stipulated deadline, and if they do not, they may face infringement proceedings before the Court of Justice of the European Union, hereafter Court of Justice or Court.[10] But if we confined ourselves to the study of directives, we would miss some important features of the EU's activities in the field of labour regulation. These include the role of EU-level agreements between trade unions and employers' associations as a source of norms,[11] and the role of EU targets and recommendations in shaping the Member States' labour market policies.[12] We could get into a discussion about whether or not to count some of these softer measures within our definition of 'law', and we will consider this a bit more in Chapter 2. But this is not central to our enterprise. Whether you think these things are law or not, a knowledge of them is still important for a rounded understanding of the subject.

Finally, putting all three terms together and thinking about 'EU labour law', it is useful to remind ourselves that the labour law provisions of the Treaty on the Functioning of the European Union (TFEU) appear under the heading of 'social policy' and Commission policy documents often refer not to EU labour law but to a broader concept of 'EU social policy'.[13] Social policy generally includes matters such as social security

---

[8] See the Posted Workers Directive (Directive 96/71/EC), discussed in Chapter 3.
[9] Article 153 TFEU.
[10] Articles 258–61 TFEU.
[11] See, for example, the Framework Agreement on Telework, 16 July 2002.
[12] See the discussion of the Europe 2020 strategy in Chapter 2.
[13] Title X TFEU. Title IX on Employment is about employment policy.

payments for those who are unemployed or unable to work, pensions, housing and healthcare. However, the EU's powers in these areas are limited and in fact, as Barnard explains, EU labour law is a big part of EU social policy.[14]

In broad terms, then, this book seeks to analyse the legal materials that fall within the scope of EU labour law. This is partly a task of describing those materials, and engaging in doctrinal analysis: assessing whether there are gaps or overlaps in the regime, defining concepts, identifying inconsistencies and uncertainties, and so on. But this book also seeks to go beyond the doctrinal level and to consider some of the big underlying policy questions of EU labour law. Our understanding of what EU labour law *is* should be increased by asking deeper questions about why it is there and what problems it faces. It is to a preliminary account of these matters that we will now turn.

EXPLAINING THE EMERGENCE OF EU LABOUR LAW

At first sight, the very existence of EU labour law is a bit of a puzzle. The Member States already had their own elaborate bodies of labour law, in most cases with strong trade union movements and constitutional guarantees of certain labour rights. And, at the beginning at least, European integration was viewed primarily in economic terms: as a means of breaking down barriers to trade between the Member States and creating a common market. EU labour law was not seen as a necessity.[15] So why did the Member States subsequently agree to allow some regulation of labour law to take place at the EU level? Our task in this section is to identify some of the arguments which have been used by the key actors – the European Commission ('Commission'), the Member States, the Court of Justice, trade unions, employers, commentators and so on – to explain and justify EU labour law.

Some caveats are in order before we begin. It is important to be clear that we are not examining these arguments with a view to determining which is the most persuasive historical explanation for the emergence of EU labour law. This book does not purport to offer a detailed history,

---

[14]   C. Barnard, 'EC "Social" Policy', in P. Craig and G. de Búrca (eds) (1999), *The Evolution of EU Law* (1st edn., Oxford University Press), 496.
[15]   This view was supported by the ILO's Committee of Experts in the 'Ohlin Report': ILO, 'The Social Aspects of European Economic Co-Operation' (1956) 74 *International Labour Review* 99.

though it will touch on the historical evidence from time to time.[16] What matters is that all of these arguments have played a role, at one time or another, in influencing the development of labour policy in the EU. They are all a *part* of the explanation. It is also important to be clear that we are not trying to determine whether any of these arguments are correct. To do this, we would need a body of empirical evidence (on the economic impact of labour law, for example, or on the utility of rights as a practical tool to protect workers) which often does not exist and the interpretation of which would in any event be hotly contested. And where there is disagreement, it is important for readers to make up their own minds. Later in the book, we will revisit these arguments, focusing in Part 2's chapters on those arguments which seem particularly pertinent to the set of legal materials under discussion.

The explanations fall into three broad categories. The first two explain the emergence of EU labour law in terms of the relationship between labour issues and the EU's economic agenda. One set of explanations regards the development of the common market as a threat to national systems of labour law, so that they need to be protected by EU regulation. The second set of arguments sees economic integration as an opportunity to advance the cause of labour law on a pan-European level. The third category focuses more on EU labour law as an end in itself, and includes both pragmatic and principled explanations. Of course, there is no bright-line division between these groups of arguments and we will consider some overlaps between them, too. But since so much of the literature makes reference to the 'European Social Model', we will begin by explaining that concept.

The European Social Model

The 'European Social Model' or ESM is used in the literature as a way of describing the Member States' shared understanding of the level and nature of the social protection their citizens enjoy.[17] It can also be used

---

16   For a detailed historical analysis, see J. Kenner (2003), *EU Employment Law: From Rome to Amsterdam and Beyond* (Oxford: Hart).

17   See, generally, B.P. ter Haar and P. Copeland, 'What are the Future Prospects for the European Social Model? An Analysis of EU Equal Opportunities and Employment Policy' (2010) 16 ELJ 273; D. Schiek, 'The European Social Model and the Services Directive', in U. Neergaard, R. Nielsen and L. Roseberry (eds) (2008), *The Services Directive: Consequences for the Welfare State and the European Social Model* (Copenhagen: Djøf). But for an argument that the ESM is a 'myth' designed to create the appearance of greater EU integration, see M. Kleinman (2002), *A European Welfare State? European Union Social Policy in Context* (Basingstoke: Palgrave), 58.

normatively, to describe the protection citizens should enjoy. We will use it in this chapter because it is a convenient shorthand, but some caveats are in order too.

The Commission has identified 'a number of shared values which form the basis of the European social model. These include democracy and individual rights, free collective bargaining, the market economy, equality of opportunity for all and social welfare and solidarity.'[18] For our purposes, it is important to be aware of two key elements of the ESM: social welfare and labour law. In terms of social welfare, under the ESM, the state takes responsibility for providing its citizens with a basic social safety net. This safety net might include unemployment benefits for people who cannot find work, access to basic healthcare services for those who are sick, and pensions in retirement. In terms of labour law, the ESM provides a set of basic protections for workers. The Commission's statement explicitly includes equal treatment and collective bargaining,[19] but we might also expect to find minimum standards on matters such as working time and health and safety. The ESM is often contrasted with the US approach to these issues.[20] So, where Europeans benefit from job security, many Americans (subject to state legislation) are employed on an 'at will' basis. And the social safety net has historically been more generous in Europe, particularly in the area of healthcare.

Importantly, though, characterising the ESM as 'European' does not mean that the ESM is laid down in EU law. Some aspects of the model are (notably in labour law), but many others, such as healthcare, are generally matters for the Member States. This leads to a further caveat. The ESM, as a 'shared' understanding of the appropriate social safety net, may mask considerable divergences between the Member States.[21] Esping-Andersen has identified four different models of welfare state provision in European countries: Anglo-Saxon, Southern, Scandinavian and Corporatist.[22] For example, the Southern and Corporatist models assume a traditional family unit with a male breadwinner, so are associated with lower levels of

---

[18] Commission, *European Social Policy – A Way Forward For The Union* (COM (94) 333 final), 2.

[19] For an understanding of the ESM heavily focused on the collective dimension, see Bercusson, above n. 7, Chapter 8.

[20] ter Haar and Copeland, above n. 17, 280.

[21] Although the 'newer' Member States have been required to adopt the *acquis communautaire* (the existing body of EU law) as a condition of accession, it is arguable that enlargement has led to much greater diversity in the EU. For discussion, see G. Majone, 'Unity in Diversity: European Integration and the Enlargement Process (2008) 33 EL Rev 457.

[22] G. Esping-Andersen, 'After the Golden Age? Welfare State Dilemmas in a Global Economy' in G. Esping-Andersen (ed.) (1996), *Welfare States in Transition* (Thousand Oaks, CA: Sage).

employment among women. The Anglo-Saxon and Scandinavian models encourage women to return to work after having children and are associated with higher levels of workforce participation among women and better provision of childcare.

It would also be possible to do some broad-brush categorisation of labour law systems within the EU.[23] For example, the 'Nordic' model of labour law involves reliance on collective bargaining between trade unions and employers' associations as the main mechanism for determining labour standards such as minimum wages or working hours, whereas other systems view collective bargaining primarily as a mechanism for elaborating or improving on basic standards set by legislation. And even within the so-called 'Nordic' model there are substantial differences between states.

In the next few sections, we will be thinking about some of the reasons why there might have been a shift from a 'shared understanding' of the ESM towards regulation of some aspects of the ESM on the EU level. For these purposes, a notion like the ESM is helpful, despite the differences it conceals. In later chapters, we will focus more precisely on specific areas of the law.

Economic Integration as a Threat to the ESM

Our task in this section is to consider claims that European economic integration might make it more difficult for the Member States to maintain the ESM. On this view, shifting some responsibility for labour law from the national level to the EU level is seen as a way of protecting the ESM. We will consider two types of threat. First, there is the well-known argument that the creation of a free market will prompt a race to the bottom in labour standards, as Member States compete with each other to become attractive locations in which firms might invest. Second, we will consider the possibility that the rules creating the free market might themselves limit the Member States' ability to set and maintain certain labour standards.

The prevention of a 'race to the bottom' is one of the classic arguments in favour of combining free trade with some regulation of labour standards.[24] Without any labour regulation, states may be tempted to lower their labour standards in order to give their firms an advantage in the

---

[23] For classification of employment models more generally, see G. Bosch and others, 'European Employment Models under Pressure to Change' (2007) 146 *International Law Review* 253.

[24] B. Hepple (2005), *Labour Laws and Global Trade* (Oxford: Hart), 13–14.

market and to attract inward investment. The claim is that this might lead to a downward spiral in labour standards across the free trade area as a whole.

However, whilst the 'race to the bottom' is commonplace in the theoretical literature, there is considerable debate on the empirical level.[25] First, it is not clear that a downward spiral in labour standards would arise in practice. States might not be able to keep reducing their labour standards, either for legal reasons (because certain rights are constitutionally protected, for example) or for political reasons (because their electorate simply would not tolerate reductions in living standards). Second, some scholars question whether states with lower labour standards are at a competitive advantage. Firms' decisions on where to locate might be influenced by a variety of factors other than labour cost, and even where labour costs are considered, they must be weighed against the workforce's level of productivity.

Nevertheless, the 'race to the bottom' view is reflected in the original Treaty of Rome and has been influential in the subsequent development of EU labour law.[26] One of the few social provisions in the Treaty was Article 119, on equal pay for men and women.[27] But this provision was included not for social reasons, but for economic ones.[28] France already had equal pay legislation, but the other Member States did not. The French government was concerned that firms in other countries would use cheap female labour to undercut French products. Similarly, it might be argued that more recent developments, such as the directive on workplace consultation,[29] reflect concerns on the part of some Member States that those Member States with very little regulation on these matters might gain a competitive advantage.

Another source of contemporary concern about undercutting is, arguably, the enlargement of the EU.[30] The EU now consists of 27 Member States. The newer Eastern European Member States generally have much lower wage levels than the 'older' Member States. This has both positive and negative consequences. For workers in the newer Member States,

---

[25]   See, for example, E. Lee, 'Globalisation and Employment: Is Anxiety Justified?' (1996) 135 *International Labour Review* 485.

[26]   See, generally, M. Weiss, 'Convergence and/or Divergence in Labor Law Systems: A European Perspective' (2006–7) 28 *Comparative Labor Law and Policy Journal* 469.

[27]   In Article 118, the Member States also undertook to co-operate on social policy, but this was largely aspirational.

[28]   Kenner, above n. 16, 2, and see Case 43/75 *Defrenne v SABENA* [1976] ECR 455 [9].

[29]   Directive establishing a general framework for informing and consulting employees (Directive 2002/14/EC).

[30]   For a useful discussion of the pressures created by enlargement, see Majone, above n. 21.

the EU presents an opportunity to travel to other countries in search of better-paid work. For the 'older' Member States, these workers bring many benefits: they fill vacancies, they may be willing to take jobs that are unpopular or poorly paid (relatively speaking), and they bring an influx of younger people into countries with ageing populations. From the perspective of EU labour law, though, they present a challenge. They may be able to undercut established workers in the 'older' Member States, giving rise to problems of unemployment and social unrest. This is sometimes referred to as 'social dumping'.[31] This term is derived from the concept of 'dumping' in economics, where a firm sells its products at a very low price in order to drive its competitors out of business and to enable it to dominate the market, at which point it will be able to charge what it likes. An important issue for EU labour law is the extent to which it should encourage, prevent or regulate competition between workers from different parts of the EU.

Another way of viewing the free market as a potential threat to national labour law is the possibility that the rules creating the free market might themselves conflict with Member States' ability to regulate their own labour markets.[32] The EU internal market is intended to be a space in which firms, services, goods and workers can move freely from one Member State to another. The creation of the internal market has involved the progressive dismantling of barriers to trade.[33] There are a variety of ways in which it might be argued that rules governing national labour markets constitute such barriers.

Let us begin with a simple example. Member State A permits only individuals who have completed a medical degree in one of its own universities to practise as doctors. Qualifications obtained elsewhere in the EU are not recognised. This rule favours Member State A's nationals over individuals from other Member States because it is much more likely that Member State A's nationals will have qualified in its education system. It can therefore be challenged as a barrier to the free movement of workers.[34] Member State A would have the opportunity to justify the rule, but it is unlikely to succeed because the need to safeguard patients by ensuring that they are treated only by suitably qualified doctors could be met by other means,

---

[31] For a definition, see H. Grossmann and G. Koopman, 'Social Standards in International Trade', in H. Sander and A. Inotai (eds) (1996), *World Trade after the Uruguay Round* (London: Routledge), 116.

[32] See, for example, F. Scharpf, 'The European Social Model: Coping with the Challenge of Diversity' (2002) 40 *Journal of Common Market Studies* 645.

[33] This gives rise to what Syrpis terms the 'integrationist' rationale for EU labour law: see P. Syrpis (2007), *EU Intervention in Domestic Labour Law* (Oxford University Press), 12–50.

[34] Article 45 TFEU.

most obviously recognising equivalent qualifications obtained in other Member States.[35] There is a long history of case-law and legislation requiring mutual recognition of qualifications and this might be thought to be an inevitable – and indeed desirable –consequence of the internal market.[36]

But there are more tricky examples. Let us imagine that a firm established in Member State A wants to move its base to Member State B where labour costs are lower. The firm's workers in Member State A will lose their jobs as a result of the move, and they organise a strike in protest. The strike is lawful under the national regulatory regime. The firm argues that the strike (which inhibits its ability to trade and thus costs it money) is a barrier to its exercise of the freedom to move its place of establishment from one Member State to another, and brings a claim against Member State A.[37] This is more difficult than our previous example in several ways. On one side of the equation, the firm's exercise of freedom of establishment is rendered more costly by the strike. On the other side of the equation, we have the union's exercise of the right to strike, a right which is constitutionally protected in the legal systems of many Member States. Strikes invariably impose costs on employers – that is how they work – so it is more difficult to determine when those costs can or cannot be justified. We will consider this set of issues in more detail in Chapter 3. For present purposes, the key point to note is the (perhaps unexpected) degree of 'bite' the internal market rules might have on traditionally national areas of regulation.

Economic Integration as an Opportunity for the ESM

Not everyone sees EU integration as a threat to the ESM. We will consider two (quite different) arguments which suggest that the creation of an internal market in the EU might be an opportunity for labour law: the argument that trade will make everyone better off, and the argument that regulatory competition between states might lead to a race to the top rather than a race to the bottom.

According to well-established economic theories, states generally gain through trade.[38] Economic growth is stunted if each state tries to be

---

[35]   The leading case is Case C–340/89 *Vlassopoulou v Ministerium für Justiz, Baden-Württemberg* [1991] ECR I–2357.

[36]   See now Directive 2005/36 on the recognition of professional qualifications.

[37]   Article 49 TFEU. This example is similar to the facts of Case C–438/05 *International Transport Workers' Federation v Viking Line* [2007] ECR I–10779.

[38]   For example, Ricardo's theory of comparative advantage: D. Ricardo (1817), *On the Principles of Political Economy and Taxation*, and the Heckscher–Ohlin model: B. Ohlin (1933), *Interregional and International Trade*.

self-sufficient in all goods and services. As trade grows, the number of jobs should increase,[39] thus reducing the number of people dependent on welfare and increasing tax revenues to pay for social benefits such as healthcare and pensions. Protective labour laws will also be more affordable: for example, the minimum wage level can be increased as the economy grows.

However, critics of this argument note that, while there might be gains from free trade in a broad sense, those gains might not necessarily be distributed fairly throughout society. So, for example, shareholders might extract more value from companies without necessarily passing on any of the gains to the workforce or (depending on their domicile and other arrangements) paying tax.

Nevertheless, the view that everyone gains through trade has played an important role in the development of EU labour law because it has acted as an important counterweight to the 'threat' approaches discussed above.[40] Those who have argued that the EU need not legislate on labour law have often invoked this argument and it may help to explain occasions on which the EU has seemed reluctant to engage fully with labour law issues. The emergence of a comprehensive EU competence to legislate on the bulk of labour law has been relatively recent and this may be a part of the reason.

The second argument which treats the EU as an opportunity for labour law is what we might term the 'race to the top' argument.[41] This reflects the view that labour law should not necessarily be seen as a disincentive to investment or an unjustifiable cost on firms. It can be argued that strong labour laws benefit firms in various different ways: for example, unfair dismissal laws can encourage loyalty, and consultation laws can encourage the free exchange of ideas to improve the firm's efficiency and productivity.[42]

On this view, the role of EU labour law might be to create the conditions in which the Member States feel free to pursue a 'race to the top'. One country acting alone may be afraid of maintaining its high labour standards because of the fear of a race to the bottom, as discussed above. But EU labour law can remove this fear by setting minimum labour standards. From this starting-point, the Member States can experiment with different

---

[39]   See, for example, J. Sachs, 'International Economics: Unlocking the Mysteries of Globalisation' (1998) 110 *Foreign Policy* 97.

[40]   This was the view taken in the Ohlin Report, above n. 15, 113.

[41]   See, generally, Hepple, above n. 24; and the discussion of the 'economic rationale' for EU labour law in Syrpis, above n. 33, 53–61.

[42]   See S. Deakin and F. Wilkinson, 'Rights vs Efficiency? The Economic Case for Transnational Labour Standards' (1994) 23 ILJ 289.

forms of protection and might even compete to raise labour standards in order to create a stable, productive and skilled workforce which will, in turn, be attractive to firms.

Again, of course, there is controversy. The 'regulating for competitiveness' theory suggests that the costs of regulation may be outweighed by the benefits, but this is difficult to prove and may work better for some firms than for others.[43] For example, it is often claimed that family-friendly policies will benefit firms (although they are costly) because they will encourage parents to stay in the labour market, thus ensuring that the parents' skills and knowledge do not go to waste. However, where a firm has an ample supply of labour, the cost of this policy will outweigh the benefits.

Nevertheless, the influence of this viewpoint on EU labour law and policy can also be traced, particularly in the Europe 2020 strategy, to be discussed further in Chapter 2. This is a mechanism for the Member States to exchange information about their labour market policies and to test their performance against targets. It is designed to provide a forum in which Member States can learn about the benefits (or disadvantages) of particular policy choices. We will also return to the 'race to the top' idea when we consider EU policy on 'flexicurity' (the idea that labour law should involve a combination of flexibility and security for workers) later in this chapter.

The ESM as an End in Itself

Since the EU began life as a common market, it is inevitable that justifications for EU activities in other areas – like labour law – will be framed in terms of their relationship with that market. However, there may be other reasons for regulating labour law at the EU level which are not so closely connected with market-related arguments.[44] We will consider some of these arguments in this section.

One way of thinking about EU labour law is simply to translate the arguments we might use to justify labour law at the national level into the EU context. Of course, there are a variety of such arguments. One of the most popular over the twentieth century has been the notion that there is an inequality of bargaining power between workers and employers.[45]

---

[43] H. Collins, 'Regulating the Employment Relation for Competitiveness' (2001) 30 ILJ 17.

[44] See the discussion of the 'social rationale' for EU labour law in Syrpis, above n. 33, 61–71.

[45] Most famously by O. Kahn-Freund, 'Legal Framework', in A. Flanders and H.A. Clegg (eds) (1954), *The System of Industrial Relations in Great Britain: Its History, Law and Institutions* (Oxford: Blackwell).

Thus, the law should intervene to redress the balance, either by providing workers with legally enforceable protection, or by creating the conditions for workers and their unions to bargain for protection. So one possible view of EU labour law is that the EU is simply another forum in which this justification can be pursued. If the Member States share a social vision (as the notion of the ESM implies that they do) then that vision could be pursued at the EU level as well as nationally.[46] The idea that EU labour law has a social justification can be found in many of the Court of Justice's judgments. For example, in *Defrenne*, the Court stated that the principle of equal pay was part of the EU's social objectives.[47] Of course, for some people, this approach fits with the view that European integration is an ongoing process with no particular limits: the idea of an 'ever-closer union'.[48] For others, there is no 'big' agenda: for the trade union movement, the EU might just be seen as offering another forum in which campaigning for workers' rights might take place. And if the national political environment is unsympathetic to workers' rights, the EU might be a viable alternative.[49]

More recently, there has been growing interest in a human rights approach to labour law (particularly in the UK), and in the argument that labour law exists to protect the fundamental rights of workers from infringement by the state and by their employers.[50] We will explore this 'constitutionalisation' trend in more depth below, because it is an important theme in contemporary EU labour law. For now, it is sufficient to note that the rights approach lends itself particularly well to being pursued at different regulatory levels, given the universal nature of human rights and the clear support for them on the part of the Member States (through instruments such as the European Convention on Human Rights). There are various examples of the Court using 'rights language' in its judgments. For example, the entitlement to paid annual leave was described in *BECTU* as a 'social right' and the UK was found to have failed to

---

[46] See the statement of the EU's values in Article 2, Treaty on European Union (TEU).

[47] *Defrenne*, above n. 28, [10].

[48] For a critique, see C. Joerges, 'What is Left of the European Economic Constitution? A Melancholic Eulogy' (2005) 30 EL Rev 461; S. Krebber, 'Status and Potential of the Regulation of Labor and Employment Law at the European Level' (2008–9) 30 *Comparative Labor Law and Policy Journal* 875.

[49] A.C.L. Davies (2009), *Perspectives on Labour Law* (2nd edn) (Cambridge University Press), 14.

[50] For discussion, see A.C.L. Davies, 'The "Constitutionalisation" of Labour Law: Possibilities and Problems' in K.S. Ziegler and P.M. Huber (eds) (forthcoming 2012), *Current Problems in the Protection of Human Rights in Germany and the UK* (Oxford, Hart).

implement the Directive properly because it had sought to derogate from the right.[51]

A rather more strategic view of EU labour law would focus on its potential role in making the EU enterprise more attractive to citizens. A problem with the EU is that there is a significant body of 'Eurosceptic' opinion in the Member States. This came into sharp focus on a number of occasions in recent years when the electorates of various Member States rejected proposed EU treaties. One way of viewing the problem is that the benefits of free trade within the EU might not be immediately apparent to individual voters, so the EU needs to show them a more human face. It is generally thought that the EU Charter of Fundamental Rights was developed – in part at least – with this in mind. It offered a way of demonstrating to voters in the Member States that the EU was committed to human rights and was not set on depriving them of constitutional safeguards. Of course, this strategy has not been entirely successful: the proposed EU Constitution did not find favour with national electorates and one reason for this was their concern at the idea of the EU as a superstate with extensive involvement in all areas of policy. Nevertheless, the task of 'selling' the EU to a sceptical citizenry might be made easier by being able to demonstrate immediate improvements in individuals' daily lives: better maternity leave provisions, for example, or greater equality between different groups in the workplace.

CURRENT ISSUES IN EU LABOUR LAW

The shape of EU labour law is determined not just by the explanations for its emergence, but also by the contemporary challenges it faces. Of course, these contemporary challenges intersect with the explanations in various ways, but it is also helpful to consider them in their own right. We will focus on three: national autonomy, constitutionalisation and the economic context.

National Autonomy

National autonomy is both a contemporary and a perpetual challenge for EU labour law.[52] Although some people might like to see the emergence

---

[51] Case C–173/99 *R v Secretary of State for Trade and Industry, ex p BECTU* [2001] ECR I–4881 [47].

[52] For the historic importance of autonomy in explaining the exclusion of labour issues from the EU's competences, see Joerges, above n. 48.

of a uniform labour code for the whole of the EU, we do not have one yet and we are not likely to have one in the foreseeable future. Labour law is a matter of 'shared competence'[53] (shared between the EU and the Member States)[54] and there is an important debate about their respective roles. The intensity of this debate in the labour law context stems not just from the usual controversy about the appropriate role of the EU (which links to the explanations for EU intervention, discussed in the previous section), but more particularly from the fact that national approaches to labour law are regarded as particularly diverse.[55]

Since 1993, the EU has formally been obliged to observe the principle of 'subsidiarity'.[56] The requirement is now laid down in Article 5(3) of the TEU:

> Under the principle of subsidiarity, in areas which do not fall within its exclusive competence, the Union shall act only if and in so far as the objectives of the proposed action cannot be sufficiently achieved by the Member States, either at central level or at regional and local level, but can rather, by reason of the scale or effects of the proposed action, be better achieved at Union level.

New legislative proposals must be justified in terms of subsidiarity, and there is a Protocol on Subsidiarity which lays down more detailed requirements.[57] An innovation in the Lisbon Treaty is the power it gives national parliaments to scrutinise legislative proposals for their compliance with subsidiarity, though it remains to be seen what effect this will have in practice.[58] The Court of Justice also has the power to annul legislation which

---

[53] Defined in Article 2(2) TFEU as follows: '[w]hen the Treaties confer on the Union a competence shared with the Member States in a specific area, the Union and the Member States may legislate and adopt legally binding acts in that area. The Member States shall exercise their competence to the extent that the Union has not exercised its competence. The Member States shall again exercise their competence to the extent that the Union has decided to cease exercising its competence.'

[54] Article 4 TFEU, though under Article 5(2) TFEU there is a power to co-ordinate the Member States' social policies. For an interesting discussion of the structure of the EU's competences after Lisbon, see R. Schutze, 'Lisbon and the Federal Order of Competences: a Prospective Analysis' (2008) 33 EL Rev 709. But as Syrpis explains, it is more helpful to refer to the detailed provisions of Titles IX and X of the Treaty to determine the EU's exact powers: P. Syrpis, 'The Treaty of Lisbon: much ado...but about what?' (2008) 37 ILJ 219, 226.

[55] See, generally, O. Kahn-Freund, 'On the Uses and Misuses of Comparative Law' (1974) 37 MLR 1.

[56] The principle was first included in the TEU as agreed at Maastricht in 1992. The Treaty entered into force in 1993.

[57] Protocol No. 2 on the application of the principles of subsidiarity and proportionality, annexed to the TEU and the TFEU.

[58] For discussion, see A. Cygan, 'The Parliamentarisation of EU Decision-Making? The Impact of the Treaty of Lisbon on National Parliaments' (2011) EL Rev 480.

does not respect the principle, though it seems unlikely that the Court will ever exercise very strict scrutiny in this regard.[59] There is a considerable debate as to the practical utility of the principle as a constraint on EU action.[60]

That said, there are a number of illustrations in EU labour law of measures which reflect national autonomy. The most striking of these is the exclusion, in Article 153 TFEU, of pay, freedom of association and the right to strike from the EU's legislative competence. The reasons for this are, of course, a matter of some speculation. But it seems likely that the exclusion of pay was for economic reasons: a Europe-wide minimum wage would be a step too far for most Member States. And on the collective front, it is probable that the wide variations in national traditions made harmonisation of the laws on trade union activity seem too difficult or too sensitive to contemplate.[61] However, as we shall see in later chapters, although the EU cannot legislate on these topics, it can affect the Member States' ability to regulate them in a variety of different ways, making the strategy of excluding them from the Treaty not entirely successful in practice.

Another much more common reflection of national autonomy within EU labour law lies in the use of directives as the preferred regulatory mechanism. The definition of a directive is that it specifies the goals to be achieved, whilst leaving to the Member States the 'choice of form and methods', thus bringing in an element of discretion.[62] Directives are a means of 'harmonisation' – co-ordinating the laws of the Member States to some extent – not of creating a uniform code. Of course, different directives afford the Member States discretion to varying degrees and some scholars have been critical of the EU's tendency to enact over-precise and rigid legislation. Some examples may help to illustrate the point.

The Directive on Fixed-Term Work contains a provision designed to combat the abuse of successive fixed-term contracts.[63] The concern is that such contracts leave workers in a precarious position, so firms should be encouraged – or forced – to make permanent jobs available unless the role in question is genuinely short-term in nature. The Directive (which enacts

---

[59]   See, for example, Case C–176/09 *Luxembourg v Council and Parliament* [2011] nyr.

[60]   See, for example, G. Davies, 'Subsidiarity: the Wrong Idea, in the Wrong Place, at the Wrong Time' (2006) 43 CMLR 63.

[61]   Though as we shall see in later chapters, some collective issues are included in the EU's competence, notably 'the information and consultation of workers' (Article 153(1)(e) TFEU) and 'representation and collective defence of the interests of workers and employers' (Article 153(1)(f) TFEU).

[62]   Article 288 TFEU.

[63]   Directive 1999/70/EC.

an agreement reached by the social partners) gives the Member States a series of options for implementation:

> To prevent abuse arising from the use of successive fixed-term employment contracts or relationships, Member States, after consultation with social partners in accordance with national law, collective agreements or practice, and/or the social partners, shall, where there are no equivalent legal measures to prevent abuse, introduce in a manner which takes account of the needs of specific sectors and/or categories of workers, one or more of the following measures:
> (a) objective reasons justifying the renewal of such contracts or relationships;
> (b) the maximum total duration of successive fixed-term employment contracts or relationships;
> (c) the number of renewals of such contracts or relationships.[64]

It is readily apparent that this gives the Member States a considerable degree of flexibility. The Directive identifies three possible regulatory options and also permits them to be used in combination, thereby increasing the range of choices. Moreover, no detail is given as to the duration or number of renewals, so that each Member State can make its own decision on this issue (subject to the Court's scrutiny as to whether it has 'effectively' implemented the Directive).[65] Perhaps not surprisingly, the Directive's critics argue that the discretion is open to abuse. We will consider this issue in more detail in Chapter 4.

Other Directives have been criticised for their rigidity. The Working Time Directive is a case in point.[66] Barnard criticises the Directive for its 'one size fits all' approach, which assumes that a 48-hour working week (on average) is appropriate for all Member States and sectors of the economy.[67] This has proved highly problematic in some areas, notably healthcare, where there is a requirement to have a doctor available on call at all times.[68] Whilst it can be argued that it is dangerous for doctors in particular to work to the point of exhaustion, there are significant financial and practical constraints. For example, shorter working weeks may make it difficult for trainee doctors to acquire the experience they need. Barnard suggests that a framework directive supplemented by a series

---

[64] Clause 5(1) of the social partner agreement annexed to Directive 1999/70/EC.

[65] On which see, for example, Case C–378/07 *Angelidaki v Organismos Nomarchiakis Autodioikisis Rethymnis* [2009] ECR I–3071.

[66] Directive 2003/88/EC.

[67] Barnard, above n. 14, 491.

[68] See, for example, Case C–303/98 *SIMAP v Conselleria de Sanidad y Consumo de la Generalidad Valenciana* [2000] ECR I–7963.

of sector-specific directives (along the lines used elsewhere in health and safety law) would have been a more attractive approach.[69]

A final example of the concern about national autonomy is the Europe 2020 strategy, to be discussed in more detail in Chapter 2. This is a mechanism for the development of labour policy, rather than labour law. It encourages the Member States to compare their performance against a series of policy objectives, such as increasing employment levels and improving the rates of participation in the labour market of under-represented groups. In theory at least, the Europe 2020 strategy is neutral as to the policy choices the Member States make. Its advocates suggest that it allows for a degree of experimentation which is beneficial where there are no 'right' answers to complex problems such as unemployment.[70] Again, though, as with all the strategies we have considered, there is a debate about the extent of the autonomy available to the Member States within the process, with some critics arguing that the targets themselves may have a tendency to push the Member States in the direction of particular policy choices.[71]

Constitutionalisation of the ESM

An emerging issue in EU labour law is the possible 'constitutionalisation' of the ESM. This is a useful umbrella term for the increasing use of rights arguments in the analysis and development of EU labour law, particularly but not exclusively in the Court of Justice. Part of the impetus for this development is the legal effect given to the EU Charter of Fundamental Rights by the Lisbon Treaty. This has proved attractive to labour lawyers because (as with similar developments at the national level) rights arguments are often afforded particular weight in legal and political argument. The protection of workers' rights may provide a stronger way of justifying EU labour law than some of the alternatives, such as redressing imbalances in bargaining power. Or – and this is an important overlap with the discussion in the previous section – it may strengthen the ESM in the face of the threats (arguably) posed by European economic integration.

As an economic union, it is not surprising that the EU began life without any kind of fundamental rights instrument. The development of

---

[69] Barnard, above n. 14.

[70] See, for example, D.M. Trubek and L.G. Trubek, 'Hard and Soft Law in the Construction of Social Europe: the Role of the Open Method of Co-ordination' (2005) 11 ELJ 343.

[71] See, for example, G. Raveaud, 'The European Employment Strategy: Towards More and Better Jobs?' (2007) 45 *Journal of Common Market Studies* 411–34.

the doctrine of supremacy of EU law over national law prompted a back-lash from national constitutional courts in some Member States, because they were unhappy that even quite minor provisions of EU law would prevail over their national constitutions. The German Constitutional Court in particular sought to preserve its own power to review EU law for its compatibility with fundamental rights. The Court of Justice's reaction in the well-known *Internationale Handelsgesellschaft* case was to insist that it would develop a fundamental rights review of its own.[72] This would draw on the constitutional traditions of the Member States and on the European Convention on Human Rights (ECHR), to which all Member States are party.

In 2000, the political actors finally 'proclaimed' a comprehensive state-ment of rights for the EU in the shape of the EU Charter of Fundamental Rights. However, this document did not have legal force and the Court of Justice was reluctant to refer to it in judgments.[73] The Lisbon Treaty has given legal effect to the Charter by inserting it into the treaty architecture, a move which has immediately resulted in a much greater willingness on the part of the Court to cite Charter rights in its decisions and even to 'rebase' its own fundamental rights jurisprudence on the Charter.[74] The Charter is a very wide-ranging statement of rights, including economic and social rights alongside civil and political rights.[75] This gives it relevance to most areas of labour law. One possible view of the changing role of the Charter is that it might result in greater prioritisation of the ESM over competing considerations (particularly economic ones) by imbuing the ESM with the force of fundamental rights. However, most commentators are sceptical about the likelihood of this happening in practice.

One set of problems relates to the drafting of the Charter. First, its scope is limited. It does not create new competences for the EU and applies to the Member States only when they are 'implementing Union law'.[76] The last phrase is far from clear and could be more or less expansively inter-preted, either to mean 'implementing' in the literal sense of transposing into domestic law, or more broadly to include any action taken in an EU

---

[72] Case 11/70 *Internationale Handelsgesellschaft* [1970] ECR 1125.

[73] The Court of First Instance (now the General Court) did cite the Charter but it was clear that the Court did not approve: Case T–177/01 *Jégo-Quéré v Commission* [2002] ECR II–2365.

[74] Case C–297/10 *Hennigs v Eisenbahn-Bundesamt* [2011] nyr.

[75] For detailed discussion see T.K. Hervey and J. Kenner (eds) (2003), *Economic and Social Rights under the EU Charter of Fundamental Rights: a Legal Perspective* (Oxford: Hart).

[76] EU Charter, Article 51(1). This aspect is emphasised by Bercusson, above n. 7, Chapter 11.

law context. Second, many of the rights are drafted with reference to EU law and national law. For example, Article 30 states that

> [e]very worker has the right to protection against unjustified dismissal, in accordance with Union law and national laws and practices.

The problem here is that the so-called right does not add very much because its content is dependent on other legal sources.

Another set of problems relates to the relationship between the Charter and other aspects of EU law.[77] Reflecting the EU's initial development as an economic union, the Court has long regarded the core principles of the internal market as the fundamental principles of EU law. So the free movement of goods, workers and services, freedom of establishment and the promotion of competition are at the heart of the EU legal order. The ESM has tended to occupy a lower position in the legal 'hierarchy'. Of course, the new legal status of the Charter may raise the profile of rights – and labour rights – in EU law. But commentators are sceptical. The Court of Justice has already been called upon to consider the relationship between labour rights and fundamental principles of EU law in the well-known *Viking* and *Laval* line of cases, which we will consider in Chapter 3.[78] In those cases, the court recognised the right to strike as a fundamental right in EU law, drawing on the Charter and other sources, but nevertheless prioritised the competing free movement principles. It is not clear that the formal change in the Charter's legal status would have led to a different outcome in these cases.[79]

Finally, for some commentators, the EU Charter might have a harmful effect on rights, and particularly labour rights, in the EU. This argument might be made in two different ways. First, the Charter contains a very long list of rights. Some of these rights have widespread international recognition in highly respected instruments such as the UN Universal Declaration and the ECHR. Others would not be regarded by many people as fundamental rights at all. For example, Article 29 sets out a 'right of access to a free placement service' but it is not clear why this should be singled out for inclusion in the Charter.[80] One possible problem,

---

[77] For an overview of this issue see S. Fredman, 'Transformation or Dilution: Fundamental Rights in the EU Social Space' (2006) 12 ELJ 41.

[78] *Viking*, above n. 37, Case C–341/05 *Laval v Svenska Byggnadsarbetareförbundet* [2007] ECR I–11767.

[79] This appears to be confirmed by some recent cases on age discrimination to be discussed in Chapter 5.

[80] Article 1(3) of the European Social Charter (1996) requires signatory states to maintain a free placement service as part of the right to work, but even this is not expressed in terms of a free-standing right for the individual worker.

then, is the 'trivialisation' of rights. By failing to pick out the most important rights, and by including some things that may not deserve the label 'rights' at all, there is a danger that the EU Charter may reduce rather than increase respect for rights.

Second, the Charter does not confine itself to rights for working people. It recognises the 'freedom' of 'every citizen of the Union' to provide services or to establish in any Member State.[81] It enshrines a right to property for 'everyone'.[82] And it recognises a 'freedom to conduct a business in accordance with Union law and national laws and practices'.[83] These represent a set of what we might call 'employer' rights. It is not clear whether they are likely to extend to legal persons (firms) as well as natural persons. The reference to 'citizen[s]' suggests only natural persons, but the other rights are more ambiguous. The recognition of 'employer' rights is controversial and gives rise to the possibility that employers might use the Charter to argue that worker rights infringe their business freedoms. Of course, this does not mean that such arguments would succeed – or that it is necessarily a bad thing for labour lawyers to have to justify their assumptions about the protections workers need – but it does mean that an instrument like the Charter should not be regarded as an unequivocally pro-worker development.

Importantly, though, the legal force given to the Charter by the Lisbon Treaty is not the only source of impetus towards 'constitutionalisation' in EU labour law. Another interesting development is the power in the Lisbon Treaty for the EU to seek accession to the ECHR.[84] It remains to be seen exactly how this would work and, in particular, how the relationship between the Court of Justice and the European Court of Human Rights (ECtHR) would be managed. As we have seen, a big issue in the Court of Justice's approach to human rights is their status in EU law: although the Court uses the term 'fundamental' to describe rights, it continues to regard the internal market rules as the most important form of EU law. It is possible that ECHR accession will challenge this, because the ECtHR is likely to regard Convention rights as the starting-point for decision making. However, this is where conflict between the two courts is likely to be at its most intense. Each court is the authority in its own field

---

[81]   EU Charter, Article 15(2).

[82]   Ibid, Article 17.

[83]   Ibid, Article 16.

[84]   Article 6(2) TEU. For discussion see, generally, J-P. Jacqué, 'The Accession of the European Union to the European Convention on Human Rights and Fundamental Freedoms' (2011) 48 CMLR 995, and C.F. Sabel and O. Gerstenberg, 'Constitutionalising an Overlapping Consensus: The ECJ and the Emergence of a Coordinate Constitutional Order' (2010) 16 ELJ 511.

– Convention rights and EU law respectively – but the crucial questions concern how these two fields of law should interrelate.

Moreover, there are limits to the possibility of 'constitutionalising' EU labour law through ECHR accession. In addition to the concern about how the two courts will relate to one another, there is the more general point that the relevance of the Convention to labour law is limited. As a statement of civil and political rights, it has relevance to equality law and collective labour law (where it has been the subject of expansive interpretation),[85] but very little to say about individual employment law.[86] Thus, although it might have a powerful impact in some areas, it is not likely to be relevant across the whole spectrum of EU labour law.

Economic Challenges

As we saw above, a big part of the explanation for the emergence of labour law at the EU level is the impact of European economic integration on the Member States' perception of their ability to regulate their own labour markets successfully, and their fears about how other Member States might behave. More generally, discussions about EU labour law nowadays take place against the background of the tough economic challenges facing the EU. It may be helpful to say something about these challenges. We will begin by considering globalisation generally, before examining the recent economic crisis.

The impact of globalisation on the economies of developed nations is, by now, a familiar theme for most people. Developments in transport and information technology mean that many firms can now choose to locate their business anywhere in the world. Their choices will often be guided by labour costs, though of course this will not be the only factor. As consumers, we benefit from the influx of cheaper goods such as clothing and electronics produced in countries with much lower wage levels than ours. But as workers, our jobs may be under threat as companies seek to relocate to low-cost destinations. The extent of relocation out of the EU – and thus the seriousness of the problem – is a matter of some debate. Nevertheless, from this perspective, the biggest challenge facing the ESM is not from European integration itself, but from global competition.

---

[85]   K.D. Ewing and J. Hendy, 'The Dramatic Implications of *Demir* and *Baykara*' (2010) 39 ILJ 2.

[86]   For an argument that the EU should accede to the European Social Charter, which contains a range of economic and social rights, see O. de Schutter, 'Anchoring the EU to the European Social Charter: the Case for Accession' in G. de Búrca and B. de Witte (eds) (2005), *Social Rights in Europe* (Oxford University Press).

In our discussion of European integration, we considered the 'race to the bottom' and 'race to the top' arguments. Faced with competition from their European neighbours, we saw that countries might be tempted either to cut costs by cutting labour standards (prompting a race to the bottom) or to promote labour standards as a way of improving productivity (prompting a race to the top). We can think about the EU's reaction to global competition using the same ideas.

One possible reaction would be for the EU to reduce the protection afforded by the ESM in order to make the EU cheaper and therefore more competitive (on a global scale) as a destination for investment.[87] As we shall see, the Commission does sometimes talk about 'modernising' the ESM and this may be a polite way of expressing this idea.[88] For example, some recent initiatives in the area of 'atypical work' have required the Member States to remove barriers to this type of work,[89] which may result in cost savings for firms.

The alternative is to argue that, although the EU is a costly location for businesses, it has compensating advantages. For many people, this is the more attractive argument because cutting labour standards is unlikely to be popular with citizens and because (given existing living standards) it may not even be possible to cut costs to a globally competitive level. Nevertheless, making this argument can be quite a challenge in itself. As we shall see, the Commission's policy documents usually focus on making European workers more attractive to firms by striving to ensure they are highly skilled, productive and adaptable to changing circumstances.[90]

An important concept in EU policy making here is 'flexicurity'.[91] This ugly word is a combination of 'flexibility' and 'security'. It is the label for a policy agenda which focuses not on traditional job security, which is about

---

[87] For an argument along these lines, see L. Funk, 'European Flexicurity Policies: A Critical Assessment' (2008) 24 *International Journal of Comparative Labour Law and Industrial Relations* 349.

[88] For example, Commission (2007), *Towards Common Principles of Flexicurity: More and Better Jobs Through Flexibility and Security* (COM(2007) 359 final), 4, and see more generally the Green Paper, Commission, *Modernising Labour Law to Meet the Challenges of the 21st Century* (COM(2006) 708 final); Commission, *Opportunities, Access and Solidarity: Towards a New Social Vision for 21st Century Europe* (COM(2007) 726 final); Commission, *Renewed Social Agenda: Opportunities, Access and Solidarity in 21st Century Europe* (COM(2008) 412 final), 15.

[89] See, for example, Directive 2008/104/EC, Article 4.

[90] See, for example, Commission (2010), *An Agenda for New Skills and Jobs: A European Contribution Towards Full Employment* (COM(2010) 682 final).

[91] Above n. 88. See, generally, P.K. Madsen, 'Flexicurity: A New Perspective on Labour Markets and Welfare States in Europe' (2007–8) 14 *Tilburg Law Review* 57, and in broader terms, S. Giubboni (2006), *Social Rights and Market Freedom in the European Constitution* (Cambridge University Press).

keeping a worker in his or her existing job, but on employment security, which is about keeping a worker in some job or other. The emphasis is on ensuring that Member States and firms have incentives to train workers so that they have high skill levels and can adapt to change. This should make them more flexible within a particular workplace (so that they can be redeployed to a variety of different tasks depending on the firm's needs) and within the labour market (so that if one job comes to an end, they are well equipped to find another).

Another temptation for states faced with the challenge of globalisation is to cut back on the generous welfare provision that is a feature of the ESM. However, the flexicurity agenda opposes this too. The argument is that workers will be more willing to accept restructuring if there is a social safety net to support them while they look for another job. The EU also provides some financial help to regions affected by job losses attributable to globalisation through the European Globalisation Adjustment Fund.[92] This is an important acknowledgement that some traditional European industries may not be able to survive globalisation and that significant effort will be needed to attract new investment and retrain workers.

The recent global financial crisis has brought the debate about the economic benefits or otherwise of the ESM into even sharper focus. As firms struggle to survive a deep recession, their demands for cost-cutting measures (including reductions in labour law protections) are bound to increase. And, as we have seen, where national economies in the Eurozone have required financial bail-outs, the level of social protection they provide to their citizens (low retirement ages, generous pension settlements and so on) have come under increasing scrutiny from the other Member States. The Commission has sought to address the crisis by focusing on financial aid – through the European Social Fund – to help affected regions to attract new jobs and investment.[93] But it remains to be seen how the ESM will survive this latest bout of intense pressure.

We will return to the flexicurity agenda at various points in the book, but for now, it is worth noting two important implications for a study of EU labour law. First, flexicurity highlights the increasing interconnectedness of labour law and employment policy. Traditionally, labour lawyers have tended to concern themselves with those in work, leaving the

---

[92] See the European Globalisation Adjustment Fund Regulation (Regulation 1927/2006) and http://ec.europa.eu/social/main.jsp?catId=326&langId=en (last visited 1 June 2011). For discussion, see M. de Vos, 'European Flexicurity and Globalization: A Critical Perspective' (2009) 25 *International Journal of Comparative Labour Law and Industrial Relations* 209.

[93] See the European Social Fund Regulation (Regulation 1081/2006), as amended, and http://ec.europa.eu/esf/home.jsp?langId=en (last visited 1 June 2011).

question of what to do about the unemployed to politicians. But flexicurity focuses on the state of the labour market as a whole and treats labour law as one part of the regulatory picture, affecting those out of work as much as those in work. Second, flexicurity is ambiguous about labour law in important ways. On one hand, it is explicitly not a deregulatory agenda and it supports labour law where this contributes to economic competitiveness. For example, its emphasis on skills suggests that workers should enjoy some degree of job security so that employers have an incentive to provide training. On the other hand, it opens up the possibility that measures which have been justified in the past on the basis of worker protection or fundamental rights (such as restrictions on the use of temporary work) may no longer be regarded as defensible now that they must be judged in economic terms. From this perspective, flexicurity is often regarded as deregulatory in practice even if not in intention.

FURTHER READING

The history of EU labour law is a fascinating subject of study. We will touch upon it at various points in this book but (due to considerations of space) we will not be able to cover it in detail. For a full account, see J. Kenner (2003), *EU Employment Law: From Rome to Amsterdam and Beyond* (Oxford: Hart). And for a concise overview, see C. Barnard, 'EU "Social" Policy: from Employment Law to Labour Market Reform', in P.P. Craig and G. de Búrca (eds) (2011), *The Evolution of EU Law* (2nd edn, Oxford University Press).

For detail on EU labour law beyond that which can be offered in this introductory volume, see C. Barnard (2006), *EC Employment Law* (3rd edn, Oxford University Press), or B. Bercusson (2009), *European Labour Law* (2nd edn, Cambridge University Press).

For a sophisticated analysis of the reasons for regulating labour law at the EU level, see P. Syrpis (2007), *EU Intervention in Domestic Labour Law* (Oxford University Press), especially Chapter 2.

2. Regulatory techniques

This chapter explains the making of EU labour law and policy. We will begin by considering the EU's competence in the field of EU labour law, before examining the process by which directives are made and implemented. We will focus in particular on the special role of the 'social partners' (the European Trade Union Confederation and a group of European employers' associations) in the negotiation and implementation of labour law directives.

In the second part of the chapter, we will consider the role of the Court of Justice as the interpreter of EU labour law in treaty articles or directives. We will examine the main ways in which cases arrive before the Court, and we will discuss some of the literature on the Court's role. The Court is often regarded as especially political and purposive in its outlook, so we will assess the evidence for and against these claims.

The third part of the chapter turns to the EU's role in co-ordinating the Member States' employment policies through what is currently labelled the Europe 2020 strategy. This involves setting EU-wide targets on matters such as reducing unemployment, translating those into targets for each Member State, and monitoring the Member States' progress towards the targets. We will examine some of the advantages and disadvantages claimed for this approach, and how it relates to EU labour law.

An important theme running through the chapter is the role of 'reflexive regulation', so it may be worth introducing this idea briefly at this point.[1] Most lawyers take for granted the idea that legislation is effective: that by requiring somebody to do something in law, we will achieve the desired result. The advocates of 'reflexive regulation' challenge this assumption. They suggest that it is harder to change people's behaviour than we might suppose, not least because everybody has his or her own preferred way of

---

[1] See, generally, G. Teubner, 'Substantive and Reflexive Elements in Modern Law' (1983) 17 *Law and Society Review* 239, and for discussion in the labour law context, J. Lenoble and M. Maesschalck, 'Renewing the Theory of Public Interest: the Quest for a Reflexive and Learning-Based Approach to Governance', in O. de Schutter and J. Lenoble (eds) (2010), *Reflexive Governance: Redefining the Public Interest in a Pluralist World* (Oxford: Hart), D. Schiek, 'Private Rule-Making and European Governance – Issues of Legitimacy' (2007) 32 EL Rev 443.

doing things. They argue that it is more effective to give people incentives to reach certain results, and to let them figure out their own solutions. Of course, this theory also has its critics: negotiating solutions to problems might be time-consuming in itself, and the outcomes might be adversely affected because the people involved have limited information about the options or because they have unequal bargaining power. The 'law versus reflexivity' debate sometimes feels a bit odd in EU labour law because directives already involve some flexibility. But reflexivity is a matter of degree and, as we shall see, the involvement of the social partners and the Europe 2020 strategy can both be regarded as situated towards the reflexive end of the spectrum.

LEGISLATION

We will be spending much of the rest of this book looking at the 'outputs' of the EU's legislative process in the field of labour law. The purpose of this section is to highlight some important features of the way labour law is made at the EU level and implemented in the Member States. We will consider the EU's competence to legislate on labour issues and the limits on its competence. We will then examine the legislative process, focusing in particular on the role of the social partners and their power to develop labour law by reaching agreements in the process known as 'social dialogue'. Finally, we will consider some aspects of the implementation of directives in the Member States, focusing again on the role of the social partners and also on the controversial issue of 'non-regression': whether the Member States are ever permitted to reduce the level of worker protection in their legal system when implementing a directive.

Competence

The EU's legislative competence in the field of labour law is set out in the Treaty on the Functioning of the EU (TFEU).[2] Most of the EU's powers to legislate in this field can be found in Article 153, but for historical and political reasons there are separate provisions governing the EU's role in equality law. The Treaty provisions on the free movement of workers, which form part of the law of the internal market, also have relevance to labour law.

---

[2] The EU can only act in accordance with the powers given to it in the Treaties. This is called the principle of 'conferral' and it is laid down in Art 5(2) TFEU.

The EU's objectives in the social policy field are set out in Article 151. This is an aspirational statement but does offer some insight into the Member States' concerns and may guide the Court in interpreting social policy legislation.[3] The first two paragraphs state:

> The Union and the Member States, having in mind fundamental social rights such as those set out in the European Social Charter signed at Turin on 18 October 1961 and in the 1989 Community Charter of the Fundamental Social Rights of Workers, shall have as their objectives the promotion of employment, improved living and working conditions, so as to make possible their harmonisation while the improvement is being maintained, proper social protection, dialogue between management and labour, the development of human resources with a view to lasting high employment and the combating of exclusion.
>
> To this end the Union and the Member States shall implement measures which take account of the diverse forms of national practices, in particular in the field of contractual relations, and the need to maintain the competitiveness of the Union's economy.

This statement captures a number of the objectives we considered in the first chapter: protecting workers' rights, improving living conditions, tackling unemployment and promoting social inclusion. It also illustrates the Member States' concerns with preserving national autonomy and the challenge of maintaining global competitiveness.

In terms of legislative competence, the starting-point is Article 153. Labour law is an area of shared competence between the EU and the Member States.[4] The list of fields in which directives can be enacted is as follows:

(a) improvement in particular of the working environment to protect workers' health and safety;
(b) working conditions;
(c) social security and social protection of workers;
(d) protection of workers where their employment contract is terminated;
(e) the information and consultation of workers;
(f) representation and collective defence of the interests of workers and employers, including co-determination . . .
(g) conditions of employment for third-country nationals legally residing in Union territory;
(h) the integration of persons excluded from the labour market . . .

---

[3] For an interesting analysis on this point, see F. Lecomte, 'Embedding Employment Rights in Europe' (2010–11) 17 *Columbia Journal of European Law* 1.
[4] See Arts 2 and 4 TFEU. For an interesting discussion of the structure of the EU's competences after Lisbon, see R. Schutze, 'Lisbon and the Federal Order of Competences: a Prospective Analysis' (2008) 33 EL Rev 709.

(i)   equality between men and women with regard to labour market
       opportunities and treatment at work . . .[5]

We will see in later chapters how this competence has been exercised.

Although Article 153(1)(i) refers to equality between men and women,
the Treaty also contains separate provisions on equality. Article 157 lays
down the principle of equal pay for men and women. This provision is
directly effective, so the Member States are obliged to comply with it
without the need for any further legislative action on the part of the EU.
Article 157(3) provides the EU with competence to legislate on equal
opportunities and equal treatment for men and women, including in the
area of pay. Article 19 TFEU gives the EU a broader competence to 'take
appropriate action to combat discrimination based on sex, racial or ethnic
origin, religion or belief, disability, age or sexual orientation'.

We will see in Chapter 3 that one of the distinctively 'EU' aspects of
EU labour law is the creation of an internal market in which workers may
move freely from one Member State to another, either in search of work
or to take up employment.[6] The principle of the free movement of workers
is laid down in Article 45, which has direct effect, and under Article 46
the EU enjoys power to enact regulations and directives to ensure the
observance of this principle. A number of other Treaty provisions are also
relevant in this area, notably the prohibition of discrimination based on
nationality in Article 18, the establishment of EU citizenship in Article 20,
and the freedom to provide services across national borders in Article 56.

Limits on Competence

In this section, we will consider some of the limits on the EU's competence:
some topics that are expressly excluded; some qualifications to the EU's
powers applicable in the labour law field; and more general limitations like
the principle of subsidiarity.

Three important areas of labour law are excluded from the EU's legislative competence. These are 'pay, the right of association, the right to strike
or the right to impose lock-outs'.[7] This explicit exclusion first came about
in 1992, in the Agreement on Social Policy annexed to the Maastricht
Treaty, and continued when the Agreement was incorporated into the
Treaty in 1997. As Ryan explains, although it seems plausible to suggest
that these matters may have been excluded in the hope of persuading the

---

[5]   Art 153(1).
[6]   This is also an area of shared competence under Arts 2 and 4 TFEU.
[7]   Art 153(5).

UK to sign up to the Maastricht Agreement, the evidence indicates that there was no support from other Member States for Community action in these fields.[8] It seems likely that these areas are simply too sensitive for the Member States to agree to their regulation at EU level. National collective bargaining systems vary widely across the Member States, and while the right to strike is merely tolerated in some countries it enjoys constitutional protection in others. Levels of pay also diverge very substantially across the EU, and matters such as the fixing of a minimum wage have important economic as well as social implications.

Having said that, it is important to note that the fact that limitations are placed on the EU's legislative competences does not necessarily mean that EU law has no relevance to these areas. Because of the principle of conferral, it is clear that the EU cannot legislate in areas in which it has no legislative power.[9] Any attempt to do so would be reviewable by the Court of Justice. But there are a variety of more indirect forms of involvement. First, areas in which the EU does have legislative competence clearly overlap with those in which it does not. For example, under Article 153(1)(e) and (f) EU labour law may address some aspects of the collective consultation and representation of workers. Second, as later chapters will demonstrate, the EU's regulation of other areas, such as the internal market, might have an impact on the Member States' ability to regulate pay and industrial action if firms argue that the States' actions impede their access to national markets. And third, the EU may involve itself indirectly in the excluded areas through softer, non-legislative means, such as the Europe 2020 strategy, to be discussed further below.

The Treaty's social policy provisions also include some more general statements about the limits of the EU's legislative competence. For example, we have already noted the reference in Article 151 to the diversity of the Member States' legal systems, which indicates a concern with their autonomy. This is reinforced by Article 153(2)(b)'s reference to 'having regard to the conditions and technical rules obtaining in each of the Member States' when enacting directives. The same provision also states that labour law directives 'shall avoid imposing administrative, financial and legal constraints in a way which would hold back the creation and development of small and medium-sized undertakings'. These statements guide the Commission when it is bringing forward proposals in the area of social policy so, for example, the Commission might address the situation of smaller firms when proposing a new directive. They may also be

---

[8]   B. Ryan, 'Pay, Trade Union Rights and European Community Law' (1997) 13 *International Journal of Comparative Labour Law and Industrial Relations* 305, 308–9.
[9]   Above n. 2.

considered by the Court when assessing a Member State's implementation of a directive,[10] or when considering the validity of the directive itself.[11]

The EU is also obliged to respect the principles of subsidiarity and proportionality when enacting legislation.[12] These principles apply in EU law generally and they guide the development of legislative proposals. They also provide grounds on which the Court of Justice might find a directive to have been outside the EU's competences to enact, though this is unusual in practice.[13]

Legislative Procedures

For a detailed account of the EU's legislative procedures, it is best to look at one of the big textbooks on EU law.[14] However, there are some interesting features of these procedures as they apply to EU labour law and we will consider those features in this section.

The TFEU brought about a significant simplification of the EU's legislative procedures. Most legislative powers are now exercised through the 'ordinary legislative procedure' laid down in Article 294. The proposed measure must be initiated by the European Commission and must receive the consent of both the European Parliament and the Council in order to become law. In some cases, a 'special legislative procedure' must be used. This is not a uniform legislative procedure but instead allows either the Parliament or the Council to legislate alone with a requirement merely to consult the other institution. Where this is used in the labour law arena, it usually takes the form of a power for the Council to legislate alone. The degree to which the Parliament is involved depends on the Treaty provision in question. The use of the special legislative procedure tends to be a sign that the topic is particularly sensitive and therefore one over which the Member States wish to retain a greater degree of control.

The EU's legislative competence under Article 153 is to be exercised in accordance with the 'ordinary legislative procedure' laid down in the Treaty, with the exception of Article 153(1)(c), (d), (f) and (g), which require unanimous voting and the use of a 'special legislative procedure'. The Council has the power to apply the ordinary legislative procedure to

---

[10] See, for example, Case C–189/91 *Kirsammer-Hack v Sidal* [1993] ECR I 6185, [32]–[35].
[11] Case C–84/94 *UK v Council* [1996] ECR I–5755, [44].
[12] See Art 5(3) and (4) TEU and Protocol No 2 on subsidiarity and proportionality.
[13] See the discussion in Chapter 1.
[14] For example, A. Dashwood and others (2011), *Wyatt and Dashwood's European Union Law* (6th edn, Oxford: Hart), Chapter 4.

paragraphs (d), (f) and (g), provided that it agrees to do so unanimously. This set of provisions indicates the high degree of sensitivity surrounding social security under paragraph (c), which is further reflected in the provision in Article 153(4) that labour law directives 'shall not affect the right of Member States to define the fundamental principles of their social security systems and must not significantly affect the financial equilibrium thereof'.

Under Article 157, there is a power to adopt 'measures' to secure observance of the principle of equal treatment for men and women using the ordinary legislative procedure. But the broader anti-discrimination provision in Article 19 requires the Council to act unanimously 'after obtaining the consent of the European Parliament'. Article 46, on free movement of workers, invokes the ordinary legislative procedure but allows for the enactment of regulations as well as directives. As we have seen, most topics in EU labour law are dealt with only through directives, but regulations laying down uniform EU-wide rules are much more common in relation to the internal market.

Many of the EU's legislative powers require the consultation of particular committees before action is taken. This is true in the labour law field too. For example, the Economic and Social Committee must be consulted prior to action under Articles 46 and 157, and the Economic and Social Committee and the Committee of the Regions must be consulted prior to action under Article 153. But labour law has its own particular brand of consultation under Article 154. The Commission is responsible for promoting the 'social dialogue'. This term has various meanings but in general it denotes discussions between representatives of management and representatives of labour.[15] Under Article 154, the Commission is obliged to consult the social partners at two stages:

> 2. . . . before submitting proposals in the social policy field, the Commission shall consult management and labour on the possible direction of Union action.
> 3. If, after such consultation, the Commission considers Union action advisable, it shall consult management and labour on the content of the envisaged proposal. Management and labour shall forward to the Commission an opinion or, where appropriate, a recommendation.

---

[15]   On the employee side, the main organisation is ETUC (the European Trade Union Confederation), with participation from two professional and managerial bodies, CEC (the European Confederation of Executives and Managerial Staff) and Eurocadres. On the employer side, the main organisation is BUSINESSEUROPE (the Confederation of European Business, formerly UNICE), with the participation of CEEP (the European Centre of Employers and Enterprises Providing Public Services) and UEAPME (the European Association of Craft, Small and Medium Sized Enterprises). Further details are available at http://ec.europa.eu/social/main.jsp?catId=479&langId=en (last visited 4 July 2011).

As we shall see in the next section, the social partners may choose to negotiate on the matter with a view to reaching an agreement themselves, but for now it is important to note that they always get an opportunity to comment both on the topics the Commission intends to pursue and on the details of Commission proposals.

Although a directive proposed by the Commission will only become law if both the Council and the European Parliament agree, the focus in practice is usually on securing the agreement of the Member States in the Council. This was particularly true under earlier versions of the treaties, which required unanimity in the Council, because it was easy for one Member State acting alone to veto proposed legislation. Now that there is much greater use of qualified majority voting in the Council, this is less of a problem, but there is still a degree of 'horse trading' before agreement is reached.[16] For example, it was widely reported that the UK's agreement to the Directive on Temporary Agency Work was only secured when the Commission agreed to drop plans to reform the Working Time Directive.[17]

Social Dialogue

Article 155(1) TFEU provides that 'should management and labour so desire, the dialogue between them at Union level may lead to contractual relations, including agreements'. This process may be initiated during the consultations provided for in Article 154. The social dialogue at this level may operate in two slightly different ways: as an alternative procedure for the enactment of legislation, or as an alternative to legislation. We will consider each version in turn.

Article 155(2) sets out the possibility of using the social dialogue as an alternative legislative procedure. The social partners may, once they have concluded an agreement, ask for it to be implemented via the legislative process, provided that it relates to an area in which the EU has competence. This involves the Commission making a proposal to the Council, which implements the social partners' agreement by a decision, and informs the European Parliament.

This procedure initially resulted in three agreements which were enacted

---

[16] For discussion of some of the resulting problems, see G. Barrett, 'Deploying the Classic "Community Method" in the Social Policy Field: The Example of the Acquired Rights Directive' (2009) 15 ELJ 198.

[17] P. Wintour, 'Agency and temporary workers win rights deal', *The Guardian*, 21 May 2008.

as directives: on parental leave (1995),[18] part-time work (1997)[19] and fixed-term contracts (1999).[20] It then fell into a period of disuse. In 2008, for example, the social partners could not reach agreement on the commencement of negotiations on the proposed revision of the European Works Councils Directive by this means.[21] However, in 2009, the social partners successfully negotiated a revision of their earlier agreement on parental leave which has now been enacted as a directive.[22] This may signal a revival of interest in the legislative version of the social dialogue, though it should be borne in mind that there may be a significant difference between revising an existing agreement and reaching an entirely new one.

In theory, the social dialogue in this sense has many benefits: it allows those most concerned with labour law, management and trade unions, to participate in the legislative process, and it is reflexive, allowing them to adapt the law to their particular needs. However, it also has disadvantages. One problem is that the negotiations can be time-consuming. The Treaty limits them to nine months (unless the parties agree to an extension)[23] but even this may seem too long if an agreement looks unlikely.

Another, more profound, problem relates to incentives. Any negotiating process will only work if the parties have an incentive to reach an agreement. In the case of collective bargaining, this is provided by the threat of industrial action. But there has never been any attempt to treat the social dialogue as a form of large-scale collective bargaining backed by industrial threats, and indeed it is not clear that such threats would be lawful in all the Member States.[24] Instead, the bargaining process takes place in the shadow of what the Commission might propose and what might be agreed in the regular legislative procedure. The employers only have an incentive to agree if they are worried that the Commission might propose more radical measures. But the unions only have an incentive to agree if they think they can improve on the Commission's likely proposals. This makes

---

[18]   Council Directive 96/34/EC on the framework agreement on parental leave concluded by UNICE, CEEP and the ETUC, extended to the UK by Council Directive 97/75/EC.

[19]   Council Directive 97/81/EC of 15 December 1997 concerning the Framework Agreement on part-time work concluded by UNICE, CEEP and the ETUC, extended to the UK by Council Directive 98/23/EC.

[20]   Council Directive 1999/70/EC of 28 June 1999 concerning the Framework Agreement on Fixed-term Work concluded by ETUC, UNICE and CEEP.

[21]   For an account, see S. Laulom, 'The Flawed Revision of the European Works Council Directive' (2010) 39 ILJ 202, 203.

[22]   Council Directive 2010/18/EU of 8 March 2010 implementing the revised Framework Agreement on parental leave concluded by BUSINESSEUROPE, UEAPME, CEEP and ETUC.

[23]   Art 154(4) TFEU.

[24]   Such action would fall outside the definition of a 'trade dispute' in the UK, for example.

it hard to see when the parties' incentives might be aligned. Moreover, it highlights the fact that, whilst the social dialogue might appear to operate as an alternative to the standard legislative procedure, its outcomes are heavily dependent on what might happen via that route. The fact that any agreements have been reached at all is, at least in part, a reflection of a political desire on the part of the Commission and the social partners to show that – despite the design flaw – social dialogue is a procedure that can be made to work.

The other possibility is that the social dialogue might be used instead of legislation. The social partners might reach an agreement and might undertake to implement it themselves, through national social dialogue. Importantly, this form of social dialogue is not constrained by the EU's legislative competences as delineated in Article 153. It has resulted in three so-called 'autonomous' agreements: on telework (2002), stress (2004) and harassment (2007).[25] One obvious objection to this form of social dialogue is that the agreements might not be implemented effectively because no legal obligations attach to them. However, this may be a 'lawyer's view' of the problem and it is possible that the social partners are in fact better equipped to regulate their own affairs through negotiation prompted by European agreements. In practice, the success of this endeavour probably depends on the effectiveness of social dialogue at the national level. This varies considerably between the Member States.

In 2008, the Commission developed a procedure for sectoral social dialogue.[26] This allows the social partners in a particular sector – railways, telecommunications, entertainment and so on – to propose to the Commission that they should be allowed to set up a sectoral social dialogue committee.[27] These committees meet to discuss topics of concern and may produce agreements or recommendations for implementation by the national social partners. Because the parties have more in common and the issues are somewhat less complex, it is possible that better progress may be made at this level. The Commission's database of social dialogue texts reveals a sizeable output from the sectoral committees,[28] some of which has led to legislation, notably on working time in the transport sector.[29]

---

[25]   Available at http://ec.europa.eu/social/main.jsp?catId=521&langId=en (last visited 4 July 2011).

[26]   Commission Decision of 20 May 1998 on the establishment of Sectoral Dialogue Committees promoting the Dialogue between the social partners at European level (Decision 98/500/EC).

[27]   Ibid, Art 1.

[28]   Above n. 25.

[29]   See Chapter 7.

A degree of concern has been expressed in the literature about the legitimacy of the social dialogue.[30] The problem is that the social partners may not be representative of workers and employers across the EU as a whole. On the worker side, the problem is that in some Member States union density is very low, with the result that national trade union federations may not be representative of the workforce as a whole, thus casting doubt on the representativeness of the ETUC. On the employer side, various employers' associations participate in the social dialogue but it has proved difficult to obtain reliable figures about their membership at the national level. The concern about representativeness is exacerbated by the fact that, when a social dialogue agreement is enacted as law, the European Parliament does not participate in the legislative process. This means that there is no possibility of arguing that the Parliament's involvement makes up for any deficiencies in the representativeness of the social partners.

Of course, one response to this might be to argue, as Bercusson has done, that the concern with representativeness is misplaced.[31] He suggests that the social dialogue should be viewed in a labour law context rather than a constitutional one.[32] On this view, the social partners might be best placed to represent the interests of management and labour even should they not have majority support in numerical terms. Indeed, any investigation into their representativeness might be in danger of infringing the important labour law principle of autonomy in bargaining.[33] However, whilst this argument may be persuasive in relation to autonomous agreements between social partners, which remain in the labour law sphere, it may be harder to sustain in relation to those agreements which are enacted as legislation. Moreover, the idea that the Council and Commission should concern themselves with the representativeness of the social partners was affirmed by the Court of First Instance in the *UEAPME* case.[34] In that case, UEAPME, an organisation representing small and medium-sized enterprises, sought the annulment of the Parental Leave Directive on the grounds that the interests of small and medium-sized enterprises had not

---

[30] See, for example, A.C.L. Davies, 'Should the EU Have the Power to Set Minimum Standards for Collective Labour Rights in the Member States?' in P. Alston (ed.) (2005), *Labour Rights as Human Rights* (Oxford University Press), 178–82.

[31] B. Bercusson, 'Democratic Legitimacy and European Labour Law' (1999) 28 ILJ 153, 159–65.

[32] For further discussion of these competing conceptualisations see S. Smismans, 'The European Social Dialogue Between Constitutional and Labour Law' (2007) 32 EL Rev 341.

[33] A principle reflected in Art 152 TFEU.

[34] Case T–135/96 *UEAPME v Council* [1998] ECR II–2335, [88]–[89].

been fully represented by the other European employers' associations. The CFI upheld the principle that representativeness was required but found that it was satisfied in that case because the other employers' associations were sufficiently representative of small businesses.[35] UEAPME dropped its appeal against this decision when it was invited to participate in the social dialogue. Whilst the CFI's judgment does not engage in a particularly deep analysis of the representativeness of the social partners, it does at least indicate that concerns about their representativeness cannot be ignored completely.

Transposition

Although it is possible for the EU to enact regulations in the area of free movement of workers, most of the EU legislation we will come across later in this book takes the form of directives. As defined in the Treaty, directives set out the goals to be achieved but leave the Member States a discretion as to the 'form and methods' to be used.[36] In practical terms, the Member States must transpose each directive into national law by the relevant deadline. There are important debates in EU law generally about the direct effect of directives and about the possibility that they might have some impact on national law prior to the deadline for transposition. We will touch on some of these issues later in this book because some of the law has been developed in the employment context.[37] This section is concerned with two particular issues about the transposition of social policy directives: first, the role of the social partners, and second, the application of so-called 'non-regression' clauses.

Social partner involvement
We saw in Chapter 1 that it is possible to group the Member States' systems of labour law into broad categories. One of the features of Scandinavian systems is that they rely heavily on collective bargaining as a means of setting minimum standards. From this perspective, a requirement for Member States to implement directives through legislation would be particularly disruptive to national ways of doing things, because it would reduce the scope for collective bargaining.

After some initial hostility,[38] the Court of Justice recognised the

---

[35]   Ibid, [99].
[36]   Art 288 TFEU.
[37]   For example, Case C–144/04 *Mangold v Helm* [2005] ECR I–9981, discussed further in Chapter 5.
[38]   Case 91/81 *Commission v Italy* [1982] ECR 2133, [11].

possibility of implementing directives through collective bargaining. This can be illustrated by the case of *Commission v Denmark*.[39] The Danish government had implemented the Equal Pay Directive by means of a law that stated, 'every person who employs men and women to work at the same place of work must pay them the same salary for the same work under this law if he is not already required to do so pursuant to a collective agreement'. The Commission argued that this was insufficient because it did not lay down a requirement to give equal pay for work of equal value. The Court upheld this argument in relation to the minority of Danish workers not protected by collective agreements and therefore subject to the protection of this law.[40] However, at the same time, the Court recognised that the directive had been properly implemented for the majority of Danish workers who were protected by collective agreements, because the collective agreements included the equal value principle.[41]

The possibility of entrusting the implementation of directives to the representatives of management and labour became a standard term in directives themselves and, eventually, in the Treaty. It can now be found in Article 153(3), which states that it is possible for the Member States to entrust management and labour 'at their request' with the task of implementing a directive. But the Member State always remains responsible for ensuring compliance, for instance if management and labour cannot agree or if some workers are outside the scope of the relevant collective agreements:

> In this case, it shall ensure that, no later than the date on which a directive or a decision must be transposed or implemented, management and labour have introduced the necessary measures by agreement, the Member State concerned being required to take any necessary measure enabling it at any time to be in a position to guarantee the results imposed by that directive or that decision.[42]

This residual responsibility remaining with the Member State was, arguably, further emphasised in the *Laval* case.[43] The case concerned the determination of wage levels for so-called 'posted' workers (people who are sent by their employer from one Member State to another to do a job on a temporary basis).[44] Instead of setting a minimum wage through

---

[39] Case 143/83 *Commission v Denmark* [1985] ECR 427.
[40] Ibid, [11].
[41] Ibid, [7].
[42] Art 153(3) TFEU.
[43] Case C–341/05 *Laval v Svenska Byggnadsarbetareförbundet* [2007] ECR I–11767.
[44] Directive 96/71/EC.

legislation or through collective agreements applicable to all employers, Sweden had allowed unions to bargain over wages with particular employers at the workplace level. The Court indicated that this did not amount to proper implementation. This seemed to be because the Court thought that negotiations might go on for a long time without reaching an agreement (which had been the case in *Laval* itself). Whilst this is no surprise to anyone familiar with collective bargaining, it does not fit very well with the Member State's obligation to secure the directive's intended result (in this case, a clear minimum wage for posted workers). Like the debate about the representativeness of the social partners, *Laval* highlights the 'culture clash' when collective bargaining is employed for legislative purposes. We will consider the case in more detail in Chapter 3.

The wholesale transposition of a directive by collective agreement is not the only way in which national-level social partners can become involved in the implementation of directives. As we shall see in later chapters, some directives provide for the details of particular provisions to be worked out through collective bargaining or workplace negotiations.[45] For example, the Working Time Directive provides in Article 4 that:[46]

> Member States shall take the measures necessary to ensure that, where the working day is longer than six hours, every worker is entitled to a rest break, the details of which, including duration and the terms on which it is granted, shall be laid down in collective agreements or agreements between the two sides of industry or, failing that, by national legislation.

More radically, some directives provide for the possibility that collective agreements might derogate from the principles they lay down. This may be illustrated by Article 5 of the Temporary Agency Work Directive.[47] This sets out the principle of equal treatment for agency workers but states in Article 5(3) that:

> Member States may, after consulting the social partners, give them, at the appropriate level and subject to the conditions laid down by the Member States, the option of upholding or concluding collective agreements which, while respecting the overall protection of temporary agency workers, may establish arrangements concerning the working and employment conditions of temporary agency workers which may differ from those referred to in paragraph 1.

---

[45]   This was also true of the Posted Workers Directive in *Laval*, above, but the Swedish government had not followed the procedures set out in the Directive.

[46]   Directive 2003/88/EC.

[47]   Directive 2008/104/EC.

What are the advantages and disadvantages of allowing the social partners to negotiate on these matters? On one hand, from a reflexive regulation perspective, the advantage is that the social partners can find solutions that make sense to them, and can adapt the law to suit particular industries and types of work. This should increase compliance and avoid the problem that a 'one size fits all' approach might have unintended harmful consequences for some workers or workplaces.

The major disadvantage of social partner involvement is the possibility that the minimum standards envisaged in the relevant directive might not be achieved in practice, for example because powerful employers' associations are able to bargain for lower levels of protection. This is a particular risk in situations in which the social partners are permitted to derogate from the directive (like the agency work example given above). It is, however, arguable that this problem is exaggerated. If workers are given a particular right by law, they will be reluctant to relinquish it unless they are offered appropriate compensation. And if no such compensation is forthcoming, the worker representatives can simply refuse to agree. This will trigger the default arrangements in the directive. So if the worker representatives are not offered adequate compensation for the employer's proposed derogations from the equal treatment principle for agency workers, they should simply refuse to agree, which would result in the application of the principle. But whilst this may be sound in theory, there might be practical problems. One is that worker representatives may be ill-informed about their rights, and may not realise what they are giving up. Another is that they may face pressure from the employer to agree, even if it is not in their best interests to do so.

Non-regression clauses
We saw in Chapter 1 that directives are designed to achieve 'harmonisation' rather than the creation of a uniform labour code for the EU. This implies an acceptance that, even after the enactment of a directive, workers in different Member States may enjoy different types and – importantly – levels of protection. For practical political reasons, it is unlikely that the Member States will agree to raise standards to the highest level available in any Member State, though they are not obliged to fix on the 'lowest common denominator' either.[48] This gives rise to two questions for Member States with higher levels of worker protection than those found in the directive: can they, or must they, maintain those levels? The 'can' question is easy to answer. Directives generally make clear that

---

[48]   See *UK v Council*, above n. 11, [17].

they do not preclude Member States from adopting or maintaining higher levels of protection if they so wish. The 'must' question depends on the interpretation of the 'non-regression' clauses included in the majority of labour law directives.[49]

Let us begin with an example of a non-regression clause. In the social partner agreement annexed to the Directive on Fixed-Term Work, we find the following statement: 'implementation of this Agreement shall not constitute valid grounds for reducing the general level of protection afforded to workers in the field of the Agreement'.[50] At first sight, this seems straightforward: where a Member State has a higher level of protection than that required by the relevant directive, it should not use the implementation of the directive as an excuse for a reduction. However, recent litigation has cast doubt on this view.[51] Whilst most of this litigation has concerned the Directive on Fixed-Term Work, it seems likely that the Court would apply the same approach in other contexts.

One issue of contention in the case-law has been the proper scope of the non-regression clause. In relation to fixed-term work, for example, does the clause apply to the Member State's regulation of fixed-term work generally, or does it apply only to the specific issues addressed by the directive (discrimination against fixed-term workers and abuse of successive fixed-term contracts)? This was addressed in *Angelidaki*.[52] The Court of Justice took a broad view, holding that even though the alleged regression had taken place in relation to the employer's first use of a fixed-term contract (and therefore not a matter addressed by the Directive) the non-regression obligation still applied.[53] However, there are limits. In *Bulicke*, the Court held that there was no regression problem where Germany implemented a shorter limitation period for bringing age discrimination claims than the one that already existed for sex discrimination claims.[54] In part, this was because age and sex discrimination were regarded as different fields of law.[55]

---

[49]   For a list, see C. Kilpatrick, 'The European Court of Justice and Labour Law in 2009' (2010) 39 ILJ 287–99, 292–3.

[50]   Directive 1999/70/EC, Framework Agreement, cl 8(3).

[51]   For discussion, see L. Corazza, 'Hard Times for Hard Bans: Fixed-Term Work and So-Called Non-Regression Clauses in the Era of Flexicurity' (2011) 17 ELJ 385–402; Kilpatrick, above n. 49, 292–4.

[52]   Case C–378/07 *Angelidaki v Organismos Nomarchiakis Autodioikisis Rethymnis* [2009] ECR I–3071.

[53]   Ibid, [120].

[54]   Case C–246/09 *Bulicke v Deutsche Büro Service* [2010] nyr. Whether this implementation complied with the general requirements for equivalence and effectiveness was left to the national court to determine.

[55]   Ibid, [45].

What about the meaning of 'non-regression'? In *Angelidaki*, the Court rejected the idea that the non-regression clause required the Member State to keep all its existing law in place. Instead, it held that a change in national provisions would only be barred by a non-regression clause if two conditions were met.[56] First, the change must be linked to the implementation of the directive in question. If the Member State could show that the change is part of an entirely separate domestic policy initiative, the clause would not bite.[57] Second, the change must significantly reduce the overall level of protection for workers in the Member State in question.[58] This condition requires the national court to consider how many workers are adversely affected by the change and also to assess whether any reduction in protection is outweighed by increases in protection elsewhere. So, for example, it was relevant in *Angelidaki* that the change only affected a small group of public sector workers and that they benefited from other aspects of the new legislation.

Finally, there is an issue about the enforcement of non-regression clauses. If these had direct effect, individuals would be able to rely on them in the national courts to challenge their Member State's implementation of directives. However, in *Angelidaki* the Court confirmed that the non-regression clause in the Directive on Fixed-Term Work did not meet the conditions for direct effect.[59] Another possibility would be for the national court to tackle the problem using its interpretative powers, but this has been restricted by the decision in *Sorge*.[60] In that case, the national court tried to reinstate limits on the use of fixed-term work which had been repealed by the legislature, but the Court held that this went beyond what the duty of compatible interpretation permitted. Thus, even if an individual can establish a breach of the clause – which seems unlikely, for the reasons just given – it may be difficult to identify a means of enforcing it in national law.

More generally, it is important to note that the concept of 'non-regression' makes sense on the assumption that the labour laws enacted by the EU are always designed to enhance worker protection.[61] It is more difficult to apply in the context of the EU's recent focus on 'flexicurity'.[62] This may involve repealing some traditional forms of worker protection in

---

[56]   *Angelidaki*, above n. 52, [126].
[57]   *Mangold v Helm* , above n. 37, [51]–[3].
[58]   *Angelidaki*, above n. 52, [140]–[42]. For critique, see Kilpatrick, above n. 49, 294.
[59]   Ibid, [208]–[12].
[60]   Case C–98/09 *Sorge v Poste Italiane* [2010] ECR I–5837, [50]–[55]. For critique, see Corazza, above n. 51, 401.
[61]   Corazza, ibid, 401–2.
[62]   See Chapter 1.

order to enhance flexibility in national labour markets. Agency work is a case in point. In the past some Member States have regarded agency work as undesirable and have restricted its use, for example by requiring firms to justify the hiring of agency workers. The flexicurity agenda regards agency work as something to be encouraged because it might be a stepping-stone to a permanent job. So the Directive on Temporary Agency Work requires Member States to reconsider the restrictions they place on firms' use of agency workers.[63] The relationship between this new agenda and the concept of 'non-regression' needs to be thought through much more carefully.

THE ROLE OF THE COURT OF JUSTICE

Much of our focus in this book will be on the EU's labour legislation. But the task of providing an interpretation of that legislation falls to the Court of Justice. In this section, we will consider some of the salient features of the Court (with a particular focus on labour law cases) with a view to examining them in more detail in later chapters.[64]

A caveat is in order before we begin. It is natural for people from a common law background to regard the decisions of the Court of Justice as a source of law. But most Member States follow the civil law tradition, in which the role of the court is to seek the solution to the case at hand from a 'code' or legislation. The Court occupies something of a middle position: its decisions clearly have normative effects (as the doctrines of direct effect and supremacy illustrate) but it does not follow a strict system of precedent in which a body of 'law' is developed incrementally from case to case. It usually decides cases consistently, and sometimes explains that it has changed its mind, but concepts like 'following', 'distinguishing' and 'overruling' are generally out of place in analysing its case-law.

The Court's Jurisdiction

There are two main types of case in which a labour law issue might arise before the Court of Justice. One is where a national court refers questions of EU law to the Court for a preliminary ruling, and the other is where the Commission brings an action against a Member State for a failure

---

[63] Directive 2008/104/EC, Art 4.

[64] For an overview of the Court's role in EU law generally, see A. Stone Sweet, 'The European Court of Justice' in P.P. Craig and G. de Búrca (eds) (2011), *The Evolution of EU Law* (2nd edn, Oxford University Press).

to implement a directive properly. We will consider each type of case in turn.

The Court's jurisdiction to give preliminary rulings is laid down in Article 267 TFEU. This is a very important part of the Court's work generally and has played a crucial role in the development of EU labour law. It has been a key mechanism for individual litigants from the Member States to drive the development of EU law, and it has been the means of encouraging national courts to think of themselves as 'EU' courts.

According to Article 267, the Court has power to rule on 'the interpretation of the Treaties' and 'the validity and interpretation of acts of the institutions, bodies, offices or agencies of the Union'. It is relatively unusual for the Court to decline jurisdiction, though it may do so where the questions referred are hypothetical,[65] or where insufficient information is provided by the referring court.[66] A reference to the Court *may* be made by a national court that considers that a ruling on a matter of EU law is 'necessary to enable it to give judgment'.[67] Where a national court of last instance finds itself in this situation, it *must* make a reference to the Court of Justice.

In theory at least, the task of the Court of Justice is to give an interpretation of EU law in answer to the questions referred by the national court. It is the role of the national court to apply that ruling to the facts of the case. However, this is a difficult line to draw and it is not surprising to find that problems have arisen in practice. The proportionality test is a key example of this. It is the task of the national court to apply the proportionality test to the facts, but in some cases the Court of Justice may give so much detailed guidance that there is no real decision left for the national court to make. For example, difficult questions have arisen in equal pay law about whether or not it is legitimate for employers to take account of a person's length of service when determining his or her pay. This is a long-established feature of many employers' pay structures but it is arguable that it disadvantages women because they are more likely to take career breaks and thus find it more difficult than men to accrue long periods of service. In *Cadman*, the Court held that it is open to the employer to use length of service as a criterion without having to justify doing so, unless the claimant can cast doubt on whether the employer's use of the criterion genuinely rewards greater experience and better job performance.[68] If the claimant can do this, the burden shifts to the employer to prove that

---

[65]   Case 104/79 *Foglia v Novello* [1980] ECR 745.
[66]   Case C–320/90 *Telemarsicabruzzo v Circostel* [1993] ECR I–393.
[67]   Article 267 TFEU.
[68]   Case C–17/05 *Cadman v Health and Safety Executive* [2006] ECR I–9583, [33]–[40].

length of service is an appropriate criterion to use in the particular situation under scrutiny. Although this ruling did not determine the outcome of *Cadman* itself, it does show the Court engaging in quite a detailed attempt to specify how the national court should approach its task.

There are, of course, advantages and disadvantages to the Court's treatment of references for preliminary rulings.[69] On one hand, the more detail the Court gives, the more uniform the application of EU law should be throughout the Member States. On the other hand, the Court is already overwhelmed with cases, and by giving detailed guidance, it may simply be making the problem worse. National courts (even courts of last resort) need not make a reference to the Court when the applicable law is clear, either because the Court has already decided the point or because the answer is obvious (the *acte claire* doctrine).[70] If the Court simply provided general tests, this doctrine would apply in more cases. But if the Court provides detailed rulings specific to particular fact situations, national courts may feel that they cannot apply the ruling to the case before them even if the facts are only slightly different. This will prompt them to make further references. Sometimes, the Court itself will decline to hear a case in full if it thinks that the answer is already governed by previous case-law, but this does not happen very often.

The other main type of labour law case to come before the Court of Justice is an action under Article 258. These cases are brought by the Commission against Member States which are in breach of their obligations in EU law. As we shall see, in most of these cases the Member State concerned has failed to implement a directive into national law by the deadline for transposition. The Commission must first notify the Member State of its alleged default by means of a 'reasoned opinion'. The Member State is then given time to put the matter right. If this fails, the Commission may bring the matter before the Court. If the Member State is found to be in breach, it is given time to implement the Court's ruling. If the Member State continues to refuse to comply, the Commission may bring the matter back to the Court for the imposition of a financial penalty.[71]

The Article 258 mechanism is an important way for the EU to ensure that the Member States comply with their obligations. Nevertheless, there are many examples of the Member States either failing to implement EU law altogether or failing to do so correctly. This seems surprising given

---

[69] For discussion with a particular focus on labour law cases, see S. O'Leary (2002), *Employment Law at the European Court of Justice* (Oxford: Hart), especially Chapter 2.

[70] Case 283/81 *CILFIT v Ministry of Health* [1982] ECR 3415, [13]–[20].

[71] Article 260 TFEU.

that the Member States have usually agreed to the measures in the first place, and given that they expect compliance from each other. However, it can occur for a variety of reasons including simple inefficiency or short-term political gain at the domestic level. Because the Commission's enforcement resources are limited, it may take some time for breaches to be identified and tackled, and some less serious ones may never be pursued at all. Importantly, Article 258 is not the only mechanism for encouraging the Member States to comply with EU law. It may also be possible for individuals who are adversely affected by a Member State's breach to bring a *Francovich* action in which they can claim damages if certain conditions are met.[72] The prospect of financial liability to a large number of individuals under *Francovich* may in some cases act as more of a spur to bring the Member State into compliance than the threat of action by the Commission.

For our purposes, Article 258 actions are important because they are another way for labour law cases to come before the Court and they may generate useful interpretative guidance. For example, in *Commission v UK*, the UK government's implementation of the Acquired Rights and Collective Redundancies Directives was challenged.[73] These Directives required consultation with representatives of the workforce. The UK implemented them by requiring consultation with trade union representatives in workplaces where the employer recognised a trade union. This was consistent with long-established tradition in which collective consultation only took place through recognised trade unions. However, it meant that there was no possibility of consultation in workplaces where the employer did not recognise a trade union. The Court held that this amounted to a failure to implement the Directives because they required that consultation be available in all workplaces. This ruling had a profound effect on the UK's 'single channel' approach to workplace representation because it required the creation of mechanisms for consultation even in workplaces with no union presence.[74]

Of course, there are other aspects to the Court's jurisdiction and we will come across some of these from time to time. For example, it is possible for a Member State to challenge EU legislation on the grounds that it is outside the EU's competence. In *UK v Council*, the UK government challenged the Working Time Directive on the ground that it was not a health and safety measure and should not have been enacted under the health

---

[72]   C–6/90 *Francovich v Italian Republic* [1991] ECR I–5357.

[73]   Case C–382/92 *Commission v UK* [1994] ECR I–2435 (transfers); Case C–383/92 *Commission v UK* [1994] ECR I–2479 (collective redundancies).

[74]   For discussion, see P. Davies, 'A Challenge to Single Channel' (1994) 23 ILJ 272.

and safety provisions of the Treaty.[75] The Court rejected the claim because it adopted a broad definition of health and safety which focused on the worker's overall wellbeing, rather than the narrow 'avoiding accidents' version favoured by the UK. However, it did accept that a provision in the Directive indicating that Sunday should normally be a rest day did fall outside the EU's health and safety competence and should be struck down.

The Court's Approach

Readers will be able to form their own judgement on the Court's approach – at least in relation to EU labour law – by the end of the book, so our task for now is to highlight some points to watch out for.[76] A widely held view of the Court is that it is 'activist', in the sense of adopting an approach which favours European integration, and 'purposive' or 'teleological', in the sense of interpreting legislation in the light of its objectives. For the Court's advocates, these are good qualities which give it an important role in the EU architecture, but for its critics, they are signs of disrespect for the interests of the Member States and for the text of the treaties and legislation. We will explore some of these issues in this section.

One of the big debates in EU law as a whole relates to the role of the Member States in relation to the EU institutions. Should the institutions be regarded as the agents of the Member States, or do they have a life of their own? One of the reasons why the Court is controversial is that it is an institution that is hard for the Member States to control. Although the Member States have control over judicial appointments, the judges act independently. And through the procedure for giving preliminary rulings, the Court interacts with national courts in a way which bypasses national governments. Of course, it is theoretically possible for the Member States to overturn unpopular judicial decisions, but this does not happen very often and has not happened with some of the most controversial rulings, like those on supremacy or direct effect. Given the complexities of the legislative process, it is often difficult to secure agreement on changes and in many cases the Member States simply choose to codify rather than overturn the Court's rulings.

Since the Court has some freedom to pursue its own agenda, what might that agenda be? The Court is usually regarded as an engine for the development of EU law even when – or perhaps especially when – the Member

---

[75] Above n. 11.

[76] For a prescient discussion, see S. Simitis, 'Dismantling or Strengthening Labour Law: The Case of the European Court of Justice' (1996) 2 ELJ 156.

States are slow to act. Since the Court is not dominated by national interests, perhaps we should not be surprised that the obvious alternative – the promotion of European integration – has emerged as a big theme in many of its judgments.

The development of the law on equal pay can be viewed as a classic example of the Court's approach. Whilst the Member States were unable to agree on new developments in EU labour law, the Court took existing powers – such as then Article 119, on equal pay[77] – and developed an elaborate jurisprudence on the matter. Of course, it is important to stress that, like any court, the Court of Justice can only decide the cases that come before it. Nevertheless, the Court's bold moves in the early cases – notably the ruling in *Defrenne* that Article 119 had direct effect,[78] despite the fact that this required some stretching of the criteria for direct effect applied in earlier case-law[79] – opened the way for further litigation. This strategy of advancing the case-law beyond what the Member States might have agreed or expected is further illustrated by the *Danfoss* case.[80] In that case, the employer operated a system of bonuses that resulted in female employees' pay being, on average, less than that of male employees. But since the system of bonuses was not transparent, the female claimants could not point to a particular criterion that was operating to their disadvantage. The Court held that, in such situations, the burden of proof could be reversed, so that it was for the employer to rebut the *prima facie* case of discrimination. This was particularly significant because the Commission had been trying to secure agreement to a directive on the burden of proof, and only succeeded in doing so once the Court had achieved the same result in *Danfoss*.[81]

A second, and related, feature of the Court's decision making often highlighted by commentators is its 'purposive' approach to construction. Importantly, in the EU context this does not denote a search for the original purposes of the drafters of the Treaty article or piece of legislation in question. The *travaux préparatoires* of the treaties have never been made available and the Court has always treated EU law as a living instrument, to be adapted to modern conditions. 'Purposive' in the EU context means a search for the aims of the legislation in policy terms, and for the interpretation most likely to advance those aims. For example, in the equal

---

[77] Now Article 157 TFEU.

[78] Case 43/75 *Defrenne v Sabena* [1976] ECR 455, [18]–[24].

[79] Case 26/62 *van Gend en Loos* [1963] ECR 1.

[80] Case 109/88 *Handels- og Kontorfunktionærernes Forbund I Danmark v Dansk Arbejdsgiverforening (Danfoss)* [1989] ECR 3199, [10]–[16].

[81] Directive 97/80/EC, extended to the UK by Directive 98/52/EC. See C. Barnard (2006), *EC Employment Law* (3rd edn, Oxford University Press), 373–5.

pay context, the Court has adopted a broad construction of 'pay' which includes any form of remuneration received from the employer, including payments made after the employment relationship has come to an end.[82] This can be seen as a purposive construction in the sense that it takes the broad purpose of Article 119 – to eliminate pay differences between men and women – and treats the concept of 'pay', not as a restriction on what is covered, but as an opportunity to expand the areas in which inequalities can be eliminated. The *Barber* decision, extending the reach of Article 119 to occupational pension schemes, is the most striking example of this.[83]

However, it is important to be aware of the fact that the Court's decisions do not follow a linear path towards ever closer integration and ever more radical interpretations of the texts. In fact, it is much more common for the Court to advance and retreat, either in the same case or in a series of cases. Both *Barber* and *Defrenne* illustrate this more mixed approach within a single case. In both of these cases, the Court significantly advanced the understanding of the requirements of equal pay. But these 'advances' were coupled with a retreat: in both cases, the Court limited the temporal effect of its judgment because of the potential for damaging economic consequences.[84] In other words, although judgments normally apply retrospectively, because they state what the law has always been (even though this is often an obvious fiction), the Court ruled that these judgments would only take effect for the future.

There are also many examples of the Court advancing and retreating in successive cases. Perhaps the most obvious is the Court's approach to the direct effect of directives. The Court decided in *Van Duyn* that directives were capable of having direct effect if the relevant conditions were met,[85] but in *Marshall*, an employment case, restricted this to vertical direct effect against the state.[86] This ruling has cast a long shadow over the law in this area. Similarly, in the *Mangold* case, the Court gave effect to the Framework Directive's provisions on age discrimination prior to the expiry of the transposition period,[87] but refused to intervene in the dispute in *Bartsch* because the transposition period had not expired.[88]

---

[82] See, for example, Case 12/81 *Garland v British Rail Engineering* [1982] ECR 359, [4]–[11].

[83] Case C–262/88 *Barber v Guardian Royal Exchange Assurance Group* [1990] ECR I–1889.

[84] *Barber*, ibid, [40]–[45]; *Defrenne*, above n. 78, [69]–[75].

[85] Case 41/74 *Van Duyn v Home Office* [1974] ECR 1337.

[86] Case 152/84 *Marshall v Southampton and South-West Hampshire AHA* [1986] ECR 723, [48].

[87] Above n. 37.

[88] Case C–427/06 *Bartsch v Bosch und Siemens* [2008] ECR I–7245, [18].

Although the later case of *Kücükdeveci* has upheld several aspects of the *Mangold* ruling, doubt still remains about whether or not it matters that the Member State still has time to transpose the directive under consideration.[89]

Even when the Court does appear to be advancing the law with each decision, some caution may still be apparent. In the *Kalanke* case, the Court was asked to consider a positive action scheme which promoted women who were equally qualified to male competitors but where women were under-represented in the relevant job category.[90] The Court ruled that the scheme was unlawful. This decision was heavily criticised by advocates of positive discrimination. In *Marschall*, the Court considered a similar scheme but with one crucial difference: the promotion of the female candidate was not automatic and the male candidate was given the opportunity to say why he should be given the job instead.[91] The Court accepted this version of the scheme. Some commentators have regarded *Marschall* as, in effect, an overruling of the *Kalanke* decision, treating the subtle difference in the facts as an excuse for a change of heart (perhaps in response to the widespread criticism of *Kalanke* by the advocates of positive action).[92] But in later cases the Court has continued to reject schemes which are more radical than *Marschall*.[93] The Court has made it clear that *Marschall* is a limited concession and it will not go further despite repeated attempts to persuade it to do so.

Another important caveat is that the Court's purposive approach to interpretation and its pro-integration agenda may not always be as closely linked as they seem. A persistent problem with EU legislation is the need to achieve agreement on the part of (now) 27 Member States with their own agendas and their own legal systems. This can lead to a rather vague approach to drafting which conceals disagreements among the Member States. This style of drafting is even more apparent in some of the social partner agreements which have been enacted as Directives.[94] These might not be thought about in terms of 'legislative drafting' at all. For the Court, purposive interpretation may not always be about advancing the European project. Sometimes it is about trying to make sense of something that would otherwise be incomprehensible. Perhaps the best example

---

[89]   Case C–555/07 *Kücükdeveci v Swedex* [2010] ECR I–365.

[90]   Case C–450/93 *Kalanke v Freie Hansestadt Bremen* [1995] ECR I–3051, [22].

[91]   Case C–409/95 *Marschall v Land Nordrhein-Westfalen* [1997] ECR I–6363, [26]–[33].

[92]   See European Commission, *On the Interpretation of the Judgment of the Court of Justice on 17 October 1995 in Case C–450/93 Kalanke v Freie Hansestadt Bremen* (COM (96) 88 final).

[93]   Case C–407/98 *Abrahamsson v Fogelqvist* [2000] ECR I–5539.

[94]   See above nn. 18, 19, 20 and 22.

of this is the Acquired Rights Directive.[95] This Directive seeks to protect the rights of workers when the firm for which they are working is transferred to new owners. The central concept of a 'transfer' was not defined in the original directive, leaving the matter to the Court to determine. And matters were further complicated by the development of 'contracting out' in the public sector, in which public bodies hired contractors to deliver public services, thus giving rise to a new set of scenarios in which the Directive might or might not apply. Of course, applying legal concepts to the facts of cases is central to the judicial role, but in this instance it is the vagueness of the concept and the variety of the fact situations confronting the Court that created particular difficulties. The Member States did not agree on a revision of the Directive until the Court had battled with it for some 20 years.[96]

CO-ORDINATION OF THE MEMBER STATES' EMPLOYMENT POLICIES

It is tempting for lawyers to focus solely on the familiar territory of Title X of the Treaty – the development of EU labour law through the enactment and implementation of directives and their interpretation by the Court of Justice. But the EU has another mechanism for getting involved in employment issues: by influencing the Member States' employment policies.[97] This is set out in Title IX of the TFEU.[98] The overriding objective is laid down in Article 145:

> Member States and the Union shall, in accordance with this Title, work towards developing a coordinated strategy for employment and particularly for promoting a skilled, trained and adaptable workforce and labour markets responsive to economic change . . .

This reflects some themes that should be familiar from our discussion, in Chapter 1, of the current challenges facing EU labour markets and the EU's policy response to those challenges: improving employment levels, promoting 'flexicurity', increasing skill levels and so on.

---

[95] Originally Directive 77/187/EEC, Art 1. For discussion, see Barrett, above n.16, and O'Leary, above n. 69, Chapter 6.

[96] For further discussion, see Chapter 8.

[97] For an in-depth analysis up to 2005, see D. Ashiagbor (2005), *The European Employment Strategy* (Oxford University Press).

[98] This is a specific type of competence within Article 2(3) TFEU and falls outside the exclusive/shared/supporting framework for competences.

The process for achieving this involves the development of objectives for the Member States through what is most conveniently labelled the European Employment Strategy (EES), and monitoring their progress towards those objectives using the Open Method of Co-ordination (OMC). We will explain these concepts in this section. Although Title IX is not a legislative process, there are at least three reasons why EU labour lawyers should be interested in it. First, as discussed in Chapter 1, on a broad definition of the subject we should be concerned with any mechanism for the regulation of labour markets in the EU. Second, the process may complement, supplement or even challenge the existing body of EU labour law. And third, the process may encourage or require the Member States to make changes to national labour law in order to achieve the EES objectives. Later in this section we will examine the debate surrounding the effectiveness or otherwise of the Title IX approach.

Regulatory Technique

This section will explain what the employment OMC involves in procedural terms.[99] The details are laid down in Article 148 TFEU. The process is cyclical, so in some respects it is difficult to identify where it starts, but for convenience we will follow the pattern laid down in the Treaty.[100] It begins with the conclusions of the European Council:

> The European Council shall each year consider the employment situation in the Union and adopt conclusions thereon, on the basis of a joint annual report by the Council and the Commission.[101]

The Council, acting on a proposal from the Commission, 'shall each year draw up guidelines which the Member States shall take into account in their employment policies' based on the European Council's conclusions.[102] These guidelines must be developed after consultation with various bodies including the European Parliament and the Employment Committee. The latter is created in accordance with Article 150 with the specific remit of monitoring the Member States' co-ordination of their

---

[99]   There are OMCs in many other policy contexts, such as economic policy, healthcare and social inclusion, but it is important to be aware that, whilst the literature often talks generally about 'the OMC', it is in fact an umbrella term covering a diverse set of procedures. For a detailed analysis of the OMC technique in employment, see Ashiagbor, above n. 97, Chapter 5.

[100]   The schedule for the process is now referred to (bizarrely) as the 'European Semester'.

[101]   Article 148(1) TFEU.

[102]   Article 148(2) TFEU.

employment policies.[103] It is obliged to consult representatives of management and labour when carrying out its tasks.

The next stage in the process is the production of annual reports by the Member States:

> Each Member State shall provide the Council and the Commission with an annual report on the principal measures taken to implement its employment policy in the light of the guidelines for employment.[104]

These reports (originally known as National Action Plans (NAPs) and now referred to as National Reform Programmes (NRPs)) are commented on by the Employment Committee and examined by the Council. The Council has the power to 'make recommendations to Member States' acting on a recommendation from the Commission.[105] Of course, the Member States themselves have an input into the Council discussions so the process can be regarded as a form of self-regulation. This makes it unlikely that the 'recommendations' will contain any very strongly worded criticism of a Member State's approach, though any criticism at this high political level would be regarded by most Member States as something to be avoided.

The process concludes with a joint report from the Council and the Commission to the European Council 'on the employment situation in the Union and on the implementation of the guidelines for employment'.[106] This is also the beginning of a new cycle because it forms the basis for the European Council's conclusions, which are the starting-point for a new set of guidelines.

Alongside these procedures, the EU also has power to adopt positive measures to encourage the Member States in their pursuit of the agreed objectives:

> The European Parliament and the Council, acting in accordance with the ordinary legislative procedure and after consulting the Economic and Social Committee and the Committee of the Regions, may adopt incentive measures designed to encourage cooperation between Member States and to support their action in the field of employment through initiatives aimed at developing exchanges of information and best practices, providing comparative analysis and advice as well as promoting innovative approaches and evaluating experiences, in particular by recourse to pilot projects.[107]

---

[103] Council Decision of 24 January 2000 establishing the Employment Committee (Decision 2000/98/EC).
[104] Article 148(3) TFEU.
[105] Article 148(4) TFEU.
[106] Article 148(5) TFEU.
[107] Article 149 TFEU.

One manifestation of this is the PROGRESS programme.[108] The current version will run from 2007 to 2013, and has a budget of €743.25 million for that time period. The programme funds a variety of initiatives including the collection of statistics on employment issues, the development of networks of employment law experts, the support of NGOs that seek to tackle discrimination at work, and publicity campaigns about employment rights. Whilst these are all worthy endeavours and may well contribute to the achievement of the EU's employment goals, it is not clear how PROGRESS in practice constitutes a set of incentives for the Member States.

Content

As an annual process, the details of the EES vary from year to year. It is not practicable to examine every single variant. Instead, for convenience, we will consider the EES in four phases: the original Luxembourg process, the EES within the Lisbon Strategy, the 'Lisbon relaunch', and Europe 2020. We will focus particularly on Europe 2020 as the current policy context for the EES. But the history is useful because, without it, it would be hard to understand some of the criticisms of today's version of the EES.

The first three phases
The first phase of the EES is often referred to as the Luxembourg process. It began in 1998, in anticipation of the entry into force of its Treaty basis in the new Employment Title of the Treaty of Amsterdam in 1999. The guidelines addressed four areas or 'pillars': improving employability, developing entrepreneurship, encouraging adaptability and promoting equality of opportunity. Various guidelines were adopted under each heading. Most were expressed in vague terms, though a few quantifiable targets were also included. For example, the Member States were required to set a target for the proportion of unemployed people offered training (under the first pillar), but merely to consider the problems faced by people with disabilities (under the fourth pillar).

In 2000, the EU launched the Lisbon Strategy. This was designed to transform the EU economy into 'the most competitive and dynamic knowledge based economy in the world'.[109] The strategy focused on

---

[108]   Decision 1672/2006 of the European Parliament and the Council establishing a Community Programme for Employment and Social Solidarity – PROGRESS. See http://ec.europa.eu/social/main.jsp?catId=327&langId=en (last visited 13 June 2011).

[109]   Lisbon Presidency Conclusions, March 2000, para 5, cited in Barnard, above n. 81, 132.

macroeconomic policies and the promotion of innovation, alongside 'modernising the European social model'. As Barnard points out, it was never made clear what exactly was meant by the European social model, but for 'modernisation' purposes the focus was on four goals: 'education and training', 'more and better jobs',[110] 'modernising social protection' and 'promoting social inclusion'. At Lisbon, the Member States also agreed on an employment target, aiming for 70 per cent employment by 2010 (with 60 per cent for women). The Luxembourg process was absorbed into this broader development and was reshaped to fit its objectives. This occurred most obviously in 2003, when the four-pillar structure was replaced by three overarching objectives (full employment, productivity and social inclusion) to be pursued in accordance with ten guidelines. The guidelines included things like promoting gender equality, making work pay and promoting lifelong learning. The Commission's Social Policy Agenda, published in 2000, fleshed out some aspects of these developments as they applied to employment matters.

By 2005, the Lisbon Strategy had come in for widespread criticism. This led to a 'relaunch' in 2005. The Lisbon relaunch did not make any very significant changes to the *content* of the employment guidelines. The familiar themes of full employment, productivity and social inclusion remained very much in evidence. However, one significant change was that the employment guidelines were linked much more closely to a similar set of guidelines which had been developed elsewhere for economic policy. These are known as the 'broad economic policy guidelines' or BEPGs. The need for the BEPGs arose out of the creation of the euro as a common currency for most of the Member States. It was recognised that if one of the Eurozone countries got into economic difficulties, for example by allowing a large budget deficit to develop, the stability of the common currency might come under threat.[111] Given the relevance of economic policy to employment levels, and the economic focus of many of the employment guidelines, it was recognised that some co-ordination between the two processes would be desirable. Thus, the Lisbon 'relaunch' involved the creation of an 'integrated' set of guidelines covering both economic and employment policies.

---

[110] For an interesting discussion of job quality in the EES and its relationship to employment levels, see L. Davoine and others, 'Monitoring Quality in Work: European Employment Strategy Indicators and Beyond' (2008) 147 *International Labour Review* 163.

[111] The recent financial crisis has shown the importance of maintaining economic stability across all the Eurozone countries, whilst at the same time casting doubt on the ability of the BEPGs to achieve the desired result. At the time of writing, the EU is seeking to develop stronger procedures for economic policy co-ordination.

The current approach

The Lisbon Strategy was intended to guide the EU's development for the decade from 2000 to 2010. The successor initiative, 'Europe 2020', builds on Lisbon but also incorporates the EU's response to the global financial crisis and ensuing recession. It sets out five targets for the EU to achieve by 2020, in the areas of employment, innovation, climate change, education and social inclusion. The employment target is to have 75 per cent of those aged 20–64 years old in employment by 2020. The targets of improving participation in education and training, and reducing poverty, are also relevant to employment policy. The education targets contribute to the idea of the EU as a high-skill economy, and the achievement of the poverty reduction target is likely to depend heavily on increasing the overall level of employment.

The Commission document *An Agenda for New Skills and Jobs: A European Contribution Towards Full Employment* develops more specific policies for achieving the Europe 2020 targets in relation to employment. This forms the basis for the Member States' development of their own targets through the EES, so it is worth examining in some detail. The *Agenda* focuses on four priorities: 'better functioning labour markets', 'a more skilled workforce', 'better job quality and working conditions' and 'stronger policies to promote job creation and demand for labour'.

The first priority, 'better functioning labour markets', focuses primarily on reinvigorating the pursuit of flexicurity in the Member States' employment policies. The Commission claims that flexicurity policies have helped the Member States to weather the economic crisis, but that more needs to be done to address the fact that vulnerable groups (such as temporary workers) have suffered disproportionately during this time. The Commission suggests various mechanisms for doing this, including more targeted training and more flexibility in social security systems so that they provide greater support during downturns. From the perspective of labour law, there is a renewed emphasis on flexible contractual arrangements. This includes the suggestion of longer probation periods with gradually increasing employment rights as a means of reducing distinctions between temporary and permanent employees, and greater use of internal flexibility within firms, such as short-time working, to preserve jobs during the recession.

In terms of skills, the Commission identifies the problem as being the persistent gap between the jobs available and the skills required. In addition to various data-collection and publicity activities, the document focuses particularly on migration. It proposes a review of the mechanisms for recognising qualifications across the Member States, in order to enhance internal migration within the EU. And it proposes better integration of migrants from third countries, noting that they often end up in jobs well below their skill level.

On job quality, the Commission reiterates the familiar argument that there is no tension between job creation and job quality, since the EU is pursuing a high-skill, high-productivity agenda. But the content of its proposals here is of particular interest to EU labour lawyers. It proposes a review of the *acquis* of EU labour law:

> to clarify the implementation or interpretation of rules, and make them easier to understand and apply by citizens and businesses; to respond to the emergence of new risks for human health and safety in the workplace; and to cut red tape. More generally, the legislative 'acquis' must be kept in tune with new working patterns and technologies, so that it helps rather than hinder workplace adaptation.[112]

The document also suggests that legislation needs to be coupled with a framework of softer measures to improve levels of awareness and compliance.

On job creation, the focus is primarily on promoting innovation and on the development of self-employment and smaller businesses. However, there is also a suggestion that 'non-wage' labour costs should be reduced as a job-creation measure. For example, Member States might consider moving away from employment taxes (such as National Insurance in the UK) and replacing them with other ways of raising revenue such as taxes on polluters.

Evaluation

We are now in a position to consider some of the advantages and disadvantages of the co-ordination of the Member States' employment policies through the EES and the OMC. We will do this in two stages. In this section, we will assess some of the claims made about the benefits of this approach. These fall into three main groups: reflexivity, subsidiarity and participation. Whilst some of these claims are made about the OMC generally, we will focus our discussion on the employment context. In the next section, we will examine the relationship between the EES and the European Social Model, or the existing *acquis* of EU labour law.

The OMC is clearly designed as a 'reflexive' regulatory technique.[113]

---

[112]   Commission, *An Agenda for New Skills and Jobs: A European Contribution Towards Full Employment* (COM(2010) 682 final), 14.

[113]   See, for example, C. Barnard and S. Deakin, 'Market Access and Regulatory Competition', in C. Barnard and J. Scott (eds) (2002), *The Law of the Single European Market* (Oxford: Hart), 218–9.

Instead of requiring the Member States to legislate in particular ways, they are given targets to achieve and the freedom to determine how best to achieve them. The reflexive approach has particular attractions in the area of employment policy. This is because the targets in question generally involve tackling highly complex problems and no-one knows how best to go about this. For example, there is no single 'right' answer to the question 'how should a state reduce the level of unemployment?' This makes it more difficult to agree on an EU-wide strategy. Of course, the Member States are likely to try different ways of tackling unemployment anyway, so the real strength of the EU's involvement through the OMC is that it provides a forum in which the Member States can compare approaches and learn what works best.

A key question here is whether the EES does in fact encourage the Member States to reconsider their policy choices. The choices national governments make are determined by a variety of complex factors, and it is important to question the idea that they approach the EES with an entirely open mind. Even if a Member State changes a particular policy, it often cannot be said with any certainty whether this resulted from discussions in the OMC, or from a shift in domestic public opinion, or a change of government, or some other cause.

An interesting study by Skidmore of the operation of the EES in Germany reveals some of the problems.[114] He focused on the EES target of increasing labour market participation among disadvantaged groups and, in particular, older workers. He found that the German National Action Plan did not even mention all of the German policies applicable to older workers at the relevant time. Some of the policies that were included were presented as incentives for workers to enter the labour market when they could also be interpreted as disincentives. These findings paint a rather bleak picture of the impact of the EES on national policy-making, suggesting that it might be more of a form-filling exercise than a genuine engagement with the policy issues at hand. However, in a study of policies to tackle unemployment in the Netherlands and the UK, Ashiagbor found a degree of enthusiasm for the EES among national governments, largely because they were already keen on the flexicurity policies being promoted at EU level.[115]

Another claim made by proponents of the EES is that it respects subsidiarity to a greater extent than the traditional legislative approach. Although directives give Member States some discretion in their imple-

---

[114]   P. Skidmore, 'The European Employment Strategy and Labour Law: a German Case Study' (2004) 29 EL Rev 52.
[115]   Ashiagbor, above n. 97, Chapter 6.

mentation, they are in practice quite specific in many cases. The policy goals of the EES are much more general, leaving the Member States more freedom to innovate. For the advocates of subsidiarity, this is seen as a good thing in itself. And it also forms an important part of the 'policy learning' agenda: if the Member States are all doing the same thing, there will be no opportunity to learn.

Again, however, there is controversy surrounding the achievement of subsidiarity through the EES. As we saw in Chapter 1, European welfare states and employment law systems can be grouped into different models. Some commentators have identified a bias in the Commission's assessments in favour of certain types of model. For example, Raveaud argues that Denmark and Sweden have fared badly in the process.[116] These systems have been criticised for their high tax levels and generous welfare provision, but Raveaud points out that they also have high levels of employment and good-quality jobs. His concern is that the focus on one or two aspects of a particular state's welfare model may undermine the logic of the model as a whole. In contrast, de la Porte rejects the idea that the Commission has any hostility towards different models, noting that, while the EES might require greater changes in Southern and corporatist welfare state models, the attempt to co-ordinate the Member States' policies on social inclusion (another OMC process) poses more of a challenge to the Southern and Anglo-Saxon models.[117]

Finally, the OMC is often hailed as a way of promoting transparency and participation in EU policy making, because it offers the prospect of policy makers engaging with civil society groups. In the labour law field, this advantage is less of an issue than it is in other fields, given the possibility of social partner consultation in the Community method or the use of social dialogue. But even in labour law, some people would argue that it is helpful to consult with a broader range of groups than just trade unions and employers' associations. Nevertheless, Szyszczak questions whether the EES has brought about any real engagement beyond the social partners and, perhaps more importantly, whether consultation with the social partners is sufficiently meaningful.[118]

Whilst most commentators would agree that civil society participation is a good thing, the democratic legitimacy of the EES and other

---

[116] G. Raveaud, 'The European Employment Strategy: Towards More and Better Jobs?' (2007) 45 *Journal of Common Market Studies* 411.

[117] C. de la Porte, 'Is the Open Method of Coordination Appropriate for Organising Activities at European Level in Sensitive Policy Areas?' (2002) 8 ELJ 38.

[118] E. Szyszczak, 'Experimental Governance: The Open Method of Coordination' (2006) 12 ELJ 486.

OMC initiatives remains problematic. There is no role for the European Parliament in these processes. Moreover, the EES might create some tension for national governments. If it were to operate as intended, national governments would be expected to reconsider their policy choices in the light of lessons learned from other Member States, but this might sometimes be difficult to reconcile with accountability to their national electorates for policy promises made during an election campaign, for example.[119]

The EES and the ESM

A particular area of controversy in the literature is the relationship between the EES and the European Social Model, both in the sense of the Member States' own social policies (to be co-ordinated through the EES) and in the sense of the existing *acquis* of EU labour law. There are various possible ways of thinking about this, and they depend not just on your view of the EES but also on your view of the traditional legislative method. It is worth noting that the debate is sometimes framed in the literature as a choice between 'hard' law (directives) and 'soft' law (the EES). But this is not particularly helpful because 'softness' and 'hardness' are difficult to pin down (directives have softer elements, for example, and allegedly 'soft' measures may seem obligatory to the Member States), so we will try to avoid this terminology.[120]

Some commentators are positive about the EES, regarding it as a complement to legislation through directives. From a reflexive regulation perspective, it can be argued that (to take gender equality as an example) simply requiring the Member States to outlaw discrimination has not achieved very much, whereas encouraging them to improve women's participation in the labour market might generate more creative solutions, such as better access to training and childcare.

Others have expressed concern that the EES might threaten the existing body of labour law (either in the Member States or at EU level). The concern is that the focus on improving the competitiveness of the EU economy might put pressure on the Member States to deregulate their

---

[119]   A. Benz, 'Accountable Multilevel Governance by the Open Method of Coordination?' (2007) 13 ELJ 505.

[120]   For discussion, see K. Armstrong and C. Kilpatrick, 'Governance, or New Governance – The Changing Open Method of Coordination' (2006–7) 13 *Columbia Journal of European Law* 649; D.M. Trubek and L.G. Trubek, 'Hard and Soft Law in the Construction of Social Europe: the Role of the Open Method of Co-ordination' (2005) 11 ELJ 343.

labour markets.[121] As we saw in Chapter 1, the EU's adoption of the policy of 'flexicurity' is designed to reconcile competiveness with the EU's traditional emphasis on worker protection, but the concern is that the EES might involve a strong push towards flexibility at the expense of the security represented by EU and national labour laws.

Commentators who take this view have focused in particular on two main features of the EES in its current form. First, whilst the theme of social inclusion has been a constant throughout the EES, its meaning appears to have shifted quite significantly in the Europe 2020 priorities. There is much more of a focus on reducing poverty and improving the integration of migrant workers. This seems to have taken the place of the traditional EU version of social inclusion which linked it closely to equality law and the integration of women and, more recently, disabled people, into the workplace. Of course, there are important overlaps between poverty reduction and improving participation of disadvantaged groups, and improving employment opportunities for women is mentioned at various points in the Europe 2020 documentation. But for some commentators, there is a worry that the EES is no longer being used to reinforce the EU's existing body of equality law. Second, there will be a review of the *acquis* of EU labour law as part of the Europe 2020 agenda. This adds to the growing concern among the advocates of EU labour law that concepts like flexicurity pose a threat to the ESM. The fear is that measures traditionally regarded as forms of worker protection may be redefined as impediments to labour market flexibility and therefore dismantled. This is already becoming apparent to some extent in the debate around atypical work and regression, discussed above.

A final school of thought regards the EES with a degree of resignation. It is becoming increasingly difficult to persuade the Member States to agree to new directives or to enhanced versions of old directives.[122] This can be illustrated by the difficulties surrounding the Directive on Temporary Agency Work and the review of the Working Time Directive, both of which we will examine in detail in later chapters. On this view, if there is to be any focus on worker protection at all in the EU, it is likely to occur through the EES rather than through legislation. But this does not mean that we should accept the EES uncritically. Our aim should therefore be to look for ways of improving the EES. One interesting suggestion is to subject the EES to the Court of Justice's jurisdiction on fundamental

---

[121] See, for example, D. Ashiagbor, 'EMU and the Shift in the European Labour Law Agenda: From "Social Policy" to "Employment Policy"' (2001) 7 ELJ 311.

[122] M. Weiss, 'European Labour Law in Transition from 1985 to 2010' (2010) 26 *International Journal of Comparative Labour Law and Industrial Relations* 3.

rights.[123] The EES appears to be unreviewable at the moment, though it might be argued that fundamental rights are so important that the Court's jurisdiction on the matter can never be excluded. Although the Court's approach to labour rights has been criticised, this might offer some constraints on the deregulatory tendencies of the EES. It could be used to lay down a 'floor of rights' which could not be challenged by the EES.

A Concluding Thought

We saw in Chapter 1 that debates about EU labour law are often framed in economic terms, using ideas such as the 'race to the top' or the 'race to the bottom'. The ESM exists in a perpetual state of tension with the EU's economic agenda. One of the more optimistic views of the OMC was that it might provide a new way of reconciling the EU's economic and social policy goals.[124] But this is precluded by the Treaty structure itself. There is a clear hierarchy in the Treaty in which the BEPGs (the economic policy guidelines the Member States must follow) are superior to the employment guidelines.[125] This suggests that if a Member State's economy was in difficulties, it would be possible to require it to reduce the level of social protection it provided to its citizens. Thus, the EES has one very important thing in common with the traditional body of EU labour law.

FURTHER READING

As we have seen, one of the distinctive features of EU labour law is the role played by the social partners. For more detail on this, see B. Bercusson (2009), *European Labour Law* (2nd edn, Cambridge University Press), Chapters 17–19. We will examine implementation of directives by the social partners in Chapters 3 and 7. It is also possible to build links between the social dialogue discussed in this chapter and EU law on worker participation, to be discussed in Chapter 8, and to think in terms of an EU law on 'collective bargaining', broadly conceived. For an example, see B. Bercusson, 'The Collective Labour Law of the European Union' (1995) 1

---

[123]   G. de Búrca, 'The Constitutional Challenge of New Governance in the European Union' (2003) 28 EL Rev 814, 833–6; S. Smismans, 'How to be Fundamental with Soft Procedures? The Open Method of Co-Ordination and Fundamental Social Rights' in G. de Búrca and B. de Witte (eds) (2005), *Social Rights in Europe* (Oxford University Press).

[124]   See, for example, O. de Schutter, 'The Democratic Experimentalist Approach to Governance: Protecting Social Rights in the EU', in de Schutter and Lenoble, above n. 1.

[125]   Article 146(1) TFEU. See M. Dawson, The Ambiguity of Social Europe in the Open Method of Coordination' (2009) 34 EL Rev 55; de Búrca, above n. 123, 831–2.

ELJ 157. Nevertheless, it is important to note that EU law also *regulates* collective bargaining through, for example, equality law: see, for example, Case C–127/92 *Enderby v Frenchay Health Authority* [1993] ECR I–5535 and Case C–447/09 *Prigge v Deutsche Lufthansa AG* [2011] nyr, [47]–[8].

On the role of the Court of Justice, S. O'Leary (2002), *Employment Law at the European Court of Justice* (Oxford: Hart) remains a useful study because it highlights the constraints within which the Court operates and the difficulties surrounding its relationship with national courts. More recent debates about the Court's role have tended to focus on the controversial rulings in *Viking* and *Laval*, to be discussed in Chapter 3, in which the Court was called upon to determine the relationship between the right to strike and the rules of the EU internal market.

There is a large literature on the EES and the OMC. For a succinct account, see G. de Búrca, 'The Constitutional Challenge of New Governance in the European Union' (2003) 28 EL Rev 814, and for an in-depth study, see D. Ashiagbor (2005), *The European Employment Strategy* (Oxford University Press). On Europe 2020, it is worth looking at Commission, *An Agenda for New Skills and Jobs: A European Contribution Towards Full Employment* (COM(2010) 682 final) for detail on the targets and proposals themselves, and for an interesting recent analysis (which builds links to the role of the Court and the *Viking* and *Laval* debate) see M. Dawson, 'Three Waves of New Governance in the European Union' (2011) 36 EL Rev 208.

PART 2

Topics in EU labour law

3. Worker migration and market integration

The founding purpose of the EU was the creation of a common market in which barriers to trade between Member States were progressively removed. Firms would be able to market their goods and services in any Member State, thereby enhancing competition and giving consumers access to lower-priced products. An elaborate body of legislation and case-law on 'free movement' has developed in the process.

Free movement has significant implications for working people. Workers have a right to move freely from one Member State to another in order to take up a job offer or to seek work. Self-employed individuals have similar rights under the rules governing freedom of establishment, which allow people to move from one Member State to another in order to set up a business.[1] But a 'free market' for labour within the EU cannot simply be established by removing barriers to migration. Since (as the ILO has long acknowledged) workers are not a 'commodity',[2] they may be unwilling to move unless their broader concerns are addressed. For example, they may want to be able to travel with their families or to put down roots in the host state. An elaborate body of rules has developed to address these issues. We will consider these rules in the first part of this chapter. Of course, all of this takes us a long way away from traditional understandings of labour law as the law governing relationships between workers and their employers. However, as we saw in Chapter 1, EU labour law can be conceived of in broader terms, as the law governing the labour market. From that perspective, the free movement rules are central to the creation of a labour market which crosses national boundaries.

In the second part of this chapter, we will explore the interactions between freedom to provide services and freedom of establishment on the one hand, and national labour law on the other hand. At first sight, these bodies of law may not appear to have much relevance to labour law.

---

[1] Throughout this chapter we will follow the common practice of using the term 'home' state to refer to the country from which the worker or firm comes, and 'host' state to denote the country to which the worker or firm is seeking to move.
[2] ILO, Declaration of Philadelphia, 1944.

But a firm which wants to provide services in another Member State may well find it cheaper and more convenient to 'post' its own workforce to that Member State for the purpose. This gives rise to a question of applicable law: should the relationship between 'posted' workers and their employer be governed by the home state's law or the host state's law? The firm might prefer home state law, because this is familiar and may give a competitive advantage over host state terms and conditions. But the host state may not want people working in its labour market who are not subject to its labour legislation, for fear that its own workers might be undercut. This has given rise to some difficult questions for the Court of Justice about the relationship between national labour law and the rules of the market.

In the third part of the chapter, we will consider a relatively new area of EU law which intersects in important ways with the free movement rules just discussed: immigration. Traditionally, the EU's competence has been confined to the movement around the EU of workers who were already citizens of one of the Member States. National governments have maintained control over who can enter their territory from outside the EU. However, in recent years, there has been growing EU involvement in immigration issues. This raises important questions about the future shape of the EU labour market as envisioned by the Europe 2020 strategy.

This chapter will provide an opportunity to explore two of the bigger themes identified in Part 1: the 'race to the bottom' and 'race to the top' arguments. On one hand, it can be argued that opening up the internal market – for workers as well as for goods and services – is about increasing wealth in the EU economy as a whole. Workers can be matched with jobs and overall prosperity will increase. On the other hand, there is a worry that workers in Member States with higher labour costs may be undercut by workers from Member States with lower labour costs (or even workers from outside the EU). As we shall see, this debate is very much a live one in today's EU.

FREE MOVEMENT FOR WORKERS AND CITIZENS

This section will focus on the body of law governing the free movement of workers. It will readily be apparent that the law extends beyond simply removing barriers to free movement. It also includes extensive facilitative rules designed to make migration more attractive. It will also be seen that the Member States have, in various ways, sought to maintain some degree of control over migration, even within the EU, and that the Court of Justice has played an important role in limiting this. Finally, this section will explore some of the ways in which the traditional focus on 'worker' status is now being replaced by an emphasis on EU citizenship.

Central Themes

There are strong (though relatively unexplored) links between migration and labour market issues. In times of strong demand for labour, governments tend to encourage economic migrants; in times of high unemployment, governments tend to limit who can access national labour markets. The creation of the internal market in the EU has removed this form of control from national governments, at least as regards migrants from other EU Member States. So why did governments agree to this?

In theory, opening up the EU labour market should lead to an efficient allocation of labour, because it enables workers to travel to where the jobs are. Free movement of workers should prevent the situation in which there is high unemployment in one Member State and demand for labour in another. It should also even out disparities in wages between different Member States. An oversupply of labour would normally drive wages down, and a labour shortage would normally drive wages up. But if those supply problems can be corrected by labour migration, wages should even out across the EU labour market as a whole. And with more people in work, prosperity should increase. On this view, everyone benefits from free movement for workers.

Of course, the reality on the ground may differ somewhat from the theory. One problem is that, because of wide variations in wage levels across the EU,[3] some countries are likely to be 'exporters' of labour while other countries are likely to be 'importers', as workers from low-wage countries seek better rewards elsewhere in the EU. This may give rise to worries in 'importing' states about the potential for migrant workers to undercut local labour. Even though this fits with the economic theory described above, it is unlikely to be popular with national electorates, so politicians may find themselves under pressure to restrict migration. One of the most obvious examples of this was the use of transitional arrangements to control migration during the process of EU enlargement.[4] When

---

[3] For example, according to Eurostat the average gross annual wage in 2007 (the most recent year for which data are available) ranges from over €50 000 per annum in Denmark to less than €5000 per annum in Bulgaria and Romania.

[4] See the Annexes to the Treaty of Accession 2003, and the Treaty of Accession of Bulgaria and Romania 2005. For discussion see A. Adinolfi, 'Free Movement and Access to Work of Citizens of the New Member States' (2005) 42 CMLR 469. Such arrangements are narrowly construed: for a recent example see Case C–546/07 *Commission v Germany* [2010] ECR I–439.

a Member State joins the EU, its workers become EU citizens with free movement rights instead of foreign nationals subject to national immigration laws. Some Member States refused to grant immediate access to their labour markets when new Member States joined because they feared an influx of migrant workers. More generally, we shall see that the Member States have struggled to agree to the removal of particular barriers to migration (particularly in the area of recognising qualifications gained in other Member States) so the Court of Justice has played an important role in tackling barriers through the case-law.

Another gap between theory and reality is that labour markets are more complex than the theory predicts, so there are lots of reasons why there might still be a mismatch between jobs and workers even within an open EU labour market. For example, the available workers may not be qualified for the available jobs, or they may not know about them or, particularly in the EU context, they may not have the language skills required to work in the country in question. This suggests that there are lots of disincentives to migration within the EU, even if barriers to free movement are removed. EU free movement policy has therefore sought to facilitate migration in a variety of different ways. These have included giving people access to other countries to look for work, not just to take up a job, allowing them to travel with their families, and giving them rights to stay in the host country even if their job comes to an end. Again, these measures have proved controversial with the Member States (particularly where they involve access to social security benefits) and the Court has played an important role in developing them.

A further issue to look out for in the discussion below is the 'constitutionalisation' theme highlighted in Chapter 1. The EU's early initiatives on free movement focused on workers: on enabling *economically active* people to move around the EU. In recent years, thanks to changes to the Treaty and the Court's developing case-law, there is more of a focus on rights attaching to citizens of the EU, regardless of their worker or work-seeker status. The emergence of the concept of citizenship can be seen as part of the development of the EU from an economic entity to one with a broader political and social agenda.

The Legal Framework

The basic right to free movement for workers is contained in Article 45 TFEU:

1. Freedom of movement for workers shall be secured within the Union.
2. Such freedom of movement shall entail the abolition of any discrimination

based on nationality between workers of the Member States as regards employment, remuneration and other conditions of work and employment.
3. It shall entail the right, subject to limitations justified on grounds of public policy, public security or public health:
    (a) to accept offers of employment actually made;
    (b) to move freely within the territory of Member States for this purpose;
    (c) to stay in a Member State for the purpose of employment in accordance with the provisions governing the employment of nationals of that State laid down by law, regulation or administrative action;
    (d) to remain in the territory of a Member State after having been employed in that State, subject to conditions which shall be embodied in regulations to be drawn up by the Commission.
4. The provisions of this Article shall not apply to employment in the public service.

Importantly, Article 45 does not apply to purely 'internal' situations: there must be a cross-border element to the individual's claim.[5] This normally arises in three main ways: when the individual moves to another Member State to look for work or to take up employment; when the individual lives in one Member State but works in another (a 'frontier' worker); and when the individual returns to his or her home state after a period working elsewhere in the EU. Article 45 has direct effect, so it can be invoked by an individual (or his or her employer) against the state.[6] It can also be invoked against non-public bodies where they regulate access to employment (like sports governing bodies or professional associations)[7] and horizontally against employers,[8] at least where they engage in obvious acts of discrimination against workers from other Member States.

The concept of EU citizenship is enshrined in Article 20 TFEU. EU citizenship is derived from national citizenship, in the sense that every citizen of a Member State is also a citizen of the EU.[9] Citizenship entails various political rights (set out in Articles 22–4) but, for our purposes, its most important features are the right not to be discriminated against on grounds of nationality,[10] and 'the right to move and reside freely within the territory of the Member States'.[11] After some initial uncertainty, the

---

[5] See, for example, Case 35/82 *Morson v Netherlands* [1982] ECR 3723. The position may be different in relation to citizenship, discussed below.

[6] Case 41–74 *Van Duyn v Home Office* [1974] ECR 1337.

[7] Case C– 415/93 *Union Royale Belge des Sociétés de Football Association ASBL v Jean-Marc Bosman* [1995] ECR I–4921.

[8] Case C–281/98 *Angonese v Cassa di Risparmio di Bolzano* [2000] ECR I–4139.

[9] Art 20(1) TFEU.

[10] Art 18 TFEU.

[11] Art 21 TFEU.

Court has confirmed that citizens can derive movement and residence rights directly from Article 21.[12] Like Article 45, the citizenship provisions might be thought not to apply to purely internal situations with no cross-border element, but some recent cases have suggested that Article 20 might be relevant even where the individual is claiming against the home state and has no plausible intention of moving.[13] This is highly controversial and the case-law here seems to be in a state of flux.

Thus, an individual might derive a right to move from one Member State to another either from Article 45, as a worker or work-seeker, or from Article 21, as a citizen. Article 21 grants the right to move 'subject to the limitations and conditions laid down in the Treaties and by the measures adopted to give them effect'. In theory, the relationship between the two provisions is clear: Article 45 grants better rights to people who can prove that they are workers, with all EU nationals able to derive some more basic rights from their status as citizens. In practice, the boundaries are somewhat blurred because the Court has interpreted 'worker' quite broadly and is also in the process of developing better rights for citizens, as the discussion below will demonstrate.[14]

Further detail is provided in the Citizens' Rights Directive (hereafter 'CRD').[15] This Directive was intended to codify the Court's case-law and to consolidate previous legislation (with some amendments) into a single point of reference for EU citizens, whether they are economically active (as workers or self-employed people) or not. As we shall see, however, since many of the rights found in the Directive are derived from the Treaty itself, the Court is not necessarily constrained by the Directive in interpreting them.[16] We will also examine some provisions of Regulation 492/2011, which governs workers' right to equal treatment in the employment sphere.

---

[12]   Case C–413/99 *Baumbast v Secretary of State for the Home Department* [2002] ECR I–7091, [80]–[94].

[13]   Case C–34/09 *Ruiz Zambrano v ONEm* [2011] nyr, [36]–[45] (for discussion see the casenote by K. Hailbronner and D. Thym (2011) 48 CMLR 1253), but cf Case C–434/09 *McCarthy v Secretary of State for the Home Department* [2011] nyr and Case C–256/11 *Dereci and Others v Bundesministerium für Inneres* [2011] nyr.

[14]   For a discussion of the developing law on citizenship, which is an important topic of enquiry in its own right, see H. de Waele, 'EU Citizenship: Revisiting its Meaning, Place and Potential' (2010) 12 *European Journal of Migration and Law* 319; M. Wind, 'Post-National Citizenship in Europe: The EU as a Welfare Rights Generator' (2009) 15 *Columbia Journal of European Law* 239.

[15]   Directive 2004/38/EC.

[16]   For an interesting discussion of the Court's approach, see K.E. Sorensen, 'Reconciling Secondary Legislation with the Treaty Rights of Free Movement' (2011) 36 EL Rev 339.

Who is Protected?

In this section, we will consider the definition of 'worker' – since the rights of economically active people are central to our concerns – and the definition of 'family member' – since EU law extends rights to workers' families too.

Workers

The use of the term 'worker' in Article 45 is liable to set alarm bells ringing for labour lawyers, given the problems associated with this concept in domestic law in particular. But these problems are much less acute in the free movement context, for three reasons. First, particularly prior to the introduction of citizenship as a concept in EU law, the Court interpreted worker very broadly in order to protect as many people as possible. Second, if an individual is not economically active, he or she may be able to fall back on citizenship rights. And third, if a person is economically active but not technically a worker (for example, because he or she is self-employed), that person will generally be covered by other aspects of the free movement regime.

In the context of Article 45, the Court has defined 'worker' in the following terms: 'the essential feature of an employment relationship . . . is that for a certain period of time a person performs services for and under the direction of another person in return for which he receives remuneration'.[17] It is clear from *Levin* that the work need not be full-time, nor is it a requirement that the individual should obtain any particular level of income from the work.[18] However, in the same case, the Court stated that the free movement rules applied 'only [to] the pursuit of effective and genuine activities, to the exclusion of activities on such a small scale as to be regarded as purely marginal and ancillary'.[19] On this basis, an individual performing work as part of a therapeutic programme for recovering drug addicts was held not to be a worker for the purposes of Article 45.[20] However, the Court has also made it clear that there is no place for an argument that the individual has taken a short-term job in

---

[17] Case 66/85 *Lawrie-Blum v Land Baden-Württemberg* [1986] ECR 2121, [17]. For a critique of the Court's approach to the definition, see C. O'Brien, 'Social Blind Spots and Monocular Policy Making: The ECJ's Migrant Worker Model' (2009) 46 CMLR 1107.

[18] Case 53/81 *Levin v Staatssecretaris van Justitie* [1982] ECR 1035, [16].

[19] Ibid, [17].

[20] Case 344/87 *Bettray v Staatssecretaris van Justitie* [1989] ECR 1621, but see also Case C– 456/02 *Trojani v CPAS* [2004] ECR I–7573.

order to acquire 'worker' status and the benefits it brings.[21] Provided the work meets the *Levin* test, it will count.

However, 'worker' status for the purposes of EU law is not co-terminous with the individual's job. This is clear from Article 45(3)(d) TFEU, which extends the right to remain in another Member State so that it applies even after the employment relationship has come to an end. Further detail is provided in Article 7(3) CRD, which allows the individual to retain worker status for the purposes of the right to longer-term residence if he or she is temporarily unable to work due to illness, is engaged in vocational training or is involuntarily unemployed (if certain conditions are met). This facilitates the exercise of free movement rights because it makes the individual's status in the host state less precarious.

Of course, it may be difficult to get a job in another Member State without being able to travel there first for the purposes of seeking work. The Court recognised this early on by holding that those seeking work also enjoy 'worker' status, and are allowed to stay for a reasonable time in the host Member State.[22] The significance of this has diminished somewhat since the introduction of Article 6 CRD, which grants all EU citizens an unconditional right to stay in another Member State for three months. But this is not the end of the story, because people who can prove they are work-seekers still get better rights in some respects. Under Article 14(4)(b) CRD, work-seekers may not be expelled after the expiry of the three-month period 'for as long as [they] can provide evidence that they are continuing to seek employment and that they have a genuine chance of being engaged'. We will discuss this further below.

If an individual is engaged in economic activity in another Member State, but does not have worker status, he or she is likely to fall within Article 56 TFEU on the provision of services or Article 49 TFEU on freedom of establishment.[23] Freedom of establishment most obviously protects companies seeking to set themselves up in other Member States, but it also covers individual working people who are self-employed and want to set themselves up in another Member State. Self-employed people who are based in one Member State and travel to another on a temporary basis to work are more likely to fall within the concept of cross-border service provision. This means that the distinction between workers and self-employed people, which is often crucial in domestic law, is not

---

[21]   Case C–413/01 *Ninni-Orasche v Bundesminister für Wissenschaft, Verkehr und Kunst* [2003] ECR I–13187, [31].

[22]   Case C–292/89 *R v Immigration Appeal Tribunal, ex p Antonissen* [1991] ECR I–745.

[23]   Case 48–75 *Royer* [1976] ECR 497.

particularly important in this context.[24] For reasons of space, our discussion will refer primarily to workers, but the rules for self-employed people are very similar in practice.

Family members

An important aspect of encouraging workers to exercise their free movement rights is to allow them to take their family with them when they move to another Member State.

Of course, family members may have their own free movement rights. A couple moving from one Member State to another, both of whom are EU citizens and both of whom are intending to work, would not need to rely on the provisions applicable to family members. These provisions become important where either the family members in question will not be economically active (most commonly, because they are children), or where they are not themselves citizens of a Member State (usually referred to as 'third-country nationals' or TCNs).

Article 2(2) of the CRD defines family member to include spouse, registered partner (where the host Member State recognises registered partnerships as equivalent to marriage), children under the age of 21 or dependent children over the age of 21, and parents or grandparents who are also dependants. The rights attaching to family members thus defined will be considered further below. Article 3(2) CRD requires the host state to 'facilitate entry and residence' for a broader category of people including family members not falling within Article 2(2) who are dependants or members of the EU citizen's household and 'the partner with whom the Union citizen has a durable relationship, duly attested'. It should be noted that Article 2(2) gives rise to some uncertainty regarding the treatment of unmarried couples (since their relationship may not be 'registered') and same-sex couples (because even if they are in a civil partnership, it may not be recognised as 'equivalent to marriage' in some Member States).[25] Although Article 3(2) addresses this to some extent, the obligation to 'facilitate' entry and residence is much less extensive. It is possible that the Court might interpret the provisions generously, but this may bring it into conflict with some Member States' desire for autonomy on these matters.

---

[24] Though it may matter in terms of transitional arrangements for new Member States and when considering questions of justification.

[25] M.B. Baraldi, 'EU Family Policies Between Domestic "Good Old Values" and Fundamental Rights: the Case of Same-Sex Families' (2008) 15 *Maastricht Journal of European and Comparative Law* 517, 528–9. See also the discussion of the *Maruko* case in Chapter 5.

Exit, Entry and Residence

The most basic aspect of free movement is the right for a person to leave his or her own country and to travel to another country to look for a job, to take up a job, or to set up a business. This involves rights against both the individual's home state and the state he or she is seeking to enter.

The citizen's right to leave one Member State is dealt with in Article 4 of the CRD, and the citizen's right to enter another Member State is dealt with in Article 5. The key point in both cases is that a valid identity card or passport should suffice for this purpose.[26] Family members who are not EU citizens may only be required to have a visa to enter another Member State (in addition to their passport) where they do not have a residence card (discussed below).[27] Citizens and their family members can only be turned away for reasons of public policy, security or health, and since these are derogations from a fundamental Treaty right the Court has construed them narrowly.[28]

The right to reside in another Member State is best considered in three stages: short-term, long-term and permanent. Union citizens and their family members are entitled as of right to reside for up to three months in another Member State.[29] There is no requirement to be economically active in order to enjoy this right. However, the CRD does draw a distinction between workers and economically inactive citizens in relation to welfare provision. Article 14(1) provides that citizens hold the right to short-term residence only 'as long as they do not become an unreasonable burden on the social assistance system of the host Member State'. But, under Article 14(4), individuals who are workers or self-employed or work-seekers with a 'genuine chance of being engaged' cannot be expelled for this reason. This is another example of the advantages attaching to worker status even within the citizenship regime.

However, some Member States were not happy with the 'unreasonable burden' rule alone as a way of managing the financial consequences of migrants' access to their welfare systems. This led to the inclusion of Article 24(2) in the CRD, which gives Member States the option of refusing to provide any 'social assistance' at all to people exercising the right to short-term residence, or to work-seekers exercising their right to stay

---

[26]   Art 4(2) and Art 5(1) CRD.

[27]   Art 5(2) CRD. For states party to the Schengen Agreement (not the UK), visa requirements are further governed by Regulation 539/2001.

[28]   These derogations are set out in Art 45(3) TFEU with further detail (codifying much of the case-law) in Arts 27–33 CRD. For an example of the Court's approach, see Case 30–77 *R v Bouchereau* [1977] ECR 1999.

[29]   Art 6 CRD.

beyond the three-month period. But the Court's interpretations of this provision appear to have significantly reduced its effect. In the pre-CRD case of *Collins*, the Court held that work-seekers were entitled to equal treatment compared with the host state's own nationals in respect of welfare payments.[30] This was limited by the proviso that the host state could require a period of residence before the work-seeker becomes entitled to such payments. Although this is indirectly discriminatory,[31] because it is harder for migrants than for host state nationals to satisfy, it can be justified (provided that the period is not too long) by the need to ensure that the migrant is not just a 'welfare tourist'. In *Vatsouras*, the Court upheld *Collins* in the post-CRD world by adopting a narrow reading of Article 24(2), in which it held that benefits 'intended to facilitate access to the labour market' do not fall within the definition of 'social assistance' and cannot therefore be excluded by the Member States.[32] This reasoning is not entirely plausible and is a good example of the Court's use of creative interpretation to defeat limits laid down by the Member States.[33]

Another advantage of 'worker' status is that in Article 10 Regulation 492/2011 provides for a right of access to education for a worker's children:

> The children of a national of a Member State who is or has been employed in the territory of another Member State shall be admitted to that State's general educational, apprenticeship and vocational training courses under the same conditions as the nationals of that State, if such children are residing in its territory.[34]

Whilst this is more likely to be relevant for workers who migrate to another Member State for longer periods of time, the provision itself is not so limited.

Under Article 7 of the CRD it is possible to enjoy a longer-term right of residence if certain conditions are met.[35] For our purposes, the most

---

[30] Case C–138/02 *Collins v Secretary of State for Work and Pensions* [2004] ECR I–2703, [54]–[73].

[31] See below for further discussion of this concept.

[32] Case C–22/08 *Vatsouras v Arbeitsgemeinschaft (ARGE) Nürnberg 900* [2009] ECR I–4585, [33]–[46].

[33] For critique, focusing particularly on the Court's reliance on what is now Art 45 TFEU rather than the citizenship provisions, see E. Fahey, 'Interpretive Legitimacy and the Distinction Between "Social Assistance" and "Work Seekers Allowance": Comment on Cases C–22/08 and C–23/08 *Vatsouras* and *Koupatantze*' (2009) 34 EL Rev 933, 948.

[34] This has been broadly interpreted to ensure that, even if the worker loses worker status, any children may remain in education and their primary carer may retain a right of residence: see Case C–480/08 *Teixeira v London Borough of Lambeth* [2010] ECR I–1107.

[35] The Member States are permitted to require compliance with certain formalities set out in Arts 8–11 CRD.

important of these is to be a worker or a self-employed person,[36] though individuals who are engaged in training,[37] or who have health insurance and sufficient resources not to become a burden on the host state's social assistance system,[38] may also enjoy this right. As we noted above, EU law takes steps to ensure that the loss of the worker's job does not result in immediate loss of the right of long-term residence. Article 7(3) therefore provides that the individual may retain worker or self-employed status even if he or she is temporarily unable to work due to sickness or injury, or is involuntarily unemployed, or embarks on vocational training. The right to longer-term residence under Article 7 is subject to fewer derogations and limitations than the right to short-term residence, with the effect that the worker is entitled to equal treatment with the host state's nationals in all matters falling within the scope of the Treaty.[39] This includes access to most benefits paid by the host state's welfare system.

If the EU citizen acquires the right to longer-term residence under Article 7, his or her family members (as defined above) enjoy the same right under Article 7(1)(d). Article 7(2) extends this right to family members who are TCNs. Family members with the right to long-term residence may themselves enter the host state's labour market as workers or self-employed people (regardless of their own nationality) under Article 23. Although family members' rights are triggered by the rights of the EU citizen, in some circumstances they may be allowed to remain in the host state even after the EU citizen on whom their rights initially depended has separated from the family, left the country or died.[40] Whilst the details of these provisions need not concern us, they are an important illustration of the lengths to which EU law goes in order to make the exercise of free movement rights attractive to workers and their families.

After five years of continuous, lawful residence in another Member State, EU citizens and their family members (including TCNs) acquire the right of permanent residence under Article 16.[41] The significance of this is that the Member State can no longer require the EU citizen either to be a worker or self-employed, or to have sufficient resources, as it can for the right of long-term residence under Article 7. People who used to have worker or self-employed status, but whose working life ended through retirement or incapacity, may be able to acquire the right of permanent

---

[36]   Art 7(1)(a) CRD.
[37]   Art 7(1)(c) CRD.
[38]   Art 7(1)(b) CRD.
[39]   Art 24 CRD.
[40]   Art 13 CRD.
[41]   The relevant formalities are set out in Arts 19–21.

residence without the need for five years' residence, under the conditions laid down in Article 17 CRD.

Opening up the EU Labour Market

The right to move from one Member State to another would not be of much assistance unless the worker had a good chance of obtaining employment in the host state. To that end, EU law prohibits discrimination in the conditions on which migrant workers can access jobs in the host state: for example, they cannot usually be required to comply with extra formalities or to have extra qualifications on top of the rules applied to host state nationals. As we shall see, the Court of Justice has taken the view that simply removing discrimination may not be enough to open up the EU's labour markets. It has also subjected to scrutiny a broader range of 'obstacles' to the free movement of workers. These can include rules in the home state as well as rules applied by the host state. This is because a worker may be deterred from going abroad to work if he or she knows that this will result in disadvantage when he or she returns home. We will consider the law on these matters first, before turning to two more specific issues: mutual recognition of qualifications, and employment in the public service. Mutual recognition of qualifications is an important aspect of realising equal treatment in the EU-wide labour market: if a worker is qualified in one Member State but his or her qualifications are only recognised in that state, his or her free movement rights become meaningless. Employment in the public service is one area in which Member States may derogate from the free movement rules and restrict certain jobs to their own nationals.

General

Article 24 CRD provides EU citizens with a right to equal treatment with nationals of the host Member State. This right extends to family members (including TCNs) who have the right of residence or permanent residence. However, the right is subject to the relevant treaty provisions (discussed further below) and secondary legislation so, in relation to workers, the most important source is Regulation 492/2011. This codifies earlier legislation and case-law.

Section I of the Regulation prohibits discrimination based on nationality in access to employment. The basic principle is set out in Article 1(1):

> Any national of a Member State shall, irrespective of his place of residence, have the right to take up an activity as an employed person, and to pursue such activity, within the territory of another Member State in accordance with the provisions laid down by law, regulation or administrative action governing the employment of nationals of that State.

Article 3 gives more specific examples of the kinds of practice that are prohibited, including special registration requirements and recruitment procedures for workers who are not nationals. Article 4 ensures that, where a
Member State requires a firm to employ a quota of its own nationals, EU
citizens also count towards the quota, and Article 6 prohibits the application of medical or vocational criteria which discriminate on grounds of
nationality.[42] The right not to be discriminated against also extends to
employers who employ workers from other Member States.[43]

There are two major exceptions to these provisions. The first is that
'conditions relating to linguistic knowledge required by reason of the
nature of the post to be filled' are not precluded.[44] In *Groener*, the Court
of Justice held that it was acceptable for a teacher in an Irish school to be
required to have some knowledge of Irish (subject to a proportionality
test) as part of the state's policy of promoting Irish as the national language, even though the teacher would not be required to use Irish in the
classroom.[45] The second is that the employer may require a non-national
to take a 'vocational test' before confirming the job offer.[46]

Discrimination on grounds of nationality is, of course, a complex
concept, and some examples from the case-law may help to illustrate the
different ways in which discrimination can arise. The most obvious form
of discrimination is direct discrimination, in which nationality is used as
a criterion for employment. Thus, in *Commission v Italy*, it was held that
Italy had failed to fulfil its Treaty obligations because Italian law restricted
employment as a private security guard to Italian nationals.[47] Nationality
criteria can only be used for jobs in the public service,[48] an exception we
will consider in more detail below.

Indirect discrimination, in which a requirement is applied equally
to nationals and to migrant workers, but is more difficult for migrant
workers to satisfy, is also prohibited by the Court's case-law under Article
45 and by Article 3(1)(b) of the Regulation.[49] This can be illustrated using
the *Scholz* case.[50] In that case, the claimant was applying for a job in Italy.
The selection process involved awarding points for previous experience.

---

[42]   The Regulation does not address recognition of qualifications obtained in other
Member States, a topic to which we will return below.
[43]   Regulation 492/2011, Art 2.
[44]   Ibid, Art 3(1).
[45]   Case C–379/87 *Groener v Minister for Education* [1989] ECR 3967, [12]–[24].
[46]   Regulation 492/2011, Art 6(2).
[47]   Case C–283/99 *Commission v Italy* [2001] ECR I–4363.
[48]   Art 45(4) TFEU; Regulation 492/2011, Art 8.
[49]   Case 152/73 *Sotgiu v Deutsche Bundespost* [1974] ECR 153, [11].
[50]   Case C–419/92 *Scholz v Opera Universitaria di Cagliari* [1994] ECR I–505.

The claimant's previous experience was in Germany, but the selectors only counted experience gained in Italy. The Court held that this constituted unlawful indirect discrimination. Whilst there is a possibility of justifying such discrimination if it pursues a legitimate aim and is proportionate, the Court found that the indirect discrimination in *Scholz* itself was unjustified.

In accordance with free movement law generally, the Court does not always consider claims through a discrimination lens. The Court sometimes chooses to focus instead on whether or not a particular measure might hinder the worker's exercise of free movement rights and, if so, whether it can be justified. An oft-cited formulation of this test comes from the *Gebhard* case, a case involving a self-employed person's freedom of establishment:

> . . . national measures liable to *hinder or make less attractive* the exercise of fundamental freedoms guaranteed by the Treaty must fulfil four conditions: they must be applied in a non-discriminatory manner[,] they must be justified by imperative requirements in the general interest[,] they must be suitable for securing the attainment of the objective which they pursue and they must not go beyond what is necessary in order to attain it . . .[51]

The *Terhoeve* case provides a useful example in the context of the free movement of workers.[52] The case concerned a Netherlands national who spent part of the year working in the UK. When he returned home, he was liable for a higher rate of social security contributions than if he had worked throughout the year in the Netherlands. The Court regarded this as an 'obstacle' to free movement and did not consider whether or not it was also discriminatory.[53] On justification, the government argued that the law in question was designed to simplify the task of collecting social security contributions and that workers who spent part of the year abroad might benefit from lower taxation in other respects. However, the Court rejected both arguments, finding that the first claim was insufficient to outweigh the breach of free movement rights and that the second claim was not established on the facts.[54]

The concept of hindering free movement is a useful tool for the Court in situations which do not fit neatly into a discrimination analysis. In

---

[51] Case C–55/94 *Gebhard v Consiglio dell'Ordine degli Avvocati e Procuratori di Milano* [1995] ECR I–4165, [37] (emphasis added).

[52] Case C–18/95 *Terhoeve v Inspecteur van de Belastingdienst Particulieren* [1999] ECR I–345.

[53] Ibid, [41].

[54] Ibid, [43]–[7].

particular, it may be a more natural way of analysing cases (like *Terhoeve*) concerning rules applied by a Member State to its own nationals that place obstacles in the way of leaving to work abroad or returning afterwards.[55] However, it also has the potential to apply very broadly indeed.[56] This is one of the examples of the worry, discussed in Chapter 1, that EU market rules might impede Member States' autonomy to regulate labour markets and other areas of national life.

One of the most extreme examples of this is *Carpenter*, a case concerning the provision of services by a self-employed person.[57] The claimant in that case was a UK national who challenged the UK's decision to deport his wife (a TCN) on the basis that this would make less attractive his provision of services as a self-employed person from his base in the UK to other Member States (he sold advertising in magazines).[58] The Court upheld the claim. This limited the UK's ability to apply its own immigration rules on the basis of what was arguably a tenuous infringement of free movement.

The case-law on workers has not gone quite so far. The *Graf* case was an attempt to make creative use of the 'hindrance' idea.[59] Graf resigned from his job in Austria to take up a position in Germany. Austrian law provided for a payment on termination of employment, but only where the employee was dismissed. Graf was not eligible for the payment because he had resigned. He tried to challenge the rule on the basis that it deterred him from exercising his free movement rights. But the Court rejected this claim, holding that the rule had not affected Graf's 'access to the labour market'.[60]

The danger for the Court is that the *Gebhard* formulation could be applied to almost any form of national regulation, including (of particular interest for our purposes) national labour laws. This may impinge too much on the Member States' regulatory autonomy and may call into question the legitimacy of the Court's activities in this area. It is arguable that the Court needs to place some limits on the case-law. One possibility, favoured by some commentators, is to focus on requirements which

---

[55] See also *Bosman*, above n. 7, and Case C–19/92 *Kraus v Land Baden-Württemberg* [1993] ECR I–1663.

[56] For discussion, linking the developments to citizenship, see E. Spaventa, 'From *Gebhard* to *Carpenter*: Towards a (Non-)Economic European Constitution' (2004) 41 CMLR 743.

[57] Case C–60/00 *Carpenter v Secretary of State for the Home Department* [2002] ECR I–6279, especially [39].

[58] Since he was asserting his spouse's right to reside against his own Member State, the CRD was not relevant to the case.

[59] Case C–190/98 *Graf v Filzmoser Maschinenbau* [2000] ECR I–493.

[60] Ibid, [23]–[5].

genuinely impede an individual's access to another labour market, as suggested by the Court in *Graf* itself.

Another area of debate is the extent to which Article 45 applies to decision makers other than national governments: in other words, does it have horizontal direct effect? It is clear from the well-known *Bosman* case that Article 45 is applicable to non-state bodies where they play a role in regulating access to employment.[61] In that case, the claimant challenged the rules on the transfer of football players between clubs which had been laid down by the sport's governing body, UEFA. In *Casteels*, the claimant was allowed to invoke Article 45 in respect of rules on pensionable service in different Member States contained in a collective agreement between his employer and a union.[62] And it is clear from *Angonese* that discrimination by employers may also be caught.[63] Angonese applied for a job with a bank in Bolzano, an area of Italy in which both Italian and German are spoken. The bank required its employees to have a certificate of bilingualism issued by the authorities in Bolzano. Angonese was bilingual but did not have the certificate. The Court held that this was indirectly discriminatory because it was easier for workers already resident in Bolzano (the vast majority of whom were Italian nationals) to obtain the certificate. Some commentators have argued that employers should only be subject to Article 45 where they have engaged in discrimination, because it would be too intrusive to require private parties to avoid hindering market access.[64]

Mutual recognition of qualifications
We saw above that Article 6 of Regulation 492/2011 prohibits the use of 'vocational criteria' where they discriminate on grounds of nationality. The Court has been alert to the possibility that a requirement to have qualifications to perform a particular job may not be necessary and may be either discriminatory or a hindrance to free movement. This was the case in *Säger*, a case concerning a German requirement that firms from other Member States providing the service of reminding people to renew their patents should employ staff qualified as patent agents.[65] The Court held that this was disproportionate since issuing reminders did not require professional knowledge.

Where qualifications are required for a particular post, there is an

---

[61] Above n. 7.
[62] Case C–379/09 *Casteels v British Airways plc* [2011] nyr.
[63] Above n. 8.
[64] For example, A. Dashwood and others (2011), *Wyatt and Dashwood's EU Law* (6th edn, London: Sweet and Maxwell), 502.
[65] Case C–76/90 *Säger v Dennemeyer* [1991] ECR I–4221.

obvious hindrance to free movement if qualifications obtained in one Member State count for nothing in another. This was anticipated in the Treaty, which provided for directives to be agreed on mutual recognition of qualifications.[66] However, since this process was politically difficult and therefore slow, the Court took matters into its own hands. The leading case is *Vlassopoulou*.[67] The claimant was a lawyer who had trained in Greece but worked in Germany, advising on Greek law and EU law. She applied to join the local German bar but was refused because she did not have the relevant German qualifications. The Court held that the national authorities were obliged to follow a three-stage process. First, it was necessary to compare her qualifications and experience with the national requirements to see whether or not they were equivalent. If they were, her qualifications and experience should be recognised by the national authorities. Second, if her qualifications and experience corresponded to national requirements only in part, it was necessary to consider whether she could show by other means (such as study or practice in the host state) that she had obtained the missing knowledge. Third, the national authorities must provide reasons for their decisions and those decisions must be subject to judicial review.

The Member States finally caught up with the Court when they agreed Directive 2005/36/EC. This consolidates several earlier directives focusing on specific professions, and three 'horizontal' or 'system' directives focusing on mutual recognition of qualifications more generally. The directive applies to 'regulated professions',[68] and to those who work as employees or on a self-employed basis.[69] According to Article 4 of the directive, it is concerned with ensuring that those who are qualified to pursue a regulated profession in one Member State have their qualifications recognised by other Member States and are thus allowed to practise their profession in those other states on the same basis as those who qualified there. The directive draws an important distinction between those who are established in one Member State and simply want to provide services in another Member State, and those who wish to establish themselves in another Member State. In the former case, the directive makes it possible for professionals to provide services on a temporary basis without the need for the host state to recognise their qualifications, though the host state is permitted to impose various regulatory requirements.[70] In the

---

[66]   Art 53 TFEU.
[67]   Case C–340/89 *Vlassopoulou v Ministerium für Justiz, Bundes- und Europaangelegenheiten Baden-Württemberg* [1991] ECR I–2357.
[68]   Directive 2005/36/EC, Art 3.
[69]   Ibid, Art 2.
[70]   Ibid, Title II.

latter case, the professional must seek recognition of his or her qualifications.[71] Consolidating the older legislation, the directive provides a three-tier approach to this. First, certain listed professions such as medicine and nursing are subject to automatic mutual recognition. Second, where the host state requires professional knowledge for the practice of a particular profession, the individual's previous experience in another Member State must be recognised provided certain conditions are met. Third, if neither of the previous two options is applicable, there are general provisions requiring the host state to recognise equivalent qualifications earned in another Member State.

Public service

An area of particular sensitivity for Member States is employment in the public service. Where a job involves national security issues, for example, a state may wish to restrict that job to its own nationals. This concern is reflected in the Treaty, which provides that employment 'in the public service' is not covered by Article 45.[72] However, the Court of Justice has played an important role in limiting this exception, holding that it must be given an EU meaning and must be construed strictly.[73] For example, in *Anker*, the claimant was a Dutch national who was denied the certificate he needed in order to captain a fishing vessel flying the German flag.[74] It was argued that captains are entitled to exercise certain public powers (for example, in maintaining order on board and dealing with deaths) so the occupation could be reserved to a Member State's own nationals. But the Court held that the mere conferral of public law powers on holders of a particular job is not sufficient unless the powers are 'in fact exercised on a regular basis by those holders and do not represent a very minor part of their activities'.[75] In this way, the Court has sought to prevent states from imposing spurious nationality restrictions on particular jobs.

Rights during Employment

Once an EU migrant worker has obtained a job in another Member State, he or she is entitled to equal treatment 'with the nationals of that Member State within the scope of the Treaty'.[76] More precise obligations can be

---

[71]   Ibid, Title III.
[72]   Art 45(4) TFEU.
[73]   Case 225/85 *Commission v Italy* [1987] ECR 2625, [7]–[8].
[74]   Case C–47/02 *Anker v Germany* [2003] ECR I–10447.
[75]   Ibid, [63].
[76]   Art 24 CRD.

found in Section 2 of Regulation 492/2011. The most important provision is Article 7:

1. A worker who is a national of a Member State may not, in the territory of another Member State, be treated differently from national workers by reason of his nationality in respect of any conditions of employment and work, in particular as regards remuneration, dismissal, and, should he become unemployed, reinstatement or re-employment.
2. He shall enjoy the same social and tax advantages as national workers.
3. He shall also, by virtue of the same right and under the same conditions as national workers, have access to training in vocational schools and retraining centres.
4. Any clause of a collective or individual agreement or of any other collective regulation concerning eligibility for employment, remuneration and other conditions of work or dismissal shall be null and void in so far as it lays down or authorises discriminatory conditions in respect of workers who are nationals of the other Member States.

Article 8 provides that workers should enjoy equal treatment as regards trade union membership and workplace participation, and Article 9 provides for equal treatment as regards access to housing. Once again, the Court has adopted a broad understanding of equality in this context, so that both direct and indirect discrimination (where the latter cannot be justified) are caught. In some cases, the Court has also applied the broader *Gebhard* formula discussed above, to catch 'obstacles' to free movement.[77] We will consider some examples relating to employment, tax and social advantages.

In the employment context, one of the commonest problems is the treatment of service accrued in other Member States (rather like *Scholz*, the access to employment case discussed above).[78] For example, in *Köbler*, the claimant was a university professor who challenged an Austrian rule granting a length-of-service bonus to individuals who had worked for more than 15 years in an Austrian university.[79] The claimant had the requisite years of service but had accrued some of it in other Member States. The Court held that the rule discriminated against individuals who were not Austrian and might also be a hindrance to free movement of Austrian professors who wished to work abroad. The Court scrutinised the Austrian government's justifications closely and held further that arguments about encouraging loyalty were not sufficient to justify the rule.

In relation to tax, a key problem is the treatment of residence, because

---

[77] Above n. 51.
[78] Above n. 50.
[79] Case C–224/01 *Köbler v Austria* [2003] ECR I–10239.

national tax systems are designed primarily with residents in mind. The *Biehl* case illustrates this.[80] That case concerned a rule of Luxembourg law that precluded non-residents from recovering overpaid taxes. Although the rule applied regardless of nationality, the Court recognised that it would have a greater impact on non-nationals than on nationals because they were more likely to enter or leave the country during the tax year. Importantly, though, the Member States may be able to justify some distinctions in this area if they pursue the legitimate aim of preserving 'the cohesion of the tax system'.[81]

In the field of social advantages, the Court has adopted a broad understanding of the types of benefit that are covered. In *Even*, it was held that the concept of 'social advantages' includes:

> all those [benefits] which, whether or not linked to a contract of employment, are generally granted to national workers primarily because of their objective status as workers or by virtue of the mere fact of their residence on the national territory and the extension of which to workers who are nationals of other Member States therefore seems suitable to facilitate their mobility within the Community.[82]

However, this does not cover every conceivable benefit: *Even* itself concerned compensation for wartime service and the Court held that this did not fall within the definition just given, because it did not relate to 'worker' status. Where a benefit is covered, it must be offered equally to nationals and migrant workers. Thus, for example, in *O'Flynn* it was held that the UK authorities could not refuse a grant for a child's funeral expenses to an Irish migrant worker on the ground that the child's funeral would take place in Ireland.[83] This rule was indirectly discriminatory, because migrant workers were more likely to want their children to be buried in their home state, and the UK's concern about costs could be dealt with in other, non-discriminatory ways, for example by limiting the sums payable.

Conclusion

There are three key points to take away from our discussion of the free movement rules. The first is that EU labour law is not fully constitutionalised, in this area at least. Although EU citizens now enjoy some of the

---

[80]   Case C–175/88 *Biehl v Administration des contributions du grand-duché de Luxembourg* [1990] ECR I–1779.
[81]   Case C–204/90 *Bachmann v Belgium* [1992] ECR I–249, [27].
[82]   Case 207/78 *Even* [1979] ECR 2019, [22].
[83]   Case C–237/94 *O'Flynn v Adjudication Officer* [1996] ECR I–2617.

rights that were initially granted only to workers, there are still significant advantages to having worker status. Thus, the free movement rules remain fundamentally economic, rather than social, in nature.

Second, we have seen that the task of creating an EU-wide labour market is an ambitious one requiring a highly developed body of EU-labour-market-creating rules. This reflects the fact that workers are unlikely to exercise their free movement rights unless the conditions for doing so are favourable: for example, they might want to take their families with them, to put their children into school, and to have some protection against immediate expulsion if they are made redundant. This has required more extensive intrusion into sensitive areas for the Member States, such as social security; and when the Member States have been reluctant to act, we have seen that the Court has pushed the law forward.

Third, we have seen that the free movement rules may come into conflict with the Member States' ability to regulate their own labour markets: to require the holders of particular jobs to hold qualifications, or to designate certain roles as public offices. For the most part, this has been about uncovering and removing (often distinctly peculiar) rules that are unjustifiable and that serve to keep out workers from other Member States. But there are risks involved in adopting an unduly broad approach to the attack on national legislation, as the *Graf* case illustrated.[84] We will pursue this theme more fully in the next section, in which we turn to consider the ways in which freedom to provide services and freedom of establishment have given rise to challenges to the Member States' labour legislation.

SERVICES, ESTABLISHMENT AND NATIONAL LABOUR LAW

In this part of this chapter, we will consider other aspects of the law on free movement in the EU, and their relationship to labour migration and to national labour law more generally. We will begin with firms' freedom to provide services in other Member States, exploring the role of EU law in determining whether home- or host-state labour law rules apply to the firm's travelling workforce. In this area, the workers' rights to move depend on their employer's right to provide services across national borders, and not on their own rights as workers or EU citizens. We will then consider the more complex interaction between national labour law and firms' freedom to establish in different Member States. This involves

---

[84]   Above n. 59.

an assessment of the extent to which national labour law rules – or industrial action by national unions – might constitute an unjustified restriction on a firm's freedom to move from one state to another.

Central Themes

The issues to be discussed in this section raise in a sharp form the worry about the negative effects of EU integration on national labour law discussed in Chapter 1. The problems we will be considering stem from the enormous wage differentials between different parts of the EU. As we saw above, this acts as a trigger for worker migration because workers from low-wage Member States may want to travel to high-wage Member States in search of a better-paying job. In this section, our focus is on the impact of wage differentials on firms, and on the Member States' likely reactions.

There are two possibilities. One is that a firm established in a high-wage state might decide to exercise its freedom of establishment by closing its operations there and moving to a low-wage state where its costs will be much reduced. This will result in job losses in high-wage states and the creation of new jobs in low-wage states. The other possibility is that firms established in low-wage states might decide to provide services in high-wage states using their own workers (often termed 'posted' workers) instead of local labour. This will enable them to provide services more cheaply than local firms. Again, this may lead to job losses in high-wage states, or to cuts in terms and conditions of employment as local firms try to compete.

One possible reaction to these developments on the part of governments in high-wage states is the 'race to the bottom'. This theory suggests that governments will try to lower their labour standards in order to discourage firms from leaving or to enable local firms to compete with service providers from low-wage Member States. This might involve reducing worker protections or cutting the level of the minimum wage. The question for the EU is whether and to what extent it should intervene to prevent such developments (subject to its competence to do so). On one hand, the prevention of a 'race to the bottom' has been used to justify some EU interventions in labour law: the right to equal pay for men and women being a classic example. On the other hand, for low-wage countries (particularly the newer Member States) a significant attraction of EU membership is their ability to develop their own economies through their competitive advantage.

The other possible reaction on the part of governments in high-wage states is to seek to protect their own economies and workers through what we might loosely label 'defensive' strategies. For example, a host state might require firms to pay host-state wage rates to their posted workers as a means of preventing those workers from undercutting local labour. The question here is whether EU law does or should permit this strategy. This is a central example of the conflict between the EU's rules on market creation and the Member States' autonomy in matters of national labour law, discussed in Chapter 1. From the market creation perspective, these 'defensive' strategies can be portrayed as a form of 'protectionism': as a means of protecting national markets from the full effects of economic integration, to the disadvantage of firms and workers from low-wage states. But from the autonomy perspective, the ability of Member States to regulate their own labour markets is significantly undermined if they cannot apply their own labour law to everyone working within their territory. Indeed, while the rules on the migration of individual workers are all about securing equality with nationals, there is a risk that the posting of workers might end up being about the creation of two-tier labour markets in which there is one set of rules for nationals and another set of rules for posted workers.

Before we delve into the details, there are two other themes to watch out for. First, the Court of Justice has played a central role in resolving these issues. The Court has drawn some very heavy fire from commentators for its pro-integration approach to the cases, but it is important to remember that the Court's involvement reflects, in part at least, the Member States' inability to come up with any very clear solutions to these problems themselves.[85] Where there is uncertainty, it is inevitable that litigation will eventually result and the Court will be called upon to decide. Second, the two most important cases in this area so far, *Viking* and *Laval*,[86] have not been straightforward examples of Member States seeking to prevent firms from leaving or to apply host state standards to posted workers. Instead, they have concerned the actions of trade unions in seeking to bring about these results through industrial action. This has meant that our 'constitutionalisation' theme is highly relevant here. The right to strike is recognised in various international human rights instruments, including the EU Charter of Fundamental Rights.[87] But it is arguable that a big test for 'constitutionalisation' in the EU is how rights might fare when they come into conflict with central principles of EU law, like the free movement rules. As we shall see, *Viking* and *Laval* present a mixed picture in this regard.

---

[85]   A.C.L. Davies, 'One Step Forward, Two Steps Back? The *Viking* and *Laval* cases in the ECJ' (2008) 37 ILJ 126, 139.

[86]   Case C–438/05 *International Transport Workers' Federation v Viking Line* [2007] ECR I–10779; Case C–341/05 *Laval v Svenska Byggnadsarbetareförbundet* [2007] ECR I–11767.

[87]   Art 28.

Freedom to Provide Services and the Treatment of Posted Workers

We will begin by considering the set of issues just identified in the context of the treatment of posted workers. Posting occurs when a firm established in one Member State is providing services to an entity in another Member State and wants to send its own workforce to the host state for that purpose. It is clear that the right to post workers is an inherent part of the freedom to provide services under Article 56 TFEU. The Court held in *Rush Portuguesa* that it was unlawful for a Member State to prohibit or restrict the use of posted workers.[88]

But this raises the more difficult question of what law is applicable to the posted workers.[89] We saw above that it may be in the interests of the host state to apply its own law to the posted workers. But firms engaged in posting will probably want to apply their home state law to their workers: they are familiar with this already and (where they are posting to a state with higher labour costs) they will be able to maintain their competitive advantage. To understand how the EU has addressed these questions, we need to consider a complex mix of the Rome I Regulation,[90] Article 56 TFEU and the Posted Workers Directive (hereafter 'PWD').[91]

Leaving aside 'labour law' for the moment, when a worker is posted to another Member State a more basic question arises: which country's law governs the contract of employment? This question is answered using 'conflict of laws' rules. Within the EU, these rules are laid down in the Rome I Regulation. There are two possibilities. First, the worker and his or her employer may have specified which country's law is applicable. This choice will be respected,[92] except that the parties will not be allowed to contract out of mandatory worker-protective legislation that would otherwise have been applicable to their relationship if they had not specified the applicable law.[93] Second, the parties might have been silent on the matter of applicable law. In that case, Article 8(2) of the Regulation states that:

---

[88] Case C–113/89 *Rush Portuguesa v Office national d'immigration* [1990] ECR I–1417, [12].

[89] On which see, generally, P. Davies, 'Posted Workers: Single Market or Protection of National Labour Law Systems?' (1997) 34 CMLR 571; E. Kolehmainen, 'The Directive Concerning the Posting of Workers: Synchronization of the Functions of National Legal Systems' (1998) 20 *Comparative Labor Law and Policy Journal* 71.

[90] Regulation 593/2008 on the law applicable to contractual obligations.

[91] Directive 96/71/EC of the European Parliament and of the Council of 16 December 1996 concerning the posting of workers in the framework of the provision of services.

[92] Regulation 593/2008, Art 3.

[93] Ibid, Art 8(1).

the contract shall be governed by the law of the country in which or, failing that, from which the employee habitually carries out his work in performance of the contract. The country where the work is habitually carried out shall not be deemed to have changed if he is temporarily employed in another country.[94]

In the case of a temporary posting to another country, this suggests that home state law will generally be applicable,[95] though a detailed assessment of the facts of each case will be required in order to determine this. Article 9 of the Regulation preserves a country's right to apply what are called 'mandatory rules of the forum' to contracts regardless of the applicable law. These are 'provisions the respect for which is regarded as crucial by a country for safeguarding its public interests'.[96] We will return to the question of what this might mean towards the end of this section.

The ability of a host state to apply national labour laws to posted workers first came before the Court in *Rush Portuguesa*, a case under the predecessor to Article 56 TFEU.[97] In holding that the freedom to provide services carries with it a right to post workers, the Court opened up the possibility of treating the application of host-state labour law to those posted workers as a hindrance to the firm's Article 56 rights. However, in a short but significant paragraph, the Court also stated that:

[EU] law does not preclude Member States from extending their legislation, or collective labour agreements entered into by both sides of industry, to any person who is employed, even temporarily, within their territory, no matter in which country the employer is established nor does [EU] law prohibit Member States from enforcing those rules by appropriate means.[98]

This bald statement was qualified and developed in subsequent cases into a two-stage, proportionality-driven approach. First, although worker protection was regarded as a legitimate aim for the host state to pursue, that state had to be able to demonstrate that its regulation conferred a genuine additional benefit on the workers in question. Thus, if the workers already enjoyed equivalent protection under their home state laws, further regulation by the host state would be unnecessary and unlawful. This is illustrated by *Arblade*, in which the Court rejected the host state's application

---

[94]   For the interpretation of this provision see Case C–29/10 *Koelzsch v Luxembourg* [2011] nyr.

[95]   Regulation 593/2008, Art 8(3) and (4) provide further possibilities if the applicable law cannot be determined by this means.

[96]   Ibid, Art 9(1).

[97]   Above n. 88.

[98]   Ibid, [18].

of laws governing the formalities associated with the employment relationship because these had already been dealt with in the home state.[99] Second, the Court held that, even where the first test was satisfied, there should also be a proportionality enquiry. For example, in *Mazzoleni*, a French firm supplied security guards to work at a shopping mall in Belgium.[100] The Belgian authorities challenged the firm for failing to pay the minimum wage. Although the application of proportionality to the facts was a matter for the national court, the Court held that the requirement to pay a minimum wage might be disproportionate where the workers were only temporarily employed in Belgium.

The Member States eventually responded to this set of developments by agreeing the PWD.[101] As Davies has argued,[102] this directive purports to pursue the aim of removing barriers to the cross-border provision of services, an aim reflected in its Treaty basis,[103] but the preservation of the host state's labour law system plays a central role in the directive's design. It should be noted that, whilst the PWD addresses substantive terms and conditions of employment, administrative formalities imposed by Member States on posted workers still fall to be considered under the Treaty using the proportionality test.[104]

The PWD defines a 'posted worker' as 'a worker who, for a limited period, carries out his work in the territory of a Member State other than the State in which he normally works'.[105] Article 1(3) of the directive identifies three situations in which a posting will be regulated by the directive: where the individual is posted to another Member State to provide services to another firm pursuant to a contract between that firm and the employer; where the individual is posted to another Member State to work for another company in the employer's group; and where the individual is employed by an agency which posts him or her to another Member State to provide services to an end user. Importantly, then, the individual must remain in an employment relationship with the original employer in the home state, and he or she must provide services to another entity in the host state. There is no posting where the individual simply moves to another Member State to become the employee of the host undertaking or where the individual moves to another Member State to work for the

---

[99] Case C–369/96 *Arblade* [1999] ECR I–8453.
[100] Case C–165/98 *Mazzoleni* [2001] ECR I–2189.
[101] Above n. 91.
[102] Above n. 89.
[103] Originally Arts 57(2) and 66 EC on services and establishment.
[104] Case C–515/08 *Palhota* [2010] nyr.
[105] Directive 96/71/EC, Art 2(1).

home state undertaking (for example, as a travelling salesperson).[106] The applicable definition of 'worker' is that used in the host state's law.[107]

The key provision of the directive is Article 3(1), which requires the host state to ensure that posted workers benefit from the host state's norms on:

(a) maximum work periods and minimum rest periods;
(b) minimum paid annual holidays;
(c) the minimum rates of pay, including overtime rates; this point does not apply to supplementary occupational retirement pension schemes;
(d) the conditions of hiring-out of workers, in particular the supply of workers by temporary employment undertakings;
(e) health, safety and hygiene at work;
(f) protective measures with regard to the terms and conditions of employment of pregnant women or women who have recently given birth, of children and of young people;
(g) equality of treatment between men and women and other provisions on non-discrimination.

The norms may be those laid down 'by law, regulation or administrative provision'.[108] Where the posted workers are engaged in the building industry, as defined in the Annex, there is a further option, to use the norms laid down in collective agreements. Such agreements must have been 'declared universally applicable' or, where no such system exists, they must be 'generally applicable to all similar undertakings in the geographical area and in the profession or industry concerned' or 'concluded by the most representative employers' and labour organizations at national level and which are applied throughout national territory'.[109]

In theory at least, the PWD is also subject to the more general possibility in EU law that a directive might be implemented by the social partners.[110] In the *Laval* case, instead of setting a minimum wage through legislation or through collective agreements applicable to all employers, Sweden had allowed unions to bargain on wages with particular employers at the workplace level. However, the Court indicated that this did not amount to proper implementation.[111] This seemed to be because the Court thought that negotiations might go on for a long time without reaching an agreement (which had been the case in *Laval* itself, with disastrous consequences for the firm doing the posting).

---

[106] Davies, above n. 89, 576.
[107] Directive 96/71/EC, Art 2(2).
[108] Ibid, Art 3(1).
[109] Ibid, Arts 3(1) and (8).
[110] See Chapter 2.
[111] Above n. 86, [71].

This does not bode well for collective bargaining as an implementation technique, whether outside the directive (as in *Laval*) or under the Annex. However, it may be explicable as a particular result of the concerns addressed by the PWD. First, it is arguable that the PWD is about certainty: if employers posting workers are required to apply some host state standards, they should be able to find out what these are. And second, where collective bargaining is used, it may be necessary to have a default option if the parties cannot agree. Otherwise, a union might be tempted to hold out for an implausibly high wage in the hope that the firm will give up on the idea of posting altogether. Indeed, this might be in the interests of host state unions since it might lead to the firm deciding to hire local labour instead.

Whilst the core of Article 3 is a mandatory requirement to apply minimum standards to posted workers, it is important to note that there are also permissive provisions which appear to give the Member States the option of imposing higher standards on workers posted to their territories. However, the scope of these provisions has been significantly reduced by the Court's interpretations.

Article 3(7) states that 'paragraphs 1 to 6 shall not prevent application of terms and conditions of employment which are more favourable to workers'. This might suggest that host states are free to extend other aspects of their labour law to posted workers. However, the decisions in *Laval* and *Rüffert* make clear that this is not the case.[112] The Court held that Article 3(7) protects posted workers where the *home* state's labour law is more protective than that of the host state: in other words, posted workers should not suffer a reduction in their terms and conditions of employment as a result of the posting. The Court also held that Article 3(7) allows the employer to agree more favourable terms with the posted workers than those provided by the host state. However, the one thing not permitted by Article 3(7) is the imposition of more protective labour law requirements by the host state.

Under Article 3(10), the Member States are given the option of applying additional standards to posted workers:

> This Directive shall not preclude the application by Member States, in compliance with the Treaty, to national undertakings and to the undertakings of other States, on a basis of equality of treatment, of: – terms and conditions of employment on matters other than those referred to in the first subparagraph of paragraph 1 in the case of public policy provisions . . .

---

[112] *Laval*, above n. 86, [80]; Case C–346/06 *Rüffert v Land Niedersachsen* [2008] ECR I–1989, [33].

At first sight, it might appear that this provision allows the Member States to apply their own national labour laws to any workers posted to their territories. This was the approach initially adopted by the UK government.[113] However, the Court held in *Commission v Luxembourg* that Article 3(10) constitutes a derogation from the Treaty provisions on freedom to provide services and should therefore be construed strictly.[114] In particular, 'public policy may be relied on only if there is a genuine and sufficiently serious threat to a fundamental interest of society'.[115] The scope of public policy 'cannot be determined unilaterally by each Member State without any control by the [EU] institutions'.[116] As a result, Luxembourg failed to establish that the labour law provisions it wanted to apply to posted workers fell within the public policy exception and, indeed, Barnard argues that it is hard to envisage any provisions that would pass the Court's test.[117] Thus, Article 3(1) is more of a ceiling than a floor in terms of protection for posted workers.

It will be recalled that the Rome I Regulation also allows the host state to apply its own rules of labour law to posted workers where these are mandatory requirements. We are now in a position to consider the meaning of this proposition. The view adopted by Davies when the PWD was passed,[118] and the view articulated by Barnard in more recent writings,[119] is that the concept of mandatory requirements in the Rome I Regulation is likely to be interpreted in the light of the PWD. Thus, only those labour law requirements laid down in Article 3(1) (plus any that satisfy Article 3(10), though this seems unlikely) can be applied by the host state's courts under the Rome regime. The same thinking seems to be applicable to Article 56 TFEU. Although this has been interpreted by the Court as laying down a proportionality requirement for the host state's labour law in a posting case, the reality of the situation is that only the Article 3(1) PWD requirements will now satisfy that test. In a reversal of the usual order of things, the Directive thus determines the construction of the Treaty Article.

When it was first enacted, Davies interpreted the PWD as a confused measure, purporting to enhance firms' freedom to provide services whilst

---

113   For example, Employment Rights Act 1996, s 204(1), and for discussion see C. Barnard, 'The UK and Posted Workers: the Effect of *Commission v Luxembourg* on the Territorial Application of British Labour Law' (2009) 38 ILJ 122.

114   Case C–319/06 *Commission v Luxembourg* [2008] ECR I–4323.

115   Ibid, [50].

116   Ibid, [50].

117   Above n. 113, 127–30.

118   Above n. 89, 579.

119   Above n. 113, 128–9.

in practice offering a considerable degree of protection to the host state's labour market.[120] Subsequent interpretation by the Court has clarified matters to some extent, but perhaps not in the way labour lawyers might have hoped. It is now clear that Article 3(1) of the PWD sets both the minimum and the maximum level of protection for posted workers. This gives greater emphasis to the policy of opening up the EU labour market. However, it does not completely disregard labour considerations: Article 3(1) covers a reasonable range of labour law provisions. So the Member States are allowed to adopt strategies to defend their labour markets against an influx of posted workers, but only within the confines of Article 3(1) PWD. From the perspective of constitutionalisation, the Court's treatment of collective bargaining and industrial action in *Laval* is unsympathetic, to say the least. But, as we noted above, this may reflect the particular circumstances of the case: the Court was more concerned to criticise Sweden's implementation of the directive than to consider the union's position, even though the case was brought against the union.

Freedom of Establishment and National Labour Law

The constitutionalisation theme comes into sharper focus when we turn to the issues surrounding freedom of establishment and the *Viking* case.[121] So far, we have been focusing on matters pertaining to worker migration; our focus here will be on the impact on workers of *firms'* ability to move around the EU.

Article 49 TFEU sets out the principle of freedom of establishment. This gives self-employed individuals and firms the possibility of setting up a permanent base for their business in the Member State of their choice. One possible consequence of this, as we discussed above, is that firms might choose to move to cheaper locations in the EU. Even if this results in job losses in the firm's state of origin, there is little the government can do about it: the Court has held that Article 49 TFEU includes a right to leave the state of origin in order to establish elsewhere.[122] But what does EU law have to say about the situation in which the firm's attempt to leave is hindered or prevented not by the government but by a trade union? This was the question addressed in *Viking*.

In that case, a shipowner operated a ferry travelling between Finland and Estonia under the Finnish flag. The shipowner wanted to re-flag the

---

[120] Above n. 89, 573.
[121] Above n. 86.
[122] Case 81/87 *R v HM Treasury, ex p Daily Mail and General Trust* [1988] ECR 5483, [16].

ferry in Estonia (an exercise of freedom of establishment within Article 49 TFEU). The Finnish trade union representing the crew, backed by the International Transport Workers' Federation (ITF), feared that this would have a detrimental impact on the crew's terms and conditions of employment. They organised a blockade of the shipowner's vessels. This blockade was highly effective and the shipowner took legal action to stop it, arguing that it was a hindrance to freedom of establishment.

The first question facing the ECJ in *Viking Line* was whether Article 49 TFEU applied horizontally against the trade unions, as well as vertically against governments. As we saw above, the case-law on workers indicates that Article 45 TFEU can apply to non-governmental organisations which regulate access to the labour market, like professional bodies or sports governing bodies, and even to private employers.[123] The Court adopted a similar approach to Article 49, though it is not entirely clear from the judgment whether it regarded the trade unions as analogous to regulatory bodies (which would be a very odd way of thinking about what trade unions do) or as analogous to private employers (which would give Article 49 a very broad reach indeed).[124]

The trade unions sought to defend their position by arguing that they were exercising a fundamental right: the right to strike. This is recognised in various international and European instruments, including the EU Charter of Fundamental Rights, and in the constitutions of many Member States. The Court recognised the right to strike – a significant move from the constitutionalisation perspective – and held that the unions were exercising it.

This brings us to the heart of the dispute: how should the Court reconcile the competing claims of the firm, seeking to exercise its freedom of establishment, and the unions, exercising their right to strike? The Court adopted what should by now be recognisable as familiar free-movement reasoning: restrictions on free movement must pursue a legitimate aim and must be proportionate. The Court accepted that worker protection was a legitimate aim, but cast doubt on the proportionality of the unions' action given that the firm had undertaken to uphold the existing workers' terms and conditions, and that the industrial action had been so strong as to prevent the firm from exercising its freedom of establishment altogether.[125] In effect, the Court's approach meant that the more effective

---

[123] *Bosman*, above n. 7; *Angonese*, above n. 8.

[124] Davies, above n. 85, 136–7.

[125] It should be noted that, although the application of the proportionality test to the facts of the case is a matter for the national court, the Court offered detailed guidance.

the blockade organised by the unions, the harder it would be for them to justify it.

The Court's decision has been heavily criticised by labour law commentators and,[126] most significantly, by the ILO.[127] While the Court's recognition of the right to strike has been welcomed, the role this played in the Court's reasoning process is more problematic. The Court did not treat the right to strike as superior to – or even equal to – freedom of establishment. Instead of considering whether any restrictions on the right to strike were proportionate (the normal method of reasoning in a fundamental rights case) the Court focused on whether the unions' exercise of the right to strike was itself proportionate.[128] This amounts to a significant restriction on the right to strike in situations with a cross-border dimension. And in terms of our constitutionalisation theme, it is not very encouraging: faced with a clash between a right and a fundamental principle of EU law, the Court did not plump for the right.

But is this really an example of the Court getting things wrong because of its pro-EU stance? As I have argued elsewhere, the problem facing the Court was that the structure of the Treaty does not lend itself to a more worker-protective decision.[129] The Treaty prioritises freedom of establishment as a fundamental principle of EU law, and there is ample case-law to support this. However, the right to strike is excluded from the EU's competences in labour law (presumably because Member States believed that this would protect their own national systems) and the human rights jurisprudence is still under development. On this view, the Court's decision is quite conservative and reflects choices made by the Member States.

Conclusion

Market integration in the EU is bound to create winners and losers. We could just regard the losers as an unfortunate side-effect of a process that will ultimately make everyone better off. But the EU's approach to this problem has, on the whole, been somewhat more subtle than this. As we saw in Chapter 1, a major reason for the existence of EU labour law is to mitigate the negative effects of opening up markets. By setting minimum

---

[126]   There is a large literature: see the further reading at the end of this chapter for a selection.

[127]   ILO, Report of the Committee of Experts on the Application of Conventions and Recommendations (99th session, 2010), commenting on the complaint by BALPA relating to Convention No 87 (1948) on Freedom of Association and Protection of the Right to Organise.

[128]   *Viking*, above n. 86, [84].

[129]   Above n. 85.

standards at EU level, there is an opportunity for the Member States to defend their labour markets against the worst effects of competition. The PWD is an interesting example of this phenomenon.

The other dimension to the problem is the effect on national trade unions of the opening-up of markets within the EU. To what extent are they able to use their 'industrial muscle', through strikes, to resist firms' decisions to close down and move elsewhere in the EU, or to bring in cheaper posted workers to perform particular tasks? On one view, we could see industrial action as just another restriction on firms' freedom of movement, analogous to national rules and regulations. At the other extreme, we could recognise the special situation of trade unions and insulate them from assessment altogether.[130] This was the approach adopted in the *Albany* case, in which the Court chose not to apply competition law to a pension fund set up by trade unions.[131] The Court took the view that there is an inevitable clash between competition law and collective bargaining in this area, so there was no point in applying competition law to the situation. Or we could try to reconcile trade unions' action with the free movement rules through some kind of proportionality or balancing approach.

The key question for the Court and the political actors after *Viking* and *Laval* is whether the decisions in those cases gave sufficient weight to the right to strike in the balancing exercise.[132] This issue may come to the fore as the EU proceeds with plans to accede to the ECHR.[133] In a series of recent decisions, the ECtHR has identified a right to strike within Article 11 (on freedom of association) which signatories must protect.[134] It seems likely that in any balancing process the ECtHR, as a human rights court, would afford greater weight to the right to strike than to EU free

---

[130]   An attempt has been made to do this in the Services Directive (Directive 2006/123/EC). For discussion see C. Barnard, 'Unravelling the Services Directive' (2008) 45 CMLR 323, 345–7; and F. Hendrickx, 'The Services Directive and Social Dumping: National Labour Law Under Strain?', in U. Neergaard, R. Nielsen and L. Roseberry (eds) (2008), *The Services Directive: Consequences for the Welfare State and the European Social Model* (Copenhagen: Djøf).

[131]   Case C–67/96 *Albany International BV v Stichting Bedrijfspensioenfonds Textielindustrie* [1999] ECR I–5751.

[132]   This balancing approach was continued in the recent case C–271/08 *Commission v Germany* [2010] nyr on collective bargaining and the procurement rules, though Syrpis points out that there are hints of a greater emphasis on collective rights in the Advocate General's opinion at least: P. Syrpis, 'Case Comment: Reconciling Economic Freedoms and Social Rights – the Potential of *Commission v Germany* (case C–271/08, judgment of 15 July 2010)' (2011) 40 ILJ 222.

[133]   See, generally, J-P. Jacqué, 'The Accession of the European Union to the European Convention on Human Rights and Fundamental Freedoms' (2011) 48 CMLR 995.

[134]   *Demir v Turkey* (2009) 48 EHRR 54; Application no 68959/01 *Enerji Yapi-Yol Sen v Turkey* (decision of 21/04/2009).

movement rules.[135] This might give rise to a conflict between the ECtHR and the Court of Justice and it remains to be seen how any such conflict might be resolved.

IMMIGRATION

Although EU law has a lot to say about freedom of movement for workers within the EU itself, it has much less to say about immigration *into* the EU for TCNs (people from non-EU countries). The EU has a shared competence on immigration set out in Article 79 TFEU, which envisages the development of a 'common immigration policy'. The aim of this section is to give a brief overview of some of the EU's emerging immigration policy, with a particular focus on measures relevant to the labour market.

Themes

The most obvious theme of EU immigration law and policy is autonomy.[136] The Member States have been very reluctant to give up their discretion in this area. The most obvious example of this is that not all Member States are covered by the common immigration policy. Article 79 forms part of Title V TFEU, on the area of freedom, security and justice. By Protocols annexed to the Treaty, the UK, Ireland and Denmark do not participate in the EU's activities under Title V.[137]

Even for the participating Member States, the measures adopted under the common immigration policy have so far been relatively limited. The Commission has been forced to adopt a strategic approach to the proposals it makes on immigration issues, focusing in particular on measures that can be 'sold' to the Member States: for example, measures that will strengthen their ability to curb illegal migration.[138]

Set against the Member States' concern for autonomy are some of the 'race to the top' arguments we considered in Chapter 1. The Europe 2020 strategy is about developing a high-skill, high-productivity economy in the EU whilst maintaining the European Social Model. But Europe faces a considerable demographic challenge: an ageing population and a declining

---

[135] For discussion see K.D. Ewing and J. Hendy, 'The Dramatic Implications of *Demir* and *Baykara*' (2010) 39 ILJ 2, 38–43.

[136] See, generally, A. Wiesbrock, 'Free Movement of Third-Country Nationals in the European Union: the Illusion of Inclusion' (2010) 35 EL Rev 455.

[137] See Protocol 21 on the UK and Ireland and Protocol 22 on Denmark.

[138] For a recent overview, see generally European Commission, *Communication on Migration* (COM(2011) 248 final).

birth-rate. The worry is that the costs of pension and social care provision are increasing, but the workforce generating the tax revenues needed to cover these costs is shrinking. The Commission clearly regards immigration as an important part of the solution to this problem.[139] Immigration offers a way of bringing younger people into the EU to keep the economy going and to plug gaps in the available workforce. On this view, there are good reasons to make the EU an attractive destination for migrant workers from third countries.

Measures to Promote Migration

In this section, we will consider some of the steps the EU has taken to encourage migrants to come to the EU to work, focusing particularly on the recent Blue Card Directive (which applies to Member States other than the UK, Ireland and Denmark).[140] We will also examine some of the challenges facing the EU in agreeing further directives on this issue.

The Blue Card Directive is intended to make it easier and more attractive for highly skilled migrant workers to move to the EU to take up employment by ensuring that the Member States deal with their applications in the same way. The Directive applies to TCNs who have completed higher education.[141] This fits neatly with the Europe 2020 objectives because it is targeted at migrants who will contribute to the 'high skills' agenda. The applicant is potentially eligible for a Blue Card if he or she has a binding offer of skilled work for at least a year, with a salary above a set threshold, and appropriate health insurance.[142] However, it is important to be clear that this does not mean that the Member State *must* grant the Blue Card. There are two highly significant limitations. First, the Member State is entitled to require employers to give priority to its own nationals, EU nationals or TCNs already on its territory before accepting a Blue Card applicant as the appropriate candidate to fill a vacancy.[143] And second, the Member States are allowed to maintain quotas for immigration by TCNs and to refuse a Blue Card application if the quota has been met.[144]

---

[139] Ibid, 12.
[140] Council Directive 2009/50/EC of 25 May 2009 on the conditions of entry and residence of third-country nationals for the purposes of highly qualified employment. For a critical discussion, see Y.K. Gümüs, 'EU Blue Card Scheme: The Right Step in the Right Direction?' (2010) 12 *European Journal of Migration and Law* 435.
[141] Directive 2009/50/EC, Art 2(g), gives Member States the option of counting five years of relevant professional experience as equivalent to higher education. Art 2(h) defines higher education for these purposes.
[142] Ibid, Art 5.
[143] Ibid, Art 8(2).
[144] Ibid, Art 6.

Another limitation on the Blue Card is that it does not necessarily entitle the holder to equal treatment with EU nationals as regards access to the labour market: Member States may opt to grant the right to equal treatment after two years, but there is no obligation to do so.[145] However, the Blue Card does provide some protection in the event that the migrant worker loses his or her job: it can only be withdrawn if he or she is unemployed for more than three months or if there is more than one period of unemployment.[146] The Blue Card also entitles the holder to equal treatment in 'working conditions' compared to EU nationals, and in relation to some aspects of social security, pensions and education.[147] After 18 months' residence in the first Member State, the Blue Card holder may move to another Member State to take up highly skilled employment, though this is not a right: when doing so he or she must apply to the second Member State for another Blue Card.[148]

Prior to the enactment of the Blue Card Directive, the EU had already taken some steps to provide TCNs who are lawfully resident in a Member State with certain rights.[149] The Family Reunification Directive applies to TCNs who hold 'a residence permit issued by a Member State for a period of validity of one year or more [and] who [have] reasonable prospects of obtaining the right of permanent residence'.[150] It requires the Member States to permit the TCN's family members to enter the EU and to reside with him or her, if certain conditions are met. The Long-Term Residence Directive provides TCNs with a right to a long-term residence permit once they have accumulated five years' lawful residence in a Member State, provided they have sufficient resources to support themselves.[151] This carries with it rights to equal treatment with nationals in various respects.[152] The Blue Card Directive enables Blue Card holders to acquire rights to family reunification and to long-term residence on slightly more favourable terms than those laid down in these measures.[153]

At the time of writing, the Commission is seeking agreement on a

---

[145] Ibid, Art 12(1).
[146] Ibid, Art 13.
[147] Ibid, Art 14.
[148] Ibid, Art 18.
[149] In addition to those granted by the free movement rules, discussed above.
[150] Council Directive 2003/86/EC of 22 September 2003 on the right to family reunification, Art 3.
[151] Council Directive 2003/109/EC of 25 November 2003 concerning the status of third-country nationals who are long-term residents, Art 4. See, generally, S. Peers, 'Implementing Equality? The Directive on Long Term Resident Third Country Nationals' (2004) 29 EL Rev 437.
[152] Directive 2003/109/EC, Art 11.
[153] Directive 2009/50/EC, Arts 15 and 16.

directive regulating seasonal work.[154] Like the Blue Card Directive, this would not constrain the Member States' discretion to determine how many TCNs could enter as seasonal workers, but it would create a single form of work permit (which would apply for more than one year, so that TCNs could come and go for several 'seasons') and would grant them certain employment rights. The Commission argues that the measure would address a need for seasonal workers in areas such as agriculture that is becoming hard to satisfy from within the EU workforce. Moreover, it would help to combat illegal immigration for this purpose and (in line with the EU's social goals) would protect vulnerable migrants against exploitation. However, it may prove difficult to persuade the Member States to agree to a measure which governs the entry of unskilled migrants, because it is harder to persuade a sceptical public of the economic benefits of this form of migration.

Measures to Control Migration

The Commission's proposals in the area of immigration are not confined to measures to promote certain types of immigration. Some attempt has also been made to address the Member States' concerns about illegal migration. From an employment perspective, the most notable example of this is the Employer Sanctions Directive, which again is not applicable in the UK.[155]

This Directive requires the Member States to prohibit the employment of 'illegally staying' TCNs.[156] They must also place an obligation on employers to require a TCN to have valid permission to be in the country and to give them a copy of the relevant documents before hiring that TCN.[157] The Directive goes on to require the imposition of 'effective, proportionate and dissuasive sanctions' on employers who breach this requirement,[158] and it gives some detail as to what those sanctions might be.

The thinking behind this directive is that, if the penalties are sufficiently severe, employers will be deterred from hiring illegal immigrants and this

---

[154]   European Commission, *Proposal for a Directive of the European Parliament and of the Council on the conditions of entry and residence of third-country nationals for the purposes of seasonal employment* (COM(2010) 379 final).

[155]   Directive 2009/52/EC of the European Parliament and of the Council of 18 June 2009 providing for minimum standards on sanctions and measures against employers of illegally staying third-country nationals.

[156]   Ibid, Art 3.

[157]   Ibid, Art 4.

[158]   Ibid, Art 5.

in turn will reduce the level of irregular migration into the EU. It remains to be seen how effective it will be in practice.

Conclusion

Immigration is a topic of considerable political controversy in most Member States. There is often a perception that immigration contributes to unemployment, as more workers chase decreasing numbers of jobs. Particularly in times of high unemployment, politicians may seek to win votes by promising to 'clamp down' on immigration and thus to enhance the job opportunities of citizens and others already resident in the country. However, in an EU with an ageing population, there may also be good economic arguments in favour of migration, which may apply not just to highly skilled migrants but also to unskilled workers in certain sectors.[159] For now at least, the Member States are keen to preserve their own autonomy in this area – whether by refusing to participate altogether or by refusing to accept new developments – and it remains to be seen whether or not the topic of migration into the EU labour market will eventually acquire a sure footing in EU labour law more generally.

FURTHER READING

The decisions in *Viking* and *Laval* gave rise to an enormous critical literature. As well as analysing the cases themselves, commentators have considered their broader implications for some of the themes we considered in Chapters 1 and 2, such as the European Social Model and its relationship with the EU's economic underpinnings, the constitutionalisation of EU labour law and the role of the Court of Justice. See, for example, C. Barnard, 'Internal Market v Labour Market: A Brief History' in M. de Vos (ed.) (2009), *European Union Internal Market and Labour Law: Friends or Foes?* (Portland, OR: Intersentia); A.C.L. Davies, 'One Step Forward, Two Steps Back? The *Viking* and *Laval* cases in the ECJ' (2008) 37 ILJ 126; C. Joerges and F. Rödl, 'Informal Politics, Formalised Law and the "Social Deficit" of European Integration: Reflections after the Judgments of the ECJ in *Viking* and *Laval*' (2009) 15 ELJ 1; C. Kilpatrick, '*Laval*'s Regulatory Conundrum: Collective Standard-Setting and the Court's New Approach to Posted Workers' (2009) 34 EL Rev

---

[159] S. Castles, 'Guestworkers in Europe: A. Resurrection?' (2006) 40 *International Migration Review* 741.

844; J. Malmberg and T. Sigeman, 'Industrial Actions and EU Economic Freedoms: the Autonomous Collective Bargaining Model Curtailed by the European Court of Justice' (2008) 45 CMLR 1115; P. Syrpis and T. Novitz, 'Economic and Social Rights in Conflict: Political and Judicial Approaches to their Reconciliation' (2008) 33 EL Rev 411.

Moving beyond these two cases, there is now some interest in whether the Court's approach might change, either of its own volition or because of the EU's ECHR accession. On the Court's most recent case-law, see P. Syrpis, 'Case Comment: Reconciling Economic Freedoms and Social Rights – the Potential of *Commission v Germany* (case C–271/08, judgment of 15 July 2010)' (2011) 40 ILJ 222, and on the ECHR, see K.D. Ewing and J. Hendy, 'The Dramatic Implications of *Demir* and *Baykara*' (2010) 39 ILJ 2, 38–43.

In relation to the free movement of workers, there is considerable interest among EU lawyers in the extent to which free movement rights now attach to citizens and not just to economically active people. Although this reading will take you outside the scope of labour law, it is an aspect of the broader 'constitutionalisation' debate: E. Spaventa, 'From *Gebhard* to *Carpenter*: Towards a (Non-)Economic European Constitution' (2004) 41 CMLR 743; H. de Waele, 'EU Citizenship: Revisiting its Meaning, Place and Potential' (2010) 12 *European Journal of Migration and Law* 319; M. Wind, 'Post-National Citizenship in Europe: The EU as a Welfare Rights Generator' (2009) 15 *Columbia Journal of European Law* 239; F. Wollenschläger, 'A New Fundamental Freedom beyond Market Integration: Union Citizenship and its Dynamics for Shifting the Economic Paradigm of European Integration' (2011) 17 ELJ 1. Although citizenship has an inclusive quality for the nationals of Member States, it has an exclusive quality for TCNs, on which see A. Wiesbrock, 'Free Movement of Third-Country Nationals in the European Union: the Illusion of Inclusion' (2010) 35 EL Rev 455. Whilst there appear to be strong economic arguments in favour of encouraging migration into the EU from third countries, the topic is politically controversial. For a good account of the context see S. Castles, 'Guestworkers in Europe: A Resurrection?' (2006) 40 *International Migration Review* 741.

4. Equality 1: women and men

This chapter and the next will explore EU equality law. The material is divided between two chapters partly because there is a lot to cover, and partly because the EU's long-established law on gender equality (discussed in this chapter) can be seen as somewhat separate to the EU's more recent expansion into other grounds of discrimination, and into techniques other than litigation by individual workers for the achievement of equality in the workplace (both of which will be considered in the next chapter).

Our discussion of EU gender equality law will focus on three main topics: equal pay, equal treatment in matters other than pay, and pregnancy and parenthood. This structure reflects the way in which EU law in this area has developed over time. Before we delve into the detail, we will identify two key themes to look out for, and give a brief account of some of the basic concepts in equality law.

KEY THEMES

This chapter will draw out two very strong themes in EU labour law generally. Indeed, it might be argued that gender equality exemplifies these themes. They are: the move from an economic rationale for EU law to a social rationale, and the role of the Court of Justice in developing the law. This section will introduce each of these themes as it applies in the equality field.

One of the things that many people know about Article 119, the provision in the original Treaty of Rome guaranteeing equal pay for men and women, is that it was *not* introduced because of a high-minded pursuit of the ideal of gender equality.[1] Instead, it was introduced for economic reasons. France already had equal pay laws and was concerned that its firms would be disadvantaged in the common market because firms in other countries with no equal pay laws would be able to use women workers as a form of cheap labour. It seems possible that Article 119 was accepted by the other signatory states in part at least because no-one

---

[1] See J. Kenner (2003), *EU Employment Law* (Oxford: Hart), 4.

realised the impact it would have.[2] In 1957, women's labour market participation was much lower than it is today, so gender equality probably seemed quite marginal. Moreover, it seems unlikely that anyone predicted the use that would be made of Article 119 in the courts (a point to which we will return below).

As with many other areas of EU law, though, what started out as a market-regulating principle has become something much more fundamental over time. EU equality law now covers social security and all aspects of employment (such as hiring and promotion) as well as pay. What started out as a focus on gender equality has been developed to provide rights for pregnant workers (by treating discrimination on grounds of pregnancy as a form of direct sex discrimination) and to provide protection for part-time workers (because discrimination against such workers is indirect sex discrimination where the majority of them are women). And, as we shall see in the next chapter, new grounds of discrimination have been added to the list.

This broader scope has been accompanied by a growing emphasis on equality as a fundamental right, not just another aspect of employment law.[3] This can be seen from the Court's statement in *Defrenne (No 3)*:

> The court has repeatedly stated that respect for fundamental personal human rights is one of the general principles of Community law, the observance of which it has a duty to ensure . . . There can be no doubt that the elimination of discrimination based on sex forms part of those fundamental rights.[4]

It can also be discerned from developments at the treaty level. The Treaty of Amsterdam amended Article 119 (then Article 141) in various ways, and new Article 13 gave the EU power to legislate to prohibit discrimination on a range of grounds as well as sex (to be discussed further in the next chapter). These provisions can now be found in Article 157 and Article 19 TFEU respectively. They had important practical consequences because they expanded the EU's competence to legislate on equality issues. Equality between men and women was also identified as one of the EU's main objectives in the Treaty of Amsterdam. These provisions can now be found in Articles 2 and 3 TEU. These provisions have symbolic value.

---

2   See C. Kilpatrick, 'Emancipation Through Law or the Emasculation of Law? The Nation-State, the EU, and Gender Equality at Work', in J. Conaghan, R.M. Fischl and K. Klare (eds) (2002), *Labour Law in an Era of Globalization* (Oxford University Press), 489–91.

3   For discussion, see M. Bell, 'The Principle of Equal Treatment: Widening and Deepening', in P.P. Craig and G. de Búrca (eds) (2011), *The Evolution of EU Law* (2nd edn, Oxford University Press).

4   Case 149/77 *Defrenne v SABENA* [1978] ECR 1365, [26]–[7].

Since Lisbon, the EU Charter of Fundamental Rights has legal effect. This contains a chapter on equality which includes a general right not to be discriminated against on a range of grounds (Article 21) and a right to equal treatment for men and women (Article 23). In its post-Lisbon case-law, the Court has tended to ground the principle of equality on the Charter, rather than on its own jurisprudence.[5]

In terms of the rationales for EU intervention that we considered in Chapter 1, EU equality law appears to have begun as a means of preventing a 'race to the bottom', or at least preventing the French government's efforts to promote equal pay from being undermined, and has now become one of the EU's core social objectives, justified as a good thing in its own right. One interesting question for consideration in this chapter is whether this transition – or transformation – is complete. To what extent have the principle's market origins remained influential over time? As we shall see, the Court does not necessarily require employers or governments to pursue equality at all costs.

A second powerful theme in this chapter is the role of the Court of Justice. Article 119 became an important tool for litigants because of two important steps in the Court's reasoning. First, it developed the doctrine of direct effect for Treaty provisions in the *van Gend* case,[6] and second, in *Defrenne (No 2)*, the Court applied it to Article 119 even though this involved stretching some of the criteria for direct effect laid down in previous case-law.[7] This provided an opportunity for trade unions, campaign groups and public bodies at the national level to use EU law to challenge inequality when national laws and practices either created it or did not do enough to stop it. Although the EU legislature has made some significant moves in the equality field, many of the biggest developments came directly from the Court itself: the application of equal pay requirements to pensions,[8] for example, or the extension of protection to individuals undergoing gender reassignment in *P v S and Cornwall*.[9] Most importantly, the gradual development of equality law has continued even during periods in which the EU legislature was unable to agree on new developments.

Of course, the Court is not without its critics. One problem (which we considered in Chapter 2) is its tendency to develop the law by taking a big

---

[5] See, for example, Case C–236/09 *Association Belge des Consommateurs Test-Achats v Council* [2011] nyr, [16]–[19].

[6] Case 26/62 *van Gend & Loos v Netherlands Inland Revenue Administration* [1963] ECR 3.

[7] Case 43–75 *Defrenne v SABENA* [1976] ECR 455.

[8] Case C–262/88 *Barber v Guardian Royal Exchange Assurance Group* [1990] ECR I–1889.

[9] Case C–13/94 *P v S and Cornwall County Council* [1996] ECR I–2143.

step forward in one case, and then to take a much more cautious stance in other apparently similar cases. For example, after the radical extension of the law on sex equality to protect people undergoing gender reassignment in *P v S and Cornwall*,[10] it came as an enormous disappointment to many people that the Court refused in the *Grant* case to make the same move to protect people who were suffering discrimination because of their sexual orientation.[11] This has now been rectified by legislation, but at the time it was frustrating for those who wanted to see the law developing more quickly. Sometimes, the Court's cautious side can be explained on economic grounds: it is concerned about the consequences of its decisions.[12] But even this can be difficult for some commentators to accept, given the importance of the equality principle.

Another concern is that the Court sometimes fails to appreciate the complexity of issues such as equality. There is a vast theoretical literature on the various concepts of equality – formal equality, equality of opportunity and equality of results – and on the limitations of equality as a guiding principle.[13] The Court's decision-making processes and reasoning style do not lend themselves to elaborate analyses of this literature, and we should not be surprised that we do not see such analyses there. However, the Court's view of equality can sometimes be rather unsophisticated. For example, as we shall see below, the Court initially adopted a formal view of equality ('treat likes alike') which regarded positive action schemes aimed at redressing the balance in favour of historically disadvantaged groups as inherently worrying and in need of special justification. It took a while for the Court to recognise that such schemes might pursue a different kind of equality altogether.

OVERVIEW

Although Article 119 featured in the original Treaty of Rome, the EU legislature did not make use of the competence it afforded until the 1970s. Two crucial directives were then adopted: Directive 75/117/EEC on equal pay, and Directive 76/207/EEC on equal treatment in other aspects of

---

[10]   Ibid.

[11]   Case C–249/96 *Grant v South-West Trains* [1998] ECR I–621. For a comparison of the two cases, see M. Bell, 'Shifting Conceptions of Sexual Discrimination at the Court of Justice: from *P v S* to *Grant v SWT*' (1999) 5 ELJ 63.

[12]   See *Barber*, above n. 8.

[13]   See, generally, S. Fredman, 'European Community Discrimination Law: A Critique' (1992) 21 ILJ 119.

employment.[14] Whilst Article 119 set out the principle of equal pay for equal work, the Equal Pay Directive was crucial in extending that principle to work of equal value: in other words, the situation in which the woman and the man are not doing exactly the same job but their jobs can be regarded as equivalent in terms of the effort or responsibility they involve.[15] The Equal Treatment Directive ensured that the principle of equality was extended beyond pay to cover other aspects of the employment relationship, such as training and promotion. Importantly, these directives have not eclipsed the Treaty article itself, not least because it has horizontal as well as vertical direct effect, so we will also find some cases decided under what is now Article 157 TFEU.

As we shall see below, a particular problem for claimants in discrimination cases is proving that discrimination has taken place. This was addressed through Directive 97/80/EC on the burden of proof in sex discrimination cases.[16] And in 2002, the Equal Treatment Directive was amended to bring it into line with the EU's legislation on other grounds of discrimination, which we will consider in more detail in the next chapter.[17] This resulted in a complex body of directives with multiple amendments, so in 2006 the Recast Directive, Directive 2006/54, was enacted.[18] This brings most of the earlier law together into a single piece of legislation.[19] This may have the effect of eliminating some of the remaining differences between EU law's treatment of pay and other matters, aside from the role of Article 157 TFEU.

Directive 86/613/EEC extended the equal treatment principle to self-employed people. This illustrates one of the ways in which equality law can be seen as a slightly different 'legal order' to traditional labour law. Whilst labour law tends not to apply to self-employed people, because they are regarded as capable of negotiating their own terms and conditions of employment, equality law transcends these traditional boundaries. The current version of this legislation is Directive 2010/41/EU on the

---

[14] Directive 79/7/EEC on social security was also adopted at this time but will not be considered in detail here.

[15] The Treaty of Amsterdam incorporated the equal value principle into then Art 141 for the first time.

[16] Extended to the UK by Directive 98/52/EC.

[17] Directive 2002/73/EC.

[18] For discussion, see N. Burrows and M. Robison, 'An Assessment of the Recast of Community Equality Laws' (2007) 13 ELJ 186.

[19] This repeals Directive 75/117/EEC on equal pay; Directive 76/207/EEC (amended by Directive 2002/73/EC) on equal treatment for men and women; Directive 86/378/EC (amended by Directive 96/97/EC) on occupational social security schemes; Directive 97/80/EC (amended by Directive 98/52/EC) on the burden of proof.

application of the principle of equal treatment between men and women engaged in an activity in a self-employed capacity.

As we shall see later in this chapter, these anti-discrimination measures were interpreted by the Court to address the situation in which a woman was discriminated against on grounds of her pregnancy. This body of case-law was supplemented by Directive 92/85/EEC, the Pregnant Workers' Directive, which made provision about the health and safety of pregnant workers and, most importantly for our purposes, laid down minimum standards about maternity leave. Parental leave (which may be used by fathers too) has been addressed quite separately through a social partner agreement concluded under the social dialogue and subsequently enacted as a directive.[20] This has recently been revised.[21]

BASIC CONCEPTS

Direct Discrimination

Direct discrimination occurs when a similarly situated man and woman are not treated alike: for example, where they are doing the same job but he is paid more than she is. Under Article 2(1)(a) of the Recast Directive, direct discrimination is defined as:

> where one person is treated less favourably on grounds of sex than another is, has been or would be treated in a comparable situation.

The key point about direct discrimination is that it cannot, in general, be justified by the employer. There are two exceptions to this. One is age discrimination, to be considered in the next chapter. The other is where a person's sex can be regarded as a qualification for doing the job in question.[22] This is illustrated by the *Sirdar* case, in which the Court held that it was justifiable for the UK government to exclude women from the Royal Marines because of the need to maintain operational effectiveness as a commando force.[23]

Importantly, there is some flexibility in determining whether or not the employer's treatment has occurred 'on grounds of sex' and thus in

---

[20]   Directive 96/34/EC.
[21]   Directive 2010/18/EU implementing the revised Framework Agreement on parental leave.
[22]   Directive 2006/54, Art 14(2).
[23]   Case C–273/97 *Sirdar v The Army Board* [1999] ECR I–7403.

delineating the boundary between direct and indirect discrimination. In *Schnorbus*, the Court adopted a formal approach.[24] The claimant challenged a rule which gave priority access to training to people who had completed military service. Military service was required of men and not women, but the Court approached the problem as one of indirect discrimination: military service, not sex, was the criterion. However, in *Maruko*, a case concerning discrimination on grounds of sexual orientation, the claimant sought payment of a widower's benefit from his same-sex partner's pension scheme after his partner's death.[25] He was refused the payment because it was only afforded to spouses. Although the law drew a distinction between spouses and civil partners, and could thus be regarded as a form of indirect discrimination on the *Schnorbus* reasoning, the Court treated the problem as one of direct discrimination. The choice is significant because it affects the availability of the justification defence.

Indirect Discrimination

Indirect discrimination occurs where the employer applies a rule equally to men and women, but the impact of doing so is to put one sex at a disadvantage. Importantly, though, the employer is given an opportunity to argue that an indirectly discriminatory measure has been adopted for a legitimate reason and can be justified. Indirect discrimination is defined in Article 2(1)(b) of the Recast Directive as follows:

> where an apparently neutral provision, criterion or practice would put persons of one sex at a particular disadvantage compared with persons of the other sex, unless that provision, criterion or practice is objectively justified by a legitimate aim, and the means of achieving that aim are appropriate and necessary.

An example may help to illustrate the point. In the classic *Bilka-Kaufhaus* case, part-time workers were only allowed to join the company's pension scheme if they had worked full-time for at least 15 years in a period of 20 years.[26] On the face of it, this rule applied equally to men and women. But in practice, it is often the case that part-time workers are mostly women, whereas full-time workers are mostly men, so a rule disadvantaging part-timers might well have a disparate impact on women.[27] This was a matter for the national court to determine on the facts. If it was the case that the

---

[24] Case C–79/99 *Schnorbus v Land Hessen* [2000] ECR I–10997.

[25] Case C–267/06 *Maruko v Versorgungsanstalt der deutschen Bühnen* [2008] ECR I–1757.

[26] Case 170/84 *Bilka-Kaufhaus v Weber von Hartz* [1986] ECR 1607.

[27] As we shall see in Chapter 6, EU law now prohibits discrimination against part-time workers regardless of sex.

rule had a disparate impact, attention would turn to the employer, who would have the opportunity of showing that the rule furthered a legitimate business aim in a proportionate way.

Although this sounds relatively straightforward, the Court has some-times found it difficult to decide what counts as disparate impact. This can be illustrated by a series of cases on the fraught issue of overtime pay for part-time workers. In *Helmig*, the claimant was a part-time worker who challenged a rule that overtime supplements were only available when a person worked more than the standard full-time working week.[28] The Court held that this situation did not demonstrate unequal treatment. If a part-timer worked more than his or her normal hours, he or she would be paid at the standard rate, just like a full-timer. And if the part-timer's hours exceeded full-time hours, he or she would get the supplement, just like a full-timer. But in *Elsner-Lakeberg*, the Court took a different approach.[29] In that case, workers (part-time or full-time) were only paid for overtime if it was in excess of three hours per week. The Court held that this was unequal treatment, because the impact on a part-timer of working an extra two hours per week was greater than the impact on a full-timer (relative to their normal weekly hours), but this was not reflected in the rules on overtime pay. The Court sought to resolve this conflict in *Voß*.[30] In that case, workers received overtime pay at a lower rate than normal pay for any hours worked above their normal contractual hours. This rule applied equally to part-time and full-time workers. However, its effect was that a part-timer who did overtime which brought his or her hours up to the full-time level would be paid for some of it at the lower overtime rate, with the result that his or her overall pay would be lower for the same number of hours. The upshot of this line of cases seems to be that the Court has moved towards an approach in which it is important to calculate the practical effect of a rule, rather than just looking at it on its face. This seems to be consistent with the underlying purpose of indirect discrimination law, to combat 'disparate impact'. However, critics might argue that the Court's approach shades over into deciding what might count as fair – not just equal – pay for part-timers, guided by the principle that there should be some kind of reward for extra hours worked.

As noted above, the employer is given an opportunity to justify rules that have a disparate impact. The Court has laid down a proportional-ity test for the national courts to use when determining this question. The application of this test will be discussed in more detail below. For

---

[28]   Case C–399/92 *Stadt Lengerich v Helmig* [1994] ECR I–5727.
[29]   Case C–285/02 *Elsner-Lakeberg v Land Nordrhein-Westfalen* [2004] ECR I–5861.
[30]   Case C–300/06 *Voß v Land Berlin* [2007] ECR I–10573.

now, it is sufficient to highlight a couple of points. First, the Court (as in many other areas) sometimes goes beyond just stating the proportionality test and seeks instead to give more detailed guidance to the national courts. Although this may be helpful to those courts, it is a mixed blessing in the sense that it encourages them to refer questions to the Court of Justice whenever a case raises slightly different issues to those previously addressed in the Court's case-law. Second, after a shaky start, the Court has now set its face against 'mere generalisations' about people and how they might behave. The employer must produce some evidence to back up its claims. Third, as we shall see below, claimants may sometimes challenge national legislation rather than their employer's decisions. In these cases, the Court has tended to be more deferential to national governments in deciding whether or not a measure is justified.

EQUAL PAY

This section will explore some of the central issues of EU equal pay law. As we shall see later in this chapter, many of the developments here have fed into EU equality law more generally. We will begin by considering the direct effect of what is now Article 157, before exploring the Court's attempts to define the concept of 'pay' and to develop the concept of equality.

Direct Effect

The Court developed the concept of direct effect for Treaty provisions in the well-known *van Gend en Loos* case.[31] Importantly, that case laid down a number of criteria for determining whether a particular treaty provision was suitable for direct effect. The focus was on whether the provision was clear enough for national courts to apply it: so a provision that required implementing measures to be adopted by the Member States could not be given direct effect. These criteria were gradually relaxed in a number of judgments, including *Defrenne (No 2)*.[32]

In *Defrenne*, the Court acknowledged that Article 119 (as it then was) was directed to the Member States, and that the principle of 'equal pay for equal work' is not always straightforward to apply, particularly in cases where the claim is that the woman's work is of equal value to that of the

---

[31] Above n. 6.
[32] Above n. 7.

man with whom she is comparing herself. However, the Court held that there are cases in which the application of the Article is clear, and that in those cases it should be found to have direct effect.[33] So in *Defrenne* itself it was directly effective because the claimant was an air hostess who did exactly the same job as male cabin stewards but was paid at a lower hourly rate.

This was a highly significant move on the part of the Court. It allowed women to bring claims for equal pay regardless of whether their Member State had implemented Article 119 in national law. Even where a Member State had taken implementing measures, claimants could try to invoke Article 119 to fill gaps in the protection thus afforded. Moreover, since Treaty articles have direct effect both vertically (against the state) and horizontally (against private parties), claimants could invoke Article 119 in litigation against private employers, thereby significantly increasing the scope for claims. This has resulted in a steady flow of cases from the national courts to the Court of Justice, via the preliminary ruling procedure. These cases have provided the Court with the opportunity it needed to develop equal pay law.

Importantly, though, the Court limited the temporal effect of the judgment in *Defrenne*.[34] This meant that claims could not be brought relating to events which had occurred prior to the date of the judgment in the case, unless litigation was already under way. Although this limited the practical effect of *Defrenne*, it shows the Court's awareness of the far-reaching economic consequences of its decision, for employers in particular. Employers might not have been aware of the possibility of litigation under Article 119, so the Court regarded it as unfair and potentially disruptive to subject them to what might have seemed like a retrospective change.

The Definition of 'Pay'

'Pay' is defined in Article 157(2) in the following terms:

> 'Pay' means the ordinary basic or minimum wage or salary and any other consideration, whether in cash or in kind, which the worker receives directly or indirectly, in respect of his employment, from his employer.

In a series of cases, the Court has adopted an expansionary interpretation of 'pay', holding that it could include benefits paid after the end of the employment relationship. For example, in *Garland*, 'pay' was found

---

[33]   Ibid, [18].
[34]   Ibid, [69]–[75].

to cover concessionary travel fares for employees after retirement.[35] In the *Barber* case, the Court extended this to cover redundancy payments (whether statutory, contractual or *ex gratia*), and 'contracted-out' occupational pension schemes.[36] The latter have an ambiguous status because, although they are privately run, employees contribute to them in place of contributing to a state-run pension scheme. And when *Barber* was decided, state-run pension schemes (which had a long history of differentiating between men and women in various ways) were exempt from EU sex discrimination law.

Importantly, though, the *Barber* case illustrates another important feature of the Court's approach: expansion is often coupled with restraint. The Court noted that it had been reasonable for Member States and employers to assume that contracted-out pension schemes would fall outside Article 119. The Court therefore decided to limit the temporal effect of its judgment, so that employers would be obliged to make changes to their schemes only for the future.[37] Critics saw this as taking away a major part of the advance made in the case. But the decision is an important illustration of the Court's awareness of the economic consequences of its decisions.

Issues of Proof

There was a time when employers were quite open about pay inequalities between men and women. Separate men's and women's grades were not uncommon. Nowadays, pay inequality – though persistent – is much less blatant. This gives rise to a significant set of concerns about proving that a pay inequality exists. The Court's approach to these concerns has generally been a cautious one, attracting criticism from some commentators, but it is alive to the practicalities faced by the national courts in applying the law, and to the concerns of employers in the market. As always with the Court, though, there have been bold moves too, notably in relation to the burden of proof. Significant changes have also been made by the EU legislature.

An unequal pay claim hinges on the claimant's ability to compare herself (usually) with a man doing the same or similar work but who is receiving more pay. This person is known as the 'comparator'. In its definition of direct discrimination, the Recast Directive allows the claimant to suggest how the comparator 'is, has been or would be treated in a comparable

---

[35]   Case 12/81 *Garland v British Rail Engineering* [1982] ECR 359.
[36]   Above n. 8.
[37]   Ibid, [40]–[45].

situation'.[38] This broad phrase allows entirely hypothetical scenarios to be constructed, in which a court decides what would have happened to a man in the claimant's situation. The Member States must make provision for this in national law. Where national law has been insufficiently protective, claimants have turned instead to Article 157, which has both vertical and horizontal direct effect. But in this context, the Court has refused to allow hypothetical comparison, holding in *Macarthys* that it is too complex an idea to be developed by judicial means.[39]

The Court has also been criticised by commentators for its development of the 'single source' rule. Identifying a real comparator can be difficult for women working for firms in sectors such as cleaning or catering, where very few men are employed. This is sometimes referred to as the problem of 'occupational segregation'.[40] This has led some theorists to suggest that women should be able to draw comparisons more widely: not just within their own workplace, but between different firms and across whole sectors of the economy.[41] The Court has resisted these suggestions. Although it has accepted that there is no need for the woman and her comparator to work for the same employer, raising the possibility of bringing a claim where, for example, the same collective agreement is applicable, it has held that there must be a 'single source' responsible for the discrimination. This is illustrated by the *Lawrence* case, in which a local council put work out to tender.[42] The successful contractor re-employed some of the council workers, but on worse terms and conditions than those they had enjoyed at the council. This resulted in a pay inequality between the female workers whose jobs had been contracted out, and various male workers who remained in the employment of the council. However, it was held that this was not a permissible comparison because the claimants' pay and the male comparators' pay did not derive from a 'single source' that could rectify the inequality. On one hand, this significantly reduces opportunities for claimants to seek equal pay, particularly in situations like *Lawrence* (and the subsequent *Allonby* case)[43] where the employer has restructured its operations at their expense. On the other hand, it reflects a concern on the part of the Court to protect employers against being held liable for another employer's decision to pay its workers at a higher rate.

---

38   Directive 2006/54, Art 2(1)(a).
39   Case 129/79 *Macarthys v Smith* [1980] ECR 1275, [15]. For discussion, see S. Fredman, 'Reforming Equal Pay Laws' (2008) 37 ILJ 193.
40   Or 'crowding': see B.R. Bergmann (1986), *The Economic Emergence of Women* (New York: Basic Books), Chapters 5 and 6.
41   See S. Fredman, 'Marginalising Equal Pay Laws' (2004) 33 ILJ 281.
42   Case C–320/00 *Lawrence v Regent Office Care* [2002] ECR I–7325.
43   Case C– 256/01 *Allonby v Accrington & Rossendale College* [2004] ECR I–873.

In relation to disparate impact claims, the law has developed through a mix of judicial activism and legislative intervention. In a disparate impact claim, the claimant must be able to show that the employer's ostensibly neutral rule works to the disadvantage of women. This can be a very data-hungry exercise. Where the challenged rule is in national legislation, the Court has expected claimants to be able to produce statistics relating to its impact on men and women across the labour market as a whole.[44] Whilst it is not inappropriate to ask a claimant to prove their case, and to demonstrate that it goes beyond a quirk in the statistics, the legislature has encouraged a more relaxed approach. The Recast Directive uses the phrase 'would put persons of one sex at a particular disadvantage', which softens the Court's previous approach in two respects.[45] First, the use of 'would' opens up the possibility of hypothetical enquiries. Second, the term 'particular disadvantage' is much less mathematical in its tone than the Court's own emphasis on evidence of a significant statistical disparity.

In relation to the burden of proof in equal pay claims, the Court has been the one to make bold moves. It has opened up the possibility for a claimant to shift the burden of proof to the employer, provided certain conditions are met.[46] In *Danfoss*, the employer paid a basic wage plus bonuses to its staff.[47] The average pay of female employees was lower than that of male employees, but the claimants were unable to determine how the bonus system worked. The Court held that where an employer's pay system was 'totally lacking in transparency' and resulted in lower pay, on average, for a large group of women, the burden shifted to the employer to prove that no discrimination was taking place.[48]

Interestingly, the Commission had been seeking the enactment of a directive on the burden of proof prior to the decision in *Danfoss*, but it was not able to secure the agreement of the Member States until after the Court's decision. Directive 97/80/EC on the burden of proof required the Member States to provide for the burden of proof to shift to the respondent if the claimant could prove 'facts from which it may be presumed that

---

[44]   Case C-167/97 *R v Secretary of State for Employment, ex p Seymour-Smith* [1999] ECR I-623.

[45]   Directive 2006/54, Art 2(1)(b).

[46]   For an example of a case in which the claimant had not done enough to shift the burden, see Case C-381/99 *Brunnhofer v Bank der österreichischen Postsparkasse* [2001] ECR I-4961.

[47]   Case 109/88 *Handels- og Kontorfunktionærernes Forbund I Danmark v Dansk Arbejdsgiverforening (on behalf of Danfoss)* [1989] ECR 3199.

[48]   Ibid, [16].

there has been direct or indirect discrimination'.[49] This requirement now features in Article 19 of the Recast Directive.

Justification

We saw above that in cases of indirect discrimination – where an ostensibly neutral criterion has been used which, in practice, disadvantages a particular group – it is possible for the employer (or the national government, in cases involving legislation) to justify the use of that criterion. In general terms, the test for justification is proportionality as laid down in *Bilka-Kaufhaus*.[50] The application of proportionality to the facts of the case is a matter for the national court, though – as is often the case – the Court of Justice has not been able to resist providing quite detailed guidance in some cases. Justification has given rise to particular problems in equal pay, so it warrants some additional discussion here. Two points are worth highlighting. First, equal pay highlights the conflict between the EU's social and market objectives in a particularly stark way. This is because employers often seek to argue that 'market forces' are the explanation for a difference in pay between two groups of workers, raising the question of how far the EU should go in regulating markets. Second, equal pay can often give rise to tensions between women's claims to equal pay and long-established structural features of the labour market, such as collective bargaining arrangements or rewards for length of service. Again, the extent to which equality law should prompt changes in these areas has proved to be a difficult question for the Court.

The 'market forces' argument was presented to the Court in the starkest form in *Enderby*.[51] In that case, a group of speech therapists working for the UK National Health Service sought pay equality with a group of pharmacists. The speech therapists were almost all female while the pharmacists were almost all male (particularly in senior positions). On the assumption that the jobs were of equal value, the Court was asked to rule on various questions including justification. One argument put forward by the employer was that pharmacists were more in demand than speech therapists, so it was necessary to pay more to attract candidates when positions were advertised. The Court held that '[t]he state of the employment market, which may lead an employer to increase the pay of a particular job in order to attract candidates, may constitute an objectively justi-

---

[49] Art 4.
[50] Above n. 26.
[51] Case C–127/92 *Enderby v Frenchay Health Authority* [1993] ECR I–5535.

fied economic ground'.[52] Importantly, though, the Court also suggested that, where it was possible to do so, the national court should consider whether the extra pay was proportionate to the need to attract candidates, opening up the possibility of finding that the employer was offering more additional pay than was genuinely necessary to combat staff shortages.

The *Enderby* decision has been strongly criticised by Fredman in particular.[53] She argues that the Court's decision fails to consider the broader question of why the two jobs were so segregated in the first place, and why the male-dominated job attracted higher levels of pay. She suggests that equal pay law should be seen as market-regulating, not market-reflecting. The employer's defence that 'the market made me do it' may show that the employer is not morally to blame for what has happened, but does not, in Fredman's view, absolve the employer or the Court from the responsibility to put the problem right once identified. However, it is easy to see why, from the Court's perspective, telling an employer that it cannot reflect (impersonal) market forces in its business decisions might seem like a step too far.

A second theme in the justification case-law is the depth of conflict between equal pay law and long-established structures in the labour market. There are various examples of this but for present purposes we will focus on two: collective bargaining and length of service. The difficult question for the Court is how far employers should be allowed to fall back on 'the way we've always done things' as a defence.

The collective bargaining issue arose in the *Enderby* case, discussed above.[54] Alongside the market forces defence, the employer also sought to argue that the collective bargaining arrangements for the speech therapists were different from those for the pharmacists. The Court was sceptical about this argument, noting that it would provide an easy way to evade the requirements of equal pay. However, the Court relaxed its stance slightly in the later *Dansk Industri* case, holding that separate collective bargaining arrangements are a factor the national court can take into account when assessing whether or not a pay differential is unrelated to sex.[55]

However, the Court has found it more difficult to address pay differentials arising out of length of service. It is very common for employers' pay schemes to reward length of service. This is seen as a way of retaining employees with firm-specific skills and experience. But critics argue that it

---

[52]   Ibid, [26].
[53]   S. Fredman, 'Equal Pay and Justification' (1994) 23 ILJ 37.
[54]   Above n. 51, [20]–[23].
[55]   Case C–400/93 *Specialarbejderforbundet i Danmark v Dansk Industri* [1995] ECR I–1275, [44]–[7].

disadvantages women because they are more likely to take career breaks, and therefore find it more difficult to build up long periods of service with the same employer. Across the labour market as a whole, it is generally the case that women have shorter periods of service than men.

The Court's initial approach to length of service was a cautious one, in which it was unwilling to disrupt employers' existing approaches. In *Danfoss*, the Court held that the employer did not have to 'provide special justification for recourse to the criterion of length of service'.[56] In *Nimz*, the Court suggested a more critical approach to length of service, in which it would be open to the national court to hold that, on the facts of the case, the employer was exaggerating the relationship between length of service and the skills or experience rewarded with extra pay.[57] The position was finally clarified in *Cadman* by weaving the *Danfoss* and *Nimz* rulings together.[58] Thus, it is open to the employer to use length of service as a criterion without having to justify this, unless the claimant can cast doubt on whether the employer's use of the criterion genuinely rewards greater experience and better job performance. If the claimant can do this, the burden shifts onto the employer to prove that length of service is an appropriate criterion to use in the particular situation under scrutiny.

This is typical of the Court's approach. It proceeds cautiously, and is careful to back-track on any particularly bold moves. But critics argue that it is too willing to accept 'traditional' approaches to pay determination, like length of service, even when there is clear evidence that they disadvantage women and contribute to entrenched inequalities in the labour market. Having said that, though, the *Cadman* decision can be criticised from the employer perspective too. It is not clear exactly what the claimant has to do in order to displace length of service as an 'assumed to be valid' criterion, or what the employer would have to do in order to defend it. Paradoxically, this uncertainty might lead some employers to abandon pay scales dependent on length of service even though the Court has tried to preserve them.

EQUAL TREATMENT

In the employment context, equal treatment of men and women in matters other than pay was first addressed in Directive 76/207, the Equal Treatment Directive. As we shall see in the next chapter, the EU has leg-

---

56 *Danfoss*, above n. 49, [24]–[5].
57 Case C–184/89 *Nimz v Freie und Hansestadt Hamburg* [1991] ECR I–297.
58 Case C–17/05 *Cadman v Health & Safety Executive* [2006] ECR I–9583.

islated more recently to address other grounds of discrimination (such as race and sexual orientation) and the drafting of these new directives left the law on sex discrimination looking rather old-fashioned. This led to the enactment of a new directive, Directive 2002/73, which amended the Equal Treatment Directive to bring it into line with these developments. The relevant law can now be found in the Recast Directive, Directive 2006/54/EC.

Scope

According to Article 14(1) of the Recast Directive:

> There shall be no direct or indirect discrimination on grounds of sex in the public or private sectors, including public bodies, in relation to:
> (a) conditions for access to employment, to self-employment or to occupation, including selection criteria and recruitment conditions, whatever the branch of activity and at all levels of the professional hierarchy, including promotion;
> (b) access to all types and to all levels of vocational guidance, vocational training, advanced vocational training and retraining, including practical work experience;
> (c) employment and working conditions, including dismissals, as well as pay as provided for in Article 141 of the Treaty;
> (d) membership of, and involvement in, an organisation of workers or employers, or any organisation whose members carry on a particular profession, including the benefits provided for by such organisations.

Thus, for example, in the *Kleist* case, it was held that it was unlawful sex discrimination for an employer to insist on the compulsory retirement of employees who reached the state pension age when this age was different for men and women.[59]

Article 14(2) lays down an exception for 'genuine occupational requirements':

> Member States may provide, as regards access to employment including the training leading thereto, that a difference of treatment which is based on a characteristic related to sex shall not constitute discrimination where, by reason of the nature of the particular occupational activities concerned or of the context in which they are carried out, such a characteristic constitutes a genuine and determining occupational requirement, provided that its objective is legitimate and the requirement is proportionate.

This allows for obvious exceptions such as employing a woman to play

---

[59]   Case C–356/09 *Pensionsversicherungsanstalt v Kleist* [2010] nyr.

the part of a female character in a play or film. It has generated litigation in the context of the armed forces because it is often the case that the Member States reserve certain roles for men. The Court has held that the exclusion of women may be justified where it is necessary for combat effectiveness,[60] but the argument must be made in relation to specific roles and cannot simply be applied in a general way to the armed forces as a whole.[61]

Harassment

A specific problem facing many women in the workplace is harassment by employers or co-workers. The Recast Directive includes harassment in its definition of discrimination under Article 2(2):

> For the purposes of this Directive, discrimination includes:
> (a)   harassment and sexual harassment, as well as any less favourable treat-
>   ment based on a person's rejection of or submission to such conduct . . .

Harassment is defined as 'where unwanted conduct related to the sex of a person occurs with the purpose or effect of violating the dignity of a person, and of creating an intimidating, hostile, degrading, humiliating or offensive environment',[62] and sexual harassment is defined as 'where any form of unwanted verbal, non-verbal or physical conduct of a sexual nature occurs, with the purpose or effect of violating the dignity of a person, in particular when creating an intimidating, hostile, degrading, humiliating or offensive environment'.[63]

It is important to note the emphasis on dignity in these provisions. Although we are generally concerned with equality in this chapter, many commentators regard dignity as either an alternative basis for the law in this area or as an important supplement to equality as the basis for the law. Dignity encourages the courts to focus on how the individual was treated and whether basic standards of fairness were met, and may be easier to deal with than complex equality inquiries into how other people (comparators) were treated or might have been treated. However, it remains the case that the harassment must be 'related to . . . sex' so some comparison may still be needed in order to prove that harassment has occurred within the definition.

---

[60]   *Sirdar*, above n. 23.
[61]   Case C–285/98 *Kreil v Germany* [2000] ECR I–69.
[62]   Directive 2006/54, Art 2(1)(c).
[63]   Ibid, Art 2(1)(d).

Positive Action

In simple terms, positive or affirmative action involves giving preference to an under-represented group when making employment decisions, such as recruitment or promotion. Commentators regard positive action schemes as a potentially important supplement to the anti-discrimination law we have considered so far in this chapter, because they provide a way of speeding up the process of achieving equality. They do not depend on individuals to bring complaints or to prove that they have been victims of discrimination. Instead, they involve identifying instances of inequality through workplace statistics, and taking positive steps to rectify the situation. Having said that, positive action schemes can also be highly controversial because they involve making employment decisions on social grounds (coupled with an assessment of the candidates' merits) and not on merit alone.[64] Those who lose out may feel that they have been treated unfairly. EU law deals with this by leaving the decision to the Member States: in other words, if Member States choose to adopt such schemes, they will not be acting unlawfully in EU law, but they are not obliged by EU law to do so.[65]

The legislative position on positive action has shifted over time.[66] The original Equal Treatment Directive presented positive action as a derogation from the equality principle, by stating that the Directive was 'without prejudice to measures which promote equal opportunity for men and women, in particular by removing existing inequalities which affect women's opportunities'.[67] A more encouraging approach can be seen in the Treaty of Amsterdam, which inserted what was then new Article 141(4). The current provision, Article 157(4) TFEU, is virtually identical:

> With a view to ensuring full equality in practice between men and women in working life, the principle of equal treatment shall not prevent any Member State from maintaining or adopting measures providing for specific advantages in order to make it easier for the underrepresented sex to pursue a vocational activity or to prevent or compensate for disadvantages in professional careers.

The Recast Directive, Article 3, refers to this provision. This newer formulation uses potentially more expansive language, in particular by

---

[64] Though the meaning of the term 'merit' is unclear: see C. McCrudden, 'Merit Principles' (1998) 18 OJLS 543.

[65] See Art 157(4) TFEU, and Directive 2006/54, Art 3.

[66] See C. Barnard (2006), *EC Employment Law* (3rd edn, Oxford University Press), 417–30.

[67] Directive 76/207, Art 2(4).

referring to the provision of 'advantages' and not just the removal of 'existing inequalities'.

The Court of Justice's early decisions on positive action were extremely hostile. In *Kalanke*, the Court considered a scheme in which preference was automatically given to the candidate from the under-represented group when the candidates competing for promotion were equally qualified.[68] It held that the scheme was unlawful. This decision came in for considerable criticism,[69] and the Court modified its stance in the *Marschall* case.[70] That case involved a scheme similar to the one in *Kalanke*, but the preference for candidates from the under-represented group was not automatic. It remained possible for the candidate who was about to be denied the promotion to argue that the particular circumstances of his case should override the positive action scheme. The Court held that this more subtle form of positive action was acceptable. In so holding, the Court noted that, even when a man and a woman were equally qualified, the woman might still lose out because of prejudices against women in the workplace.[71]

The shift in the Court's attitude became most obvious in the *Abrahamsson* case, in which the Court (unusually) made a passing reference to the underlying concepts of equality:

> The clear aim of [the use of criteria generally favouring women] is to achieve substantive, rather than formal, equality by reducing de facto inequalities which may arise in society and, thus, in accordance with Article 141(4) EC, to prevent or compensate for disadvantages in the professional career of persons belonging to the under-represented sex.[72]

This formulation has been repeated in subsequent cases including, recently, *Roca Álvarez*.[73] It suggests that the Court now regards positive action schemes not as an exception to the basic principle of formal equality, but as a legitimate way of pursuing a different objective of equality of results.

Nevertheless, the Court still subjects positive action schemes to careful scrutiny using the proportionality test. As regards schemes relating to hiring and promotion, the ruling in *Marschall* remains authoritative. The

---

[68]   Case C–450/93 *Kalanke v Freie Hansestadt Bremen* [1995] ECR I–3051.

[69]   See European Commission, *On the Interpretation of the Judgment of the Court of Justice on 17 October 1995 in Case C–450/93 Kalanke v Freie Hansestadt Bremen* (COM (96) 88 final).

[70]   Case C–409/95 *Marschall v Land Nordrhein-Westfalen* [1997] ECR I–6363. For background to these cases, see D. Schiek, 'Sex Equality Law After *Kalanke* and *Marschall*' (1998) 4 ELJ 148.

[71]   Ibid, [29].

[72]   Case C–407/98 *Abrahamsson v Fogelqvist* [2000] ECR I–5539, [48].

[73]   Case C–104/09 *Roca Álvarez v Sesa Start España* [2010] nyr, [34].

Court appeared to place an outer limit on what the Member States could do in the *Abrahamsson* case.[74] In that case, the positive action scheme allowed a 'sufficiently' qualified person from a disadvantaged group to be promoted, even where she was less well-qualified than her competitors. This seemed to go too far against the Court's underlying view that jobs should be allocated primarily on merit, so the Court found it to be disproportionate.

The position in relation to childcare advantages has proved more problematic. On one hand, by giving better nursery access or parental leave to women, employers or Member States may believe that they are providing advantages which may help to increase women's labour market participation. On the other hand, there is a danger of entrenching a stereotype that women have particular responsibility for childcare. This tension can be seen in two cases, *Lommers* and *Roca Álvarez*. In *Lommers*, the Court upheld a scheme which gave priority in the allocation of workplace nursery places to the children of female workers.[75] The scheme did not exclude male workers altogether, because they could apply for places in an emergency or if they were single parents. The Court noted that the scheme might entrench the stereotype that women have particular responsibility for childcare, but countered this view with the argument that the scheme only related to the workplace nursery, and not to access to childcare generally. Since demand exceeded supply, some of the female staff would have to look elsewhere for their childcare. In *Roca Álvarez*, national law provided that a woman with a child under the age of 9 months could take an hour off work each day to care for the child.[76] This leave was also available to fathers where both mother and father were employed. The claimant complained of discrimination because his partner was self-employed so he was not able to take the leave. The Spanish government sought to defend the law on the basis that it provided a positive benefit for women, but the Court rejected this view, stating that it was 'liable to perpetuate a traditional distribution of the roles of men and women by keeping men in a role subsidiary to that of women in relation to the exercise of their parental duties'.[77]

It is inherent in the nature of individual litigation that positive action schemes are developed at the national level and then challenged before the Court. This leaves the Member States with the responsibility for figuring

---

[74] Above n. 72, [53].
[75] Case C-476/99 *Lommers v Minister van Landbouw, Natuurbeheer en Visserij* [2002] ECR I-2891.
[76] Above n. 73.
[77] Ibid, [36].

out from the Court's case-law what it might be willing to permit. This may also seem rather discouraging for governments because they are only told what is not allowed. And since there is no obligation to develop positive action schemes, it may seem easier not to bother. As we shall see in the next chapter, the focus of much of the equality literature has shifted away from positive action towards 'mainstreaming' approaches, in which governments and (perhaps) firms are encouraged to consider the equality impact of their decision making in more general terms. Nevertheless, there may yet be interesting developments in positive action. For example, Caruso argues that the legislation on other grounds of discrimination – which also permits positive action – will require the Court to develop a much more sophisticated understanding of equality in order to cope with the more complex claims that are likely to arise.[78] A positive action scheme which sought to redress the balance between a range of different disadvantaged groups might not lend itself to the easy application of a proportionality test.

Justification

As we saw above in the discussion of equal pay, indirect discrimination is regarded as justified where it demonstrably pursues a legitimate aim and is proportionate. Much of what was said there about the justification of employers' pay practices is also applicable in the equal treatment field. But it is also important to remember that an individual might bring a challenge to national legislation where it gives rise to unequal pay or treatment. The Court's approach to such cases seems to be subtly different.

One of the best-known examples of this is the *Seymour-Smith* case, in which female workers challenged the UK requirement that a worker must have completed a two-year 'qualifying period' of continuous work for the same employer before any entitlement to claim unfair dismissal would arise.[79] They argued that women tended to stay with the same employer for shorter periods of time than men. The Court doubted on the facts whether the statistical difference between men's and women's ability to satisfy the two-year requirement was sufficient to show indirect discrimination. Nevertheless, it had interesting things to say about justification. The Court appeared to make reference to the proportionality test, following its earlier decision in *Rinner-Kühn*:[80]

---

[78]   D. Caruso, 'Limits of the Classic Method: Positive Action in the European Union After the New Equality Directives' (2003) 44 *Harvard International Law Journal* 331.
[79]   Above n. 44.
[80]   Case 171/88 *Rinner-Kühn v FWW Spezial-Gebäudereinigung* [1989] ECR 2743.

Mere generalisations concerning the capacity of a specific measure to encourage recruitment are not enough to show that the aim of the disputed rule is unrelated to any discrimination based on sex nor to provide evidence on the basis of which it could reasonably be considered that the means chosen were suitable for achieving that aim.[81]

However, Barnard notes that the use of the word 'reasonably' in this paragraph may suggest that the proportionality test as applied to the Member States is a bit softer than that applied to employers.[82]

The solution may lie in the reference, in the preceding paragraph, to the Member State's margin of appreciation on social policy issues. The Court made it clear that this could not be used to defeat fundamental principles of EU law, such as equality. However, the objectives likely to be cited by the Member States include large-scale economic and social policy considerations, such as reducing unemployment, and these are the kinds of policy factor that are most likely to attract judicial deference. This is true both of the Court itself and, more importantly, the national courts whose job it is to apply the proportionality test to the facts of cases. So, provided the Member States advance arguments that go beyond 'mere generalisations', they are likely to be scrutinised with a relatively 'light touch'. We will return to this point when considering some of the other grounds of discrimination, since it has been important in the age discrimination case-law in particular.

PREGNANCY

The EU legislature did not make specific provision for pregnant workers until the enactment of Directive 92/85/EEC, the Pregnant Workers Directive (PrWD). The Equal Treatment Directive simply stated, in Article 2(3), that it was without prejudice to national legislation protecting women in respect of pregnancy and maternity.[83] Thus, in the early years at least, it was left to the Court of Justice to develop the concept of pregnancy discrimination.[84] And even today, equality law remains relevant because the PrWD does not deal comprehensively with the issues. Maternity

---

[81] Above n. 44, [76].
[82] Barnard, above n. 66, 368–71.
[83] Above n. 67.
[84] For a detailed analysis of the early case-law, see A. Masselot and E. Caracciolo di Torella, 'Pregnancy, Maternity and the Organisation of Family Life: an Attempt to Classify the Case Law of the Court of Justice' (2001) 26 EL Rev 239.

leave is now recognised as a right in Article 33(2) of the EU Charter of
Fundamental Rights.

The Case-law

On a very literal view of equality, in which a woman must compare herself
with a similarly situated man, pregnancy is difficult to deal with, because
there are no similarly situated men. The Court's first significant move, in
the *Dekker* case, was to hold that, since pregnancy only affects women,
decisions made on the ground that a woman is pregnant are a form of
sex discrimination without the need to make comparisons.[85] The case-law
since *Dekker* has been concerned in a broad sense with determining exactly
what counts as a decision made 'on grounds of pregnancy'.

An early line of defence adopted by employers was to suggest that their
decision had been made on the grounds that the pregnant woman would
not be available to perform her duties, and not on the grounds that she
was pregnant per se. To accept this argument would render the protection
afforded by *Dekker* nugatory because it is inherent in pregnancy that it
will involve spending some time away from work. However, the argument did present difficulties where the employer argued that the worker
was required for a particular time and would not be available for that
time. This argument first emerged in *Webb*, in which a woman was hired
to cover another woman's maternity leave.[86] She then found that she was
pregnant and the employer dismissed her. The Court held that this was
discriminatory. On the facts, though, Ms Webb had been engaged on an
indefinite contract, so this cast doubt on the employer's claim that she had
been hired for the sole purpose of covering the other employee's maternity
leave. In the *Tele Danmark* case, the Court had an opportunity to clarify
its position.[87] In that case, a woman on a fixed-term contract was dismissed when it was discovered that she was pregnant. The Court held (in
no uncertain terms) that this constituted discrimination:

> Since the dismissal of a worker on account of pregnancy constitutes direct dis-
> crimination on grounds of sex, whatever the nature and extent of the economic
> loss incurred by the employer as a result of her absence because of pregnancy,
> whether the contract of employment was concluded for a fixed or an indefinite
> period has no bearing on the discriminatory character of the dismissal. In either

---

[85]   Case C–177/88 *Dekker v VJV-Centrum* [1990] ECR I–3941, [12].
[86]   Case C–32/93 *Webb v EMO Air Cargo* [1994] ECR I–3567.
[87]   Case C–109/00 *Tele Danmark v Handels- og Kontorfunktionærernes Forbund i Danmark*
[2001] ECR I–6993.

case the employee's inability to perform her contract of employment is due to pregnancy.[88]

Thus it was established that dismissal because a woman is pregnant is never acceptable, regardless of any arguments that the 'true reason' is her unavailability for work.

It is always possible for the employer to argue that the reason for dismissing a pregnant worker is unrelated to the pregnancy: redundancy, for example. But from the beginning of the pregnancy to the end of the maternity leave, it seems clear in practice that the employer will need to have very strong evidence to support the claim that the woman's pregnancy was not the reason for dismissal. The decision in *Paquay* extends the protection even further.[89] In that case, a woman was notified of her dismissal when she returned to work after maternity leave. However, it was established on the facts that the employer had decided to dismiss her and had taken steps to recruit her replacement while she was on maternity leave. The Court held that this fell foul of the prohibition on dismissal in Article 10 of the PrWD (to be discussed further below).

The Court also developed some principles for maternity pay prior to the enactment of the PrWD. It has held that there is no obligation on the state to arrange for a pregnant woman to receive full pay during her maternity leave.[90] But any reduction in pay must not render the pay (plus other benefits) 'so low as to undermine the purpose of maternity leave'.[91] In *Gillespie*, where the employer had calculated the employees' maternity pay based on full pay, the Court held that the employees on maternity leave were entitled to benefit from a pay rise afforded to the rest of the workforce while they were absent, because to do otherwise would amount to discrimination.[92]

An area of particular difficulty has been the extent to which the protection against discrimination on grounds of pregnancy covers illness attributable to the pregnancy. The Court's approach here has been broadly protective of pregnant workers, on the basis that pregnancy-related illness does not affect men and cannot be compared with other types of illness. However, it has placed limits on the protection it affords. A pregnant worker is protected against dismissal during the pregnancy because of

---

[88]   Ibid, [31].
[89]   Case C–460/06 *Paquay v Société d'architectes Hoet & Minne* [2007] ECR I–8511.
[90]   Case C–342/93 *Gillespie and others v Northern Health and Social Services Boards* [1996] ECR I–475, [20].
[91]   Ibid.
[92]   Ibid, [21]–[2].

absence due to pregnancy-related illness.[93] During any such periods of absence, it is usually permissible for her to receive reduced pay, provided she is treated in the same way as a man who is off sick.[94] During maternity leave, the worker is protected against dismissal in any event. In *Hertz* (which predated the PrWD), the Court held that the Member States were obliged to ensure that the maternity leave period was long enough to cover what the Court described as 'the period in which the disorders inherent in pregnancy and confinement occur'.[95] However, once the maternity leave period has ended, an employer may terminate a worker's contract for absence owing to pregnancy-related illness in the same way as it would for any other type of sickness absence. The Court took the view that any other approach would be too uncertain for employers and might have harmful consequences in relation to women's employment.[96]

The Pregnant Workers Directive

The PrWD is primarily a health and safety measure.[97] It is an individual directive within the meaning of Article 16(1) of Directive 89/391/EEC, the Framework Directive on Health and Safety. Thus, a large part of the PrWD is given over to a requirement on the employer to conduct a risk assessment of the potential hazards facing pregnant workers at the workplace,[98] such as exposure to dangerous chemicals.[99] There is also a requirement on the Member States to ensure that pregnant workers are not obliged to undertake night-time working.[100] Since we are not concerned with health and safety law in this book, our main focus will be on the provisions governing maternity leave and protection against dismissal.

Article 9 of the Directive requires the Member States to grant a right to paid time off to attend antenatal examinations where these take place during working hours. Article 8 requires Member States to provide a right to 14 weeks' maternity leave. When the leave can be taken is to be determined in accordance with national law and practice. Although 14 weeks is not particularly generous compared with the leave already available in

---

[93] Case C–394/96 *Brown v Rentokil* [1998] ECR I–4185.
[94] Case C–191/03 *North Western Health Board v McKenna* [2005] ECR I–7631.
[95] Case C–179/88 *Handels- og Kontorfunktionaerernes Forbund i Danmark (on behalf of Hertz) v Dansk Arbejdsgiverforening* [1990] ECR I–3979, [15].
[96] Ibid, [9].
[97] Directive 92/85/EEC.
[98] Ibid, Art 2, leaving definitions to national law.
[99] Ibid, Arts 3–6.
[100] Ibid, Art 7.

some Member States, Article 1(3) contains a non-regression clause. During the leave the pregnant worker must receive either pay or an 'adequate' allowance which is at least equivalent to that she would receive if she was off work due to illness.[101] Apart from pay, the worker's other rights under her employment contract must be maintained during the leave.[102]

Finally, Article 10 requires the Member States to provide protection against dismissal:

> Member States shall take the necessary measures to prohibit the dismissal of workers, within the meaning of Article 2, during the period from the beginning of their pregnancy to the end of the maternity leave referred to in Article 8(1), save in exceptional cases not connected with their condition which are permitted under national legislation and/or practice . . .

Article 10 is directly effective;[103] it has been held to apply to both fixed-term and indefinite contracts.[104] This had been an issue of some controversy because, as we saw above, employers had sought to argue that it was legitimate to dismiss a pregnant worker on a fixed-term contract since she would be unavailable for work at the required time. The right to return to work after maternity leave was inserted into the Equal Treatment Directive in 2002,[105] and can now be found in the Recast Directive, Article 15:

> A woman on maternity leave shall be entitled, after the end of her period of maternity leave, to return to her job or to an equivalent post on terms and conditions which are no less favourable to her and to benefit from any improvement in working conditions to which she would have been entitled during her absence.

The obligation to ensure that the worker benefits from improvements, such as pay rises, awarded during her absence codifies some of the Court's case-law on the matter, discussed above.[106]

In 2008, the Commission proposed an amendment to the Directive that would have seen maternity leave increased from 14 weeks to 18 weeks.[107]

---

[101] Ibid, Art 11(2) and (3). The Member States may make this conditional including on a qualifying period of employment but such period may not exceed 12 months.
[102] Ibid, Art 11(2).
[103] Case C–438/99 *Jiménez Melgar v Ayuntamiento de Los Barrios* [2001] ECR I–6915.
[104] See *Tele Danmark*, above n. 87, and *Jiménez Melgar*, ibid.
[105] Directive 2002/73/EC, inserting new Art 2 into Directive 76/207.
[106] *Gillespie*, above n. 90.
[107] European Commission, *Proposal for a Directive of the European Parliament and of the Council amending Council Directive 92/85/EEC on the introduction of measures to encourage improvements in the safety and health at work of pregnant workers and workers who have recently given birth or are breastfeeding* (COM (2008) 637).

The European Parliament supported this move and indeed proposed that leave should be set at 20 weeks.[108] However, these plans were rejected by the Council.

Parental Leave

So far, our focus has been predominantly on women: on legislation and case-law enabling them to challenge instances of discrimination, and on employment protection during pregnancy. Despite these various measures, it is generally accepted that full equality for men and women at work has yet to be achieved. For many commentators, one of the most significant reasons for this is that women still tend to have a greater share of the responsibility for looking after children and doing other household tasks alongside their paid work in the labour market. One challenge therefore is to make it easier to reconcile work and family life, and (where children are raised by a couple) to encourage men to get more involved in parenting.[109] And one way to do this might be through the provision of parental leave to both male and female workers.

One approach by which EU law can influence the provision of parental leave is by ensuring that arrangements put in place by the Member States are scrutinised through an equality lens. As we saw above, special protection for pregnant women has always been allowed in EU law as a derogation from the equal treatment principle.[110] This is clear from the *Hofmann* case, in which the Court stated that:

> [t]he Directive recognizes the legitimacy, in terms of the principle of equal treatment, of protecting a woman's needs in two respects. First, it is legitimate to ensure the protection of a woman's biological condition during pregnancy and thereafter until such time as her physiological and mental functions have returned to normal after childbirth; secondly, it is legitimate to protect the special relationship between a woman and her child over the period which follows pregnancy and childbirth, by preventing that relationship from being disturbed by the multiple burdens which would result from the simultaneous pursuit of employment.[111]

However, over time, the Court has become more willing to scrutinise whether a period of leave is genuinely designed to protect women who

---

[108]   See http://ec.europa.eu/social/main.jsp?catId=89&langId=en&newsId=930&further News=yes (last visited 23 August 2011).

[109]   See, generally, E. Caracciolo di Torella and A. Masselot (2010), *Reconciling Work and Family Life in EU Law and Policy* (Basingstoke: Palgrave Macmillan).

[110]   Directive 2006/54, Art 28.

[111]   Case 184/83 *Hofmann v Barmer Ersatzkasse* [1984] ECR 3047, [25].

have just given birth. For example, we saw above that in *Roca Álvarez*, the Court examined a Spanish scheme which allowed both women and men to take an hour off work each day to be with a very young child, but placed more obstacles in the way of men seeking to take advantage of the scheme.[112] The Court noted that, historically, the scheme had been designed to assist women who were breastfeeding, but that more recently it had become a way of enabling either parent to care for their child. On that view, the leave should be afforded to men on the same terms as it was afforded to women. Thus, EU law is now playing a role in ensuring that national parental leave is granted equally to men and women unless it is strictly related to pregnancy.

EU law has also put in place minimum standards relating to parental leave. The Parental Leave Directive was enacted in 1996 to implement the social partners' first agreement under the social dialogue procedure.[113] The social partners negotiated a revised agreement on the subject in 2009, and a new Directive was enacted in 2010 to give effect to this.[114] Parental leave is recognised as a fundamental right in Article 33(2) of the EU Charter of Fundamental Rights.[115]

The agreement applies equally to male and female workers. One of the new features of the revised agreement is that it applies explicitly to part-time, fixed-term and agency workers,[116] though the definition of 'worker' remains a matter for national law.[117] The basic right it affords is to four months' parental leave (an increase from the previous entitlement to three months' leave) for every parent.[118] This right is not conferred on the children themselves and there is no obligation on the Member State to provide double the leave when the parents have twins.[119] The Member States are obliged to ensure that at least one month out of the four is not transferable to the other parent, as a means of encouraging both parents to make use of the leave.[120] Many of the practical details of taking leave are for the Member States to determine, such as the imposition of a qualifying period of service (which may not exceed one year), the circumstances in

---

[112] Above n. 73.
[113] Directive 96/34/EC implementing the framework agreement on parental leave concluded by UNICE, CEEP and the ETUC, extended to the UK by Directive 97/75/EC.
[114] Directive 2010/18/EU implementing the revised Framework Agreement on parental leave concluded by BUSINESSEUROPE, UEAPME, CEEP and ETUC and repealing Directive 96/34/EC.
[115] Cited in Case C–149/10 *Chatzi v Ypourgos Oikonomikon* [2010] nyr, [63].
[116] Directive 2010/18/EU, Annex, cl 1(3).
[117] Ibid, cl 1(2).
[118] Ibid, cl 2.
[119] *Chatzi*, above n. 115.
[120] Directive 2010/18/EU, Annex, cl 2(2).

which the employer can postpone the leave for business reasons, and the form in which leave can be taken (in longer or shorter blocks of time, for example).[121]

Clause 5 of the Agreement requires that workers taking parental leave be afforded the right to return to the same or an equivalent job afterwards. Their contractual rights should be maintained, so that, for example, any pay rises awarded during their leave should be applied to them on their return. The clause also requires the Member States to ensure that those taking or seeking to take parental leave are protected against dismissal and other detrimental treatment on this ground (the latter being a new addition to the revised Agreement).

The Parental Leave Directive requires the Member States to put in place two other rights in addition to the right to parental leave itself. One of these is the right to 'emergency leave' in clause 7(1):

> Member States and/or social partners shall take the necessary measures to entitle workers to time off from work, in accordance with national legislation, collective agreements and/or practice, on grounds of force majeure for urgent family reasons in cases of sickness or accident making the immediate presence of the worker indispensable.

The Member States may place conditions on this form of leave, which may include limiting it to a certain amount of time per year. The other right, which is new in the revised Agreement, is a right to request changes to working arrangements in clause 6(1):

> In order to promote better reconciliation, Member States and/or social partners shall take the necessary measures to ensure that workers, when returning from parental leave, may request changes to their working hours and/or patterns for a set period of time. Employers shall consider and respond to such requests, taking into account both employers' and workers' needs.
>
> The modalities of this paragraph shall be determined in accordance with national law, collective agreements and/or practice.

This right has considerable potential to help workers of both sexes to achieve a better work/life balance. For example, it could enable a worker to opt for part-time working, so that work could be fitted around his or her children's school day. However, there are some significant limitations. First, the right is not free-standing. It only applies on the worker's 'return' from parental leave. This means that the worker must exercise the right to parental leave before he or she can make a request. This limits workers'

---

[121]   Ibid, cl 3.

choices, because some people might prefer to adjust their hours instead of taking parental leave. Also, most worryingly, it means that the right to request a change in hours may not be available to those who cannot afford to take parental leave (because there is no obligation on the Member States to ensure that periods of parental leave are paid). And second, it is only a right to make a 'request', so the employer may refuse. Of course, there is a need to ensure that the legitimate interests of firms can also be taken into account here, but much will depend on how the Member States implement the provisions. For example, the right will be more effective where the law controls the reasons for which employers can refuse a request.

Despite these criticisms, it is worth noting that the revised Parental Leave Directive does represent an improvement on the position under the original directive. It illustrates the gradual improvement in rights over time in the field of equality, and shows that this can take place through legislation as well as through case-law. It has also demonstrated that the social partners are still capable of successful use of the cross-industry social dialogue procedure, even if this is only to revise an existing agreement rather than to tackle a new subject area.

FURTHER READING

EU gender equality law is a very substantial body of law, and you may find it helpful to refer to one of the many specialist texts on the subject for a more detailed account.

There is a powerful feminist critique of 'traditional' gender equality law in the EU: see S. Fredman, 'European Community Discrimination Law: A Critique' (1992) 21 ILJ 119. As we shall see in the next chapter, recent developments have sought to address some aspects of this critique, but whether or not they have succeeded is open to debate.

One of the themes picked out in this chapter was the role of the Court of Justice. For a detailed analysis, see C. Kilpatrick 'Emancipation through Law or the Emasculation of Law? The Nation-State, the EU and Gender Equality at Work' in J. Conaghan, R.M. Fischl and K. Klare (eds) (2002), *Labour Law in an Era of Globalization: Transformative Practices and Possibilities* (Oxford University Press). Another fascinating piece by the same author explores in depth the neglected topic of the role of national courts: C. Kilpatrick, 'Community or Communities of Courts in European Integration? Sex Equality Dialogues Between UK Courts and the ECJ' (1998) 4 ELJ 121.

In view of the EU's proposed accession to the ECHR, interesting questions arise as to the relationship between the case-law of the Court of

Justice and that of the ECtHR. These are explored in S. Besson, 'Gender Discrimination under EU and ECHR Law: Never Shall the Twain Meet?' (2008) 8 *Human Rights Law Review* 647.

Our focus in this chapter has been on equality in the employment sphere, but the issue of gender equality in other spheres of life is also important. To get a flavour of the discussion, see S. Millns, 'Gender Equality, Citizenship, and the EU's Constitutional Future' (2007) 13 ELJ 218, and A. Masselot, 'The State of Gender Equality Law in the European Union' (2007) 13 ELJ 152. And from an even broader perspective, it is also possible to locate gender equality within a broader notion of equality in EU law generally: see, for example, G. More 'The Principle of Equal Treatment: from Market Unifier to Fundamental Right' in P.P. Craig and G. de Búrca (eds) (1999), *The Evolution of EU Law* (Oxford University Press).

5. Equality 2: new grounds, new techniques

Now that we have got to grips with the basics of equality law in the EU, through analysis of the provisions on gender equality, we are in a position to assess some of the more recent developments in EU equality law. We will focus on two main areas: the enlargement of the EU's competence to legislate on grounds of discrimination other than gender, and the emergence of new techniques for enforcing or promoting equality alongside individual litigation.

NEW GROUNDS

The EU's heavy focus on gender equality has come to seem slightly anomalous in modern times, given the general acceptance of the fact that there are many other forms of discrimination in society and in the workplace. Moreover, the EU's relative effectiveness in addressing sex discrimination has made it an obvious target for pressure groups campaigning for legal action to combat other types of discrimination.

Article 21(1) of the EU Charter of Fundamental Rights identifies a long list of prohibited grounds of discrimination:

> Any discrimination based on any ground such as sex, race, colour, ethnic or social origin, genetic features, language, religion or belief, political or any other opinion, membership of a national minority, property, birth, disability, age or sexual orientation shall be prohibited.

Moreover, this list is illustrative and would not preclude the recognition of other grounds. However, as is well known, the EU Charter does not create legislative competences for the EU. For the EU's power to legislate on discrimination, we need to look to the treaties. The Treaty of Amsterdam inserted a new Article 13 into the EC Treaty which is now Article 19(1) TFEU:

> Without prejudice to the other provisions of the Treaties and within the limits of the powers conferred by them upon the Union, the Council, acting

unanimously in accordance with a special legislative procedure and after obtaining the consent of the European Parliament, may take appropriate action to combat discrimination based on sex, racial or ethnic origin, religion or belief, disability, age or sexual orientation.

The EU made use of this new provision to enact two directives,[1] one on race discrimination[2] and the so-called 'framework directive' covering the other grounds.[3] This expansion of grounds has led to new challenges, particularly for the Court of Justice, in elaborating their scope. We will consider these new directives below.

One question which has arisen in some of the cases is whether the Court might be willing to expand the EU's competences in the field of equality beyond the grounds listed in Article 13. However, it does not look as if this will occur. In *Chacón Navas*, for example, the claimant had been dismissed on grounds of sickness.[4] The case focused on the definition of disability discrimination, but once the Court had established that sickness and disability were two different things, the claimant sought to argue that discrimination on grounds of sickness should also be prohibited by EU law. The Court rejected this argument. Thus, while there may be some room for expansionist interpretations of the grounds listed in Article 13 (as we shall see) there does not appear to be any scope for argument that the categories of discrimination addressed by EU law are open.[5]

Race

The EU's first use of its new power to legislate on grounds of discrimination other than sex after the Treaty of Amsterdam was the enactment of the Race Directive, Directive 2000/43.[6] Although our focus will be on the

---

[1] For an interesting argument that Article 13 was not the correct Treaty basis for the Framework Directive, because it is an employment measure, see M. Bell and R. Whittle, 'Between Social Policy and Union Citizenship: the Framework Directive on Equal Treatment in Employment' (2002) 27 EL Rev 677.

[2] Directive 2000/43 implementing the principle of equal treatment between persons irrespective of racial or ethnic origin.

[3] Directive 2000/78/EC establishing a general framework for equal treatment in employment and occupation. For a critical overview, see D. Schiek, 'A New Framework on Equal Treatment of Persons in EC Law?': Directives 2000/43/EC, 2000/78/EC and 2002/73/EC changing Directive 76/207/EEC in Context' (2002) 8 ELJ 290.

[4] Case C–13/05 *Chacón Navas v Eurest Colectividades* [2006] ECR I–6467, [53]–[7]. For discussion see D.L. Hosking, 'A High Bar for EU Disability Rights' (2007) 36 ILJ 228.

[5] See also Case C–217/08 *Mariano v INAIL* [2009] ECR I–35; Case C–310/10 *Ministerul Justiiei i Libertilor Ceteneti v Agafiei* [2011] nyr.

[6] For an overview and comparison with Council of Europe initiatives on race equality, see E. Howard, 'Anti Race Discrimination Measures in Europe: An Attack on Two Fronts'

employment aspects of the Directive, one of its most significant features is that – in contrast to the Framework Directive[7] – it extends beyond the employment field and applies in many other areas, such as access to education and the supply of goods and services.[8]

Defining 'racial or ethnic origin'

The Race Directive prohibits discrimination on the ground of 'racial or ethnic origin'.[9] Importantly, this phrase is not limited to the claimant's racial or ethnic origin, so the Member States are required to ensure that, for example, discrimination based on the ethnicity of the claimant's friends or family is also precluded when implementing the Directive.

The Race Directive does not define the terms 'racial or ethnic origin'. This leaves the matter in the hands of the Court. Although the definition of 'racial or ethnic origin' is unlikely to pose very many problems, it may prove difficult to determine where 'race' ends and other related concepts, such as religion and nationality, begin. In an ideal world, these distinctions would not matter: claimants often face multiple forms of discrimination and should not necessarily be expected to be able to specify the precise ground on which they are claiming. However, in EU law the distinctions are important because race, religion and nationality attract different levels of protection and because protection against nationality discrimination is only available to EU citizens. Thus, it is important to think about where the lines between them might be drawn.

Race discrimination and religious discrimination overlap where a particular religious group also has a shared ethnic origin. For example, in English law Sikhs were able to claim under race discrimination legislation (prior to the enactment of legislation prohibiting religious discrimination) because their group had a shared ethnic origin as well as a shared faith.[10] As yet, it is unclear whether the same approach will be taken by the Court of Justice. As we shall see below, religious discrimination is also prohibited

---

(2005) 11 ELJ 468. For a detailed account of EU law on race generally, see M. Bell (2009), *Racism and Equality in the European Union* (Oxford University Press).

[7] The Commission has proposed extending the law here but agreement has not yet been reached: see European Commission, *Proposal for a Council Directive on Implementing the Principle of Equal Treatment Between Persons Irrespective of Religion or Belief, Disability, Age or Sexual Orientation* (COM(2008) 426 final). For discussion, see L. Waddington, 'Future Prospects for EU Equality Law: Lessons to be Learnt from the Proposed Equal Treatment Directive' (2011) 36 EL Rev 163.

[8] Directive 2000/43, Art 3(1). EU law on gender equality extends beyond employment but not as far as the Race Directive: see Directive 2004/113 on goods and services, and the provisions on social security discussed in Chapter 6.

[9] Directive 2000/43, Art 1.

[10] *Mandla v Dowell Lee* [1983] 2 AC 548.

in EU law, though this prohibition is confined to the employment context and has more exceptions than the prohibition on race discrimination. It may therefore be more attractive for claimants to present their claims as relating to race discrimination rather than religious discrimination when both are arguable.

Another possible area of overlap is discrimination on grounds of nationality or national origin. It is not difficult to imagine situations in which the unequal treatment experienced by an individual might have been on grounds of race or on grounds of nationality. The treatment of nationality discrimination in EU law is much more controversial and has led to some significant criticism of the Race Directive.[11] Of course, in one sense, the prohibition of discrimination on grounds of *nationality* has long been a central part of the European project. The rules of the internal market have forced the Member States to dismantle barriers to workers from other Member States. And, as we saw in Chapter 3, citizens of the EU have some rights even when they are economically inactive. However, the development of EU citizenship brings with it another distinction: between those who are citizens and those who are not (often referred to as 'third-country nationals' or TCNs). In relation to TCNs, the Member States remain keen to preserve their ability to control migration from non-EU countries: indeed, governments' inability to control migration within the EU may have enhanced the demand for secure external borders. This has resulted in a situation in which EU nationals enjoy considerable protection against nationality discrimination whereas TCNs do not.

This distinction emerges from the structure of the Treaty. Article 18 TFEU prohibits discrimination on the grounds of nationality 'within the scope of the Treaties'. This is generally taken to mean that it applies only to EU citizens. Article 19 TFEU empowers the EU to legislate to prohibit discrimination on various grounds including 'racial or ethnic origin' but does not mention nationality. It is generally thought that this provision does apply to TCNs and that the omission of nationality as a prohibited ground is deliberate. The EU Charter of Fundamental Rights reinforces the distinction. Article 21(1) contains a prohibition on discrimination which is broader than that found in Article 19 TFEU, but importantly, Article 21(2) separates out nationality as a ground and states that it is covered 'within the scope of application of the Treaties and without prejudice to any of their specific provisions'. Under the Treaties and the Charter, EU citizens enjoy additional rights which are not applicable to TCNs.

---

[11]   See, generally, B. Hepple, 'Race and Law in Fortress Europe' (2004) 67 MLR 1, and S.B. Lahuerta, 'Race Equality and TCNs, or How to Fight Discrimination with A Discriminatory Law' (2009) 15 ELJ 738.

Most significantly for present purposes, nationality discrimination is clearly excluded from the Race Directive by Article 3(2):

> This Directive does not cover difference of treatment based on nationality and is without prejudice to provisions and conditions relating to the entry into and residence of third-country nationals and stateless persons on the territory of Member States, and to any treatment which arises from the legal status of the third-country nationals and stateless persons concerned.

Of course, the subject of immigration control is, itself, controversial, but this is not the place for a full discussion. For present purposes, what is significant is the extent of this exclusion. Can TCNs be treated differently in employment situations because of their status as non-citizens? Some commentators have suggested that this provision should be construed as applying only to the Member States' activities in the immigration field, but the wording is quite broad, referring as it does to 'any treatment'.[12] However, the Court's decision in the *Firma Feryn* case offers some encouragement.[13] The case concerned statements in the media by an employer to the effect that he did not want to employ 'immigrants' because his customers would not trust them in their homes. It might have been arguable that the case was one of nationality rather than race discrimination, since the employer's statements referred to 'immigrants', but this issue was not raised and the case was treated as a straightforward example of race discrimination. This suggests that the Court may prefer not to apply the Article 3(2) exclusion strictly and may not be interested in drawing technical distinctions in this area.

Direct and indirect discrimination
The Race Directive prohibits direct and indirect discrimination and harassment, defined in the usual way.[14] The *Firma Feryn* case exposed a possible gap in these provisions.[15] As noted above, the case concerned statements by an employer that he did not wish to employ 'immigrants'. The claim was brought by a Belgian NGO concerned with race discrimination issues, but no individual victim of the discrimination could be discovered. The Court held that the employer's statement was sufficient to give rise to a *prima facie* case of direct discrimination, even though there was no identifiable victim. The employer could rebut the *prima facie* case

---

[12] For discussion, see Hepple, ibid.
[13] Case C–54/07 *Centrum voor gelijkheid van kansen en voor racismebestrijding v Firma Feryn* [2008] ECR I–5187.
[14] Directive 2000/43, Art 2.
[15] Above n. 13.

by showing that its recruitment practices did not correspond to its public statements.

As Krause explains, the Court adopted an expansive interpretation of the Directive's provisions but, unusually, did not do so by invoking rights arguments or broad statements about general principles of EU law.[16] Instead, the Court focused on arguments about 'fostering . . . a socially inclusive labour market'.[17] He points out that a rights argument would not have been helpful in the context of 'victimless' discrimination because there was no-one to argue that his or her rights had been violated. The Court's focus on access to the labour market was a more appropriate basis for its teleological interpretation.

Importantly, though, there is a limit to the Court's decision. The Directive does not require the Member States to provide anyone other than the victim with a right to sue. This is clear from Article 7. The first paragraph of Article 7 requires the Member State to provide judicial or administrative enforcement procedures for people who claim to be victims of discrimination. Article 7(2) further states that:

> Member States shall ensure that associations, organisations or other legal entities, which have, in accordance with the criteria laid down by their national law, a legitimate interest in ensuring that the provisions of this Directive are complied with, may engage, either on behalf or in support of the complainant, with his or her approval, in any judicial and/or administrative procedure provided for the enforcement of obligations under this Directive.

This provision only requires the Member State to allow NGOs to participate in judicial or administrative procedures 'on behalf of or in support of the complainant', and does not require that they be allowed to bring complaints in their own name. As it happened, Belgian law did provide this opportunity so the NGO was able to bring the case. But the possibility of other actions like *Firma Feryn* will depend on whether other Member States are willing to go beyond the provision of the minimum remedies required by the Directive.

Race equality bodies
The Race Directive requires each Member State to set up a body to promote race equality in accordance with Article 13. The minimum requirements for such a body are:

---

[16]   R. Krause, 'Case C–54/07, *Centrum voor Gelijkheid van kansen en voor racismebestrijding v Firma Feryn NV*' (2010) 47 CMLR 917.
[17]   *Firma Feryn*, above n. 13, [24].

– . . . providing independent assistance to victims of discrimination in pursuing their complaints about discrimination,
– conducting independent surveys concerning discrimination,
– publishing independent reports and making recommendations on any issue relating to such discrimination.

This was an innovation for EU law at the time, though a similar requirement now applies in sex discrimination law.[18] It represents an important conceptual shift in discrimination law, in the sense that it acknowledges some responsibility on the part of the state to help victims and to take steps to identify and combat discrimination more generally. Traditionally, discrimination law has relied on individuals to come forward and litigate, so this is an important acknowledgement of the limitations of that approach, a point we will consider in greater detail in the second part of this chapter.

Religion or Belief

The Framework Directive prohibits discrimination on grounds of 'religion or belief', without defining either concept.[19] Although there has been very little litigation so far, this may give rise to some difficulties of interpretation. In particular, it is not clear whether the definition of religion should be subjective or objective, or how far the concept of 'belief' extends beyond beliefs which are related to religion, such as atheism or agnosticism. Some guidance is available from the ECtHR jurisprudence under Article 9 of the ECHR, though some may question whether courts in general are best qualified to determine such matters.

Article 4 of the Directive creates an exception to the rules on direct and indirect discrimination where the individual's characteristic (such as religion or belief) is a 'genuine occupational requirement'.[20] Where this can be established, it is not unlawful to take account of the individual's characteristic when making employment decisions. This is a particular issue for religious bodies and other organisations based on a particular belief, since they may want to reserve key positions in the organisation for individuals who share the relevant religion or belief. The particular sensitivity of this

---

[18] Art 20, Recast Directive; originally new Art 8a inserted into Directive 76/207 by Directive 2002/73.

[19] Directive 2000/78, Art 1.

[20] Art 15 contains further exceptions to deal with the particular situation in Northern Ireland with regards to school teachers and the police, given the historical conflict between the Protestant and Catholic communities.

issue clearly resulted in pressure on the EU legislature to include further detail in Article 4(2):

> Member States may maintain national legislation in force at the date of adoption of this Directive or provide for future legislation incorporating national practices existing at the date of adoption of this Directive pursuant to which, in the case of occupational activities within churches and other public or private organisations the ethos of which is based on religion or belief, a difference of treatment based on a person's religion or belief shall not constitute discrimination where, by reason of the nature of these activities or of the context in which they are carried out, a person's religion or belief constitute a genuine, legitimate and justified occupational requirement, having regard to the organisation's ethos. This difference of treatment shall be implemented taking account of Member States' constitutional provisions and principles, as well as the general principles of Community law, and should not justify discrimination on another ground.
>
> Provided that its provisions are otherwise complied with, this Directive shall thus not prejudice the right of churches and other public or private organisations, the ethos of which is based on religion or belief, acting in conformity with national constitutions and laws, to require individuals working for them to act in good faith and with loyalty to the organisation's ethos.

There are a number of interesting points to note about this provision. First, it clearly allows Member States to permit religious groups and other expressive associations to use religion or belief as a criterion for employment. This is apparent from the first paragraph. Second, though, it goes further by stating that organisations based on religion or belief may 'require individuals working for them to act in good faith and with loyalty to the organisation's ethos'. In most organisations based on religion or belief, there may be some job roles that are not immediately connected with the organisation's ethos. For these roles, it would not be justified to insist that the individuals performing them share the relevant religion or belief. For example, it may not be necessary for a person who is a church cleaner to be a Christian. But the 'loyalty' requirement may enable religious and other similar organisations to require people in these non-central roles to avoid open hostility towards their beliefs. Third, and perhaps most importantly, the religious occupational requirement may 'not justify discrimination on another ground'. This may prove to be a source of tension given the blurred boundaries between decisions taken on the basis of religious beliefs and decisions taken on other grounds. For example, in the *JFS* case in the UK, a school's decision not to admit a pupil on the grounds that he was not Jewish by matrilineal descent was held by the Supreme Court to be a decision based on ethnic origin rather than religion, and therefore not protected by national law.[21]

---

[21]   *R (E) v JFS Governing Body* [2009] UKSC 15, [2010] 2 AC 728.

Disability

The Framework Directive prohibits discrimination on grounds of disability.[22] Alongside the usual concepts of direct and indirect discrimination,[23] the Directive also creates a duty to provide 'reasonable accommodation' for disabled people.[24] Although various criticisms can be made of the 'reasonable accommodation' approach, it does provide an opportunity to think in positive ways about how workplaces can be adapted so that they no longer pose barriers to people with disabilities. We will examine this issue after considering how the term 'disability' should be interpreted.

The Directive does not contain a definition of disability. The literature generally divides definitions of disability into two types: medical and social. Medical definitions focus on the impairments suffered by particular individuals. Social definitions focus on the barriers disabled people encounter when they seek to participate in a particular area of life: in our case, in the labour market. Most commentators favour interpretations of the latter kind because they draw attention to the need to adapt society to disabled people. Medical definitions have a tendency to portray disabled people as in need of special help and can seem patronising or disempowering.

The EU's policy pronouncements on disability have tended towards the social definition. For example, the Commission's Action Plan published in 2003 explicitly stated that disability was a 'social construct'.[25] However, the Court has been much more cautious. In *Chacón-Navas*, it appeared to adopt a medical definition.[26] The claimant in that case was dismissed while she was off work due to what was described as 'sickness'. The question raised was whether her dismissal constituted discrimination on grounds of disability. The Court said that in the context of the Framework Directive 'the concept of "disability" must be understood as referring to a limitation

---

[22] Directive 2000/78, Art 1. For a critical overview, see D.L. Hosking, 'Great Expectations: Protection from Discrimination Because of Disability in Community Law' (2006) 31 EL Rev 667, and R. Whittle, 'The Framework Directive for Equal Treatment in Employment and Occupation: an Analysis from a Disability Rights Perspective' (2002) 27 EL Rev 303. Note that 'disability' is not confined to the claimant's disability, but may also cover 'discrimination by association' with a disabled person: Case C–303/06 *Coleman v Attridge Law* [2008] ECR I–5603.

[23] Directive 2000/78, Art 2(2), addresses the overlap between indirect discrimination and the duty to provide 'reasonable accommodation'.

[24] Directive 2000/78, Art 5.

[25] European Commission, *Equal Opportunities for People with Disabilities: A European Action Plan* (COM (2003) 650 final), 4.

[26] Above n. 4.

which results in particular from physical, mental or psychological impairments and which hinders the participation of the person concerned in professional life'.[27] The Court further stated that 'disability' cannot be equated with sickness,[28] and only covers impairments which last, or would probably last, for 'a long time'.[29] The decision in *Chacón-Navas* is problematic. The referring court gave virtually no detail about the claimant's medical circumstances. Although the application of EU law to the facts is a matter for national courts, the distinction between sickness and disability which the Court treated as obvious may not be so in a particular case. Further detail might have enabled the Court to give a more nuanced ruling.[30] For example, a condition such as cancer might be described as a sickness or as a disability, or perhaps as either depending on the type of cancer, the prognosis for the affected individual, and the duration of any resulting impairment.

The decision in *Chacón-Navas* presents a striking contrast with some of the Court's other discrimination decisions, notably *Mangold*,[31] discussed further below. Various explanations have been suggested for the Court's approach. One possibility is cost: perhaps there is a concern to limit the obligations imposed on employers by the Directive in this area. Another possibility is a concern with subsidiarity: perhaps the Court wanted to adopt a minimalist definition of disability given that disability discrimination law was a new development for many Member States.[32] Of course, despite the Court's comments about its definition of disability being 'uniform',[33] it is arguable that the Member States remain free to provide broader protection.[34] And those with such protection already in place should not in theory use the Directive as an excuse to reduce it because there is a non-regression clause.[35] Moreover, some commentators have suggested that the Court may have to revise its view in the light of the UN Convention on the Rights of Persons with Disabilities, to which the EU is a signatory, because this adopts a social definition of disability.[36]

---

[27]   Ibid, [43].

[28]   Ibid, [44].

[29]   Ibid, [45].

[30]   See Hosking, above n. 4.

[31]   Case C–144/04 *Mangold v Helm* [2005] ECR I–9981.

[32]   Hosking, above n. 4, 237.

[33]   Above n. 4, [40].

[34]   See Directive 2000/78, Art 8(1), and L. Waddington, 'Case Comment: Case C–13/05, *Chacón Navas v Eurest Colectividades SA'* (2007) 44 CMLR 487, 494–6.

[35]   Directive 2000/78, Art 8(2).

[36]   UN Convention on the Rights of Persons with Disabilities (2006), Art 1, ratified by the EU in 2010. For background see G. de Búrca, 'The European Union in the Negotiation of the UN Disability Convention' (2010) 35 EL Rev 174. For discussion see Waddington, above n. 35, 498–9.

However, so far at least, it does not appear that the Court has been presented with a suitable case in which to reconsider the issue.

An important difference between disability and the other grounds of discrimination included in the Framework Directive is the use of the concept of 'reasonable accommodation'. This is set out in Article 5:

> In order to guarantee compliance with the principle of equal treatment in relation to persons with disabilities, reasonable accommodation shall be provided. This means that employers shall take appropriate measures, where needed in a particular case, to enable a person with a disability to have access to, participate in, or advance in employment, or to undergo training, unless such measures would impose a disproportionate burden on the employer. This burden shall not be disproportionate when it is sufficiently remedied by measures existing within the framework of the disability policy of the Member State concerned.

The duty requires positive action on the part of the employer to ensure that barriers to the claimant's participation are removed. In that respect, it requires more creative thinking than the traditional concepts of direct and indirect discrimination. However, the duty is limited by the employer's 'disproportionate burden' defence, and it remains to be seen how the Court will interpret this provision.[37] There are two main criticisms of 'reasonable accommodation'. First, on a general level, while its focus on the individual claimant helps to ensure that he or she receives tailored support, this does not necessarily result in higher standards of accessibility in workplaces generally. As we shall see in the second part of this chapter, this is true of anti-discrimination law more generally and reflects the need to couple such legislation with other policies designed to promote equality. Second, with particular reference to the Directive, there is a problem regarding the relationship between reasonable accommodation and indirect discrimination. As Waddington and Hendriks explain, an employer may use the fact that reasonable accommodations have been made as a defence to a claim of indirect discrimination.[38] However, this may leave the claimant 'accommodated' but unequal: for example, where essential areas of the workplace are made accessible to a physically disabled

---

[37] For an interesting account of how this has been implemented in the Member States, see L. Waddington, 'When It Is Reasonable for Europeans to be Confused: Understanding When a Disability Accommodation Is Reasonable from a Comparative Perspective' (2008) 29 *Comparative Labor Law & Policy Journal* 317.

[38] Directive 2000/78, Art 2(2)(b)(ii), and see L. Waddington and A. Hendriks, 'The Expanding Concept of Employment Discrimination in Europe: From Direct and Indirect Discrimination to Reasonable Accommodation Discrimination' (2002) 18 *International Journal of Comparative Labour Law and Industrial Relations* 403.

claimant but he or she remains unable to move freely around the building like other employees.[39]

Age

Of all the new grounds, age has given rise to the greatest difficulty and to the largest volume of litigation.[40] This is because, traditionally, age has featured heavily in employers' decision making, for good reasons or bad. For example, a job might be reserved for younger candidates because substantial training is involved and the employer wants time to recoup the benefits, or because the employer thinks that younger staff are more suited to certain roles, such as youth work or fashion retail. At the other 'end' of the labour market, it is common in many Member States for it to be compulsory for employees to retire at a particular age, usually when they become entitled to a state pension. Age is often considered in the employment context in indirect ways, too. For example, it is common for experience, seniority or length of service to be taken into account in determining an employee's pay, but such arrangements generally mean that older workers will earn more than younger ones. Since age as a ground of discrimination is a relatively new idea, it requires us to reconsider many of our assumptions about how labour markets should work, and to ask ourselves whether traditional practices should be dismantled because, from this novel perspective, they are discriminatory. The Directive reflects some of this ambivalence by allowing Member States and employers to justify direct as well as indirect age discrimination.[41] This opens up the possibility that age may still be used as a criterion in employment decisions. In turn, this creates an important role for the Court in determining when age-based decisions can be justified.

The relationship between age discrimination and sex discrimination
Before examining the case-law on age discrimination, it is important to note that EU law has historically had some influence over the issue indirectly through the law on sex discrimination. For example, in the recent *Kleist* case, the employer required workers to retire when they became entitled to a state retirement pension.[42] This occurred at 60 for women and

---

[39] Waddington and Hendriks, ibid, 415–6.
[40] For an analysis of the recent case-law, see C. Kilpatrick, 'The Court of Justice and Labour Law in 2010: A New EU Discrimination Law Architecture' (2011) 40 ILJ 280, and D. Schiek, 'Age Discrimination Before the ECJ – Conceptual and Theoretical Issues' (2011) 48 CMLR 777.
[41] Directive 2000/78, Art 6.
[42] Case C–356/09 *Pensionsversicherungsanstalt v Kleist* [2010] nyr.

at 65 for men.[43] The Court held, consistently with its previous case-law, that the question of dismissal should be treated separately from the question of pension entitlement. On that basis, the employer's action constituted direct discrimination on grounds of sex and was therefore unlawful.

Another potential overlap between age and sex discrimination is in the area of seniority. Employers often base their pay determinations on an individual's length of service or experience. It is generally argued that this rewards the bigger contribution to the employing enterprise made by more knowledgeable workers. However, it may also constitute age discrimination, since older workers will find it easier to accumulate years of service and will therefore be paid more than younger workers under a regime of this kind. EU law has already begun to address the issue through the lens of sex discrimination: on average, women tend to have shorter periods of service than men, probably because they take more breaks from the labour market for family reasons, making it possible to claim that pay scales based on seniority involve indirect discrimination on grounds of sex. In *Cadman*, the Court took a middle course in which it held that pay based on seniority was generally acceptable, but that it would be possible in a particular case for a claimant to cast doubt on the employer's use of the criterion, so that the employer would then be required to provide further justification.[44] In more practical terms, this probably means that the employer would not be allowed to use seniority where its pay scheme rewarded long periods of service beyond what could reasonably be regarded as necessary to gain experience.

Non-discrimination on grounds of age as a general principle of EU law

There has been some debate in the case-law about the exact status of the principle of non-discrimination on grounds of age in EU law.[45] This arose out of the Court's decision in *Mangold*.[46] That case concerned provisions of German law which allowed employers to conclude successive fixed-term contracts with workers over the age of 52. The German government's aim was to promote the continued employment of older workers by allowing employers a greater degree of flexibility. The Court found that

---

[43]   See Directive 79/7, Art 7, on state pension ages.

[44]   Case C–17/05 *Cadman v Health & Safety Executive* [2006] ECR I–9583.

[45]   This has given rise to a large literature in both labour law and EU law. See, for example, P. Craig, 'The Legal Effect of Directives: Policy, Rules and Exceptions' (2009) 24 EL Rev 349, and T. Papadopoulos, 'Criticising the Horizontal Direct Effect of the EU General Principle of Equality' [2011] *European Human Rights Law Review* 437.

[46]   Above n. 32. For discussion see D. Schiek, 'The ECJ Decision in *Mangold*: a Further Twist on Effects of Directives and Constitutional Relevance of Community Equality Legislation' (2006) 35 ILJ 329.

the measure was disproportionate because it had the potential to deprive all older workers of stable employment, regardless of their individual situations. However, the Court faced two serious technical difficulties with this ruling. First, the transposition period for Directive 2000/78 had not elapsed at the relevant time. It was therefore arguable that no obligations had yet arisen under the Directive. The Court addressed this problem by holding that 'the principle of non-discrimination on grounds of age must ... be regarded as a general principle of Community law'.[47] By avoiding any reliance on the Directive, the Court could then hold that the transposition period did not matter. Second, the case was 'horizontal' in the sense that the claimant had challenged the fixed-term provision in his contract in proceedings against his employer. This meant that the claimant could not base a claim on the Directive because of the well-known (but controversial) rule that directives do not have horizontal effect. Here, the Court held that the national court was obliged to do what it could to bring national law into line with the principle, including disapplying inconsistent provisions if necessary.[48]

The *Mangold* ruling has proved highly controversial in EU law generally, because it gives some legal effects to directives before their transposition period has expired, and because it does so by extending the already much debated principle of incidental direct effect, in which a national court can disapply a provision of national law which is incompatible with EU law even in a horizontal case.[49] But from the labour law perspective the most interesting feature of the decision is the ruling that age discrimination is a fundamental principle of EU law. That raises interesting questions about what this might mean in terms of its status relative to other legal principles, and about whether this move is confined to age discrimination or might extend more broadly.

The later case-law has clarified some, but by no means all, of these matters. In *Bartsch*, the claimant challenged a rule of German law which denied a widow's pension to widows who were more than 15 years younger than their deceased husbands.[50] Again, the case arose before the time limit for transposing Directive 2000/78 had expired. However, the Court held that the situation did not fall within the scope of EU law for precisely that reason. This appeared to suggest a retreat from *Mangold*. However, in

---

[47]   Mangold, above n. 32, [75].

[48]   Ibid, [77].

[49]   See M. de Mol, 'The Novel Approach of the CJEU on the Horizontal Direct Effect of the EU Principle of Non-Discrimination: (Unbridled) Expansionism of EU Law?' (2011) 1/2 *Maastricht Journal of European and Comparative Law* 109.

[50]   Case C–427/06 *Bartsch v Bosch und Siemens* [2008] ECR I–7245.

Kücükdeveci, the Court steered a middle course between these two previous cases.[51] It reaffirmed the status of non-discrimination on grounds of age as a general principle of EU law and held that the purpose of Directive 2000/78 was to elaborate – and not to lay down – that principle. It appears from the judgment that this general principle forms part of a broader general principle of non-discrimination in employment and occupation. In *Hennigs*, the Court based this general principle on the equality right in Article 21 of the EU Charter of Fundamental Rights.[52] This seems to be part of a general trend of 'rebasing' the Court's fundamental rights jurisprudence on the Charter. The Court in *Kücükdeveci* further held that where the national court could not interpret national law compatibly with EU law it was obliged to disapply the inconsistent national law. This is the controversial 'incidental direct effect' from *Mangold*. Importantly, though, the Court followed *Bartsch* in holding that the facts of the case must fall within the scope of EU law. In *Kücükdeveci* this was satisfied because the case had arisen after the transposition period had expired. This suggests that the Court will be less likely to seek a way around a transposition deadline in the future.[53]

Justification

A significant danger in the discussion of 'general principles' is that we might form the view that non-discrimination (on grounds of age or otherwise) is somehow fundamental in that it trumps other considerations. Nothing could be further from the truth. First, in contrast to other grounds of discrimination, the Directive permits justification to be offered for direct as well as indirect age discrimination. Second, for some commentators at least, the Court's approach to the justification test has not been tough enough. We will examine each of these issues in turn. The next section will consider some exceptions to the principle of non-discrimination on grounds of age.

The possibility of justifying direct age discrimination is provided for in Article 6(1) of the Directive:

---

[51] Case C–555/07 *Kücükdeveci v Swedex* [2010] nyr. For discussion, see G. Thüsing and S. Horler, 'Case C–555/07, *Seda Kücükdeveci v Swedex*, Judgment of the Court (Grand Chamber) of 19 January 2010' (2010) 47 CMLR 1161, and S. Peers, 'Supremacy, Equality and Human Rights: Comment on *Kücükdeveci* (C–555/07)' (2010) 35 EL Rev 849.

[52] Case C–297/10 *Hennigs v Eisenbahn-Bundesamt* [2011] nyr.

[53] See also Case C–147/08 *Römer v Freie und Hansestadt Hamburg* [2011] nyr, [53]–[64]. This casts doubt on whether *Mangold* itself would now be regarded as falling within the scope of EU law, though Kilpatrick (above n. 41, 283–7) argues that the fixed-term work dimension of the case (not Directive 2000/78) can be relied on for this purpose.

> Notwithstanding Article 2(2), Member States may provide that differences
> of treatment on grounds of age shall not constitute discrimination, if, within
> the context of national law, they are objectively and reasonably justified by
> a legitimate aim, including legitimate employment policy, labour market and
> vocational training objectives, and if the means of achieving that aim are
> appropriate and necessary.

The provision goes on to give various examples of differences in treatment,
including 'the setting of special conditions on access to employment',[54]
'the fixing of minimum conditions of age, professional experience or seniority in service for access to employment or to certain advantages linked
to employment',[55] and 'the fixing of a maximum age for recruitment which
is based on the training requirements of the post in question or the need
for a reasonable period of employment before retirement'.[56] It is noticeable that the phrasing of Article 6(1) differs slightly from that of Article
2(2), the justification for indirect discrimination, but in the *Age Concern*
case the Court held that 'no particular significance' should be attached to
this.[57]

The Court's approach to justification has followed the usual reasoning
structure to be found in other cases of this kind. It considers whether or
not the approach taken by the Member State is in pursuit of a legitimate
aim, and then whether it is appropriate or necessary to achieve that aim.
However, the Court's degree of scrutiny is variable and difficult to predict.
On one hand, it often emphasises that the Member States 'enjoy broad
discretion in their choice of the measures capable of attaining their objectives in the field of social and employment policy'.[58] On the other hand, it
is concerned to ensure that the Member States do not rely on 'mere generalisations'[59] and sometimes makes a point of insisting that the national
court should find particular facts to support the claims being made. For
example, in *Georgiev*, the Court accepted in general terms the justifications
for the compulsory retirement of university professors being put forward
by the Member State but held that it was for the national court to ascer-
tain whether those arguments were applicable in the national context.[60]
It is probably too early to identify any very clear trends in the Court's
case-law but, so far at least, it seems that retirement ages are attracting

---

[54]   Directive 2000/78, Art 6(1)(a).
[55]   Ibid, Art 6(1)(b).
[56]   Ibid, Art 6(1)(c).
[57]   Case C–388/07 R *(Age Concern England) v Secretary of State for Business, Enterprise and Regulatory Reform* [2009] ECR I–1569, [65].
[58]   *Mangold*, above n. 32, [63].
[59]   *Age Concern*, above n. 58, [51].
[60]   Case C–250/09 *Georgiev v Tehnicheski universitet – Sofia* [2010] nyr.

relatively sympathetic treatment whereas discrimination against younger workers is not. We will consider some examples of each.

In *Hütter* and *Kücükdeveci*, younger workers were disadvantaged by national rules that did not 'count' all of their service. In *Kücükdeveci*, the claimant received notice of termination calculated on the basis of three years' service for her employer.[61] She had worked for the firm for ten years, but national law provided that service before the age of 25 did not count. The national government argued that the rule protected the job security of older workers and reflected the greater flexibility of younger workers. The Court disagreed, pointing out that the rule did not apply equally to younger workers because it disadvantaged those who entered the labour market early. And it operated to reduce the notice given to workers who entered the labour market before the age of 25 regardless of their age at the time of dismissal, so it did not protect the job security of older workers. In *Hütter*, the claimant's starting salary in the public service was determined only on the basis of experience acquired after the age of 18, even though he had largely completed his apprenticeship before attaining that age.[62] The government argued that this encouraged young people to stay in general secondary education for longer, and gave employers an incentive to hire workers with vocational training because they would be cheaper. The Court found these two objectives to be inconsistent: the first sought to promote secondary education whereas the second might have the effect of making vocational education more advantageous. Moreover, the Court held that the policy did not encourage a particular type of education because it disregarded work experience regardless of a person's choice of education. Nor did it promote the employment of younger workers because it applied to exclude workers' early experience regardless of their age at the time of recruitment. However, this does not mean that all rules treating younger workers differently will necessarily be found to be discriminatory. In *Hütter*, the Court hinted that lower minimum wages for younger workers might be justified as a measure to promote their integration into the labour market.[63]

As we noted above, rules that discriminate on grounds of age are common in the workplace and it may take some time to eliminate them. The Court has been sympathetic in this regard. For example, in *Hennigs*, the claimant challenged an age-related pay scale for civil servants in which a person's salary on recruitment was determined by the grade attached to

---

[61] Above n. 52.
[62] Case C–88/08 *Hütter v Technische Universität Graz* [2009] ECR I–5325.
[63] Ibid, [49].

their job and by their age.[64] The Court held that this was discriminatory and rejected an argument that age could be used as a proxy for experience.[65] The Court went on to consider the applicable collective agreement, which was designed to remove the age-related pay scale and to replace it with non-discriminatory criteria. This involved some continuing age discrimination during a transitional period because it protected the income of those workers who would lose out when the age-related scale was removed (sometimes known as 'red-circling'). The Court held that this was justifiable because it was only a temporary measure.

Most of the cases have concerned older workers and the policies that affect them around retirement. Recital 14 of the Directive states that it is 'without prejudice' to compulsory retirement ages, but in the seminal case of *Palacios* the Court held that rules laying down retirement ages were subject to review.[66] Nevertheless, on the whole, the Court has been sympathetic to the idea of a compulsory retirement age, and although it has insisted on the possibility of review, that review has been relatively light-touch. In *Palacios*, the Court accepted the argument that retirement ages were necessary in order to share employment opportunities across the generations. It appears that there may be two possible qualifications to this. First, in *Palacios* the retiring employees were eligible for a pension. The Court saw this as a safeguard for them and would probably be unsympathetic to the compulsory retirement of workers who would not receive a pension, though in *Rosenbladt* it rejected an argument that the pension on offer was insufficient.[67] Second, in *Palacios* and *Rosenbladt*, the retirement rules were determined by collective agreement. The Court seemed attracted to this because it allowed for the specific situation of particular types of job to be taken into account.[68] Kilpatrick notes that the Court's sudden enthusiasm for collective bargaining contrasts with its approach in the sex discrimination case-law, in which the presence of a collective agreement has never been regarded as a reason to accept a discriminatory outcome.[69] However, it may be that it is the context-specific nature of collective bargaining, rather than any particular deference to collective agreements per se, that is at work in the age cases.[70] This would fit with

---

[64] Above n. 53.

[65] See Chapter 4 for a discussion of the Court's case-law on experience.

[66] Case C–411/05 *Palacios de la Villa v Cortefiel Servicios* [2007] ECR I–8531.

[67] Case C–45/09 *Rosenbladt v Oellerking Gebäudereinigungsges* [2010] nyr.

[68] Ibid, [49].

[69] Kilpatrick, above n. 41, 295–6, and cf in the sex discrimination context Case C–127/92 *Enderby v Frenchay Health Authority* [1993] ECR I–5535.

[70] Case C–447/09 *Prigge v Deutsche Lufthansa AG* [2011] nyr, [47]–[8] would appear to confirm this.

the Court's general caution in its approach to retirement issues. In *Age Concern*, the Court was keen to stress that the final decision on proportionality lay with the national court and – for once – did not try to dictate the outcome.[71] The *Georgiev* case (discussed above) also opened up the possibility for context-specific reasoning by the national court.[72]

Other types of policy concerning older workers have met with less sympathy from the Court. In *Mangold*, national law allowed firms to conclude successive fixed-term contracts with workers over the age of 52.[73] It was argued that this would promote employment among older workers. But the Court rejected this claim, pointing out that the legislation did not apply only to those who were unemployed and seeking to enter the labour market, but also to those who were already in work. The legislation deprived workers in the latter group of job security and was found not to be proportionate. Similarly, in *Ingeniørforeningen i Danmark (Andersen)*, national law provided that workers who were dismissed were not entitled to a severance payment if they were old enough to take their pension.[74] The Court found this to be disproportionate because it did not take account of the possibility that some older workers might want to look for a new job rather than retiring and might therefore benefit from the severance payment.

Exceptions

In addition to the possibility of justifying age discrimination using Article 6(1) of the Directive, there are two exceptions to the principle of equal treatment on grounds of age which have also been invoked in the case-law. These are the claim that age may be a 'genuine occupational requirement' within Article 4(1), and the public policy exception (which does not apply in race or gender cases) in Article 2(5). The latter provides that:

> [t]his Directive shall be without prejudice to measures laid down by national law which, in a democratic society, are necessary for public security, for the maintenance of public order and the prevention of criminal offences, for the protection of health and for the protection of the rights and freedoms of others.

We will consider some examples of each.

The 'genuine occupational requirement' concept was successfully invoked in the *Wolf* case.[75] The claimant challenged a rule laying down 30

---

[71] Above n. 58, [52].
[72] Above n. 61. See also Case C–159/10 *Fuchs v Land Hessen* [2011] nyr.
[73] Above n. 32.
[74] Case C–499/08 *Ingeniørforeningen i Danmark (on behalf of Andersen) v Region Syddanmark* [2010] nyr.
[75] Case C–229/08 *Wolf v Stadt Frankfurt am Main* [2010] ECR I–1.

as the maximum age for recruitment to the fire service. The government argued that the limit was necessary because fire-fighting requires considerable physical strength and stamina, and fire-fighters were transferred to administrative duties at the age of 45 or 50. It was claimed that the rule ensured a balance within the fire service between those engaged on active service and those performing administrative duties. The Court accepted these arguments and did not seem concerned about the use of age as a proxy for physical capabilities, even though these might vary from person to person.

The 'public policy' exception was considered in *Petersen* and *Prigge*.[76] In both cases, arguments were made that a retirement rule was justified on safety grounds: in *Petersen*, a retirement age of 68 for dentists on grounds of patient safety, and in *Prigge*, a collectively agreed retirement age of 60 for airline pilots on grounds of passenger safety. However, in both cases, the argument failed: in *Petersen* because there are many situations in which dentists could continue working after the age of 68, and in *Prigge* because national and international law set 65 as the retirement age for pilots. Nevertheless, the cases are noteworthy because they increase the range of options for Member States seeking to defend the ongoing use of age-related criteria.[77]

Conclusion

As noted above, we should probably be cautious about our conclusions from this relatively small body of case-law. Although the Court seems reluctant to tackle age discrimination in some cases, perhaps the most promising trend is towards the dismantling of general rules on age in favour of rules that are more nuanced and that take account of the variety of facts and circumstances. This trend is an interesting one. On one hand, it reduces age discrimination by discouraging the use of over-inclusive blanket rules. On the other hand, it makes life unpredictable. If the justification of a compulsory retirement age depends on the economic situation in the relevant sector, it may be difficult to know in advance what the retirement age might be. It will also be interesting to see whether the Court's current deference to national courts will continue over the longer term. In other areas, national courts have continued to refer cases to the Court of Justice for guidance on the application of proportionality and the Court has tended to oblige. A detailed body of case-law might well develop. Moreover, it is possible that, whilst age-related criteria are

---

[76] Case C–341/08 *Petersen v Berufungsausschuss für Zahnärzte für den Bezirk Westfalen-Lippe* [2010] ECR I–47; *Prigge*, above n. 71.
[77] See Kilpatrick, above n. 41, 299–300.

currently a familiar and accepted feature of labour markets, the law may develop and social attitudes may change such that age discrimination becomes as unacceptable as discrimination on other grounds.

Sexual Orientation

After the decision in *P v S and Cornwall CC*, considered in the previous chapter, which broadened the scope of 'sex' to include transgender discrimination, many commentators thought that the next step would be to extend 'sex' to include discrimination on grounds of sexual orientation.[78] However, in the *Grant* case, the Court rejected the argument that existing law on sex discrimination also protected those who were discriminated against on grounds of sexual orientation.[79] Grant argued that she had been discriminated against on grounds of sex because her female partner was not given travel benefits by her employer. Had Grant been a man with a female partner, the partner would have received the travel benefit. The Court took a different view of the situation. It characterised the claimant as a woman with a same-sex partner and therefore compared her to a man with a same-sex partner. Since the man would not have received travel benefits for his same-sex partner, he would have been treated in the same way as Grant had been treated and there was no discrimination on grounds of sex. The Court further held that, since neither the ECtHR nor the laws of most of the Member States at the relevant time regarded same-sex relationships as equivalent to marriage, it was not appropriate for the Court itself to take that step.

The Framework Directive was therefore essential to ensure that sexual orientation discrimination was included in EU law.[80] So far at least, the provision has not given rise to much litigation, suggesting that it has not caused particular problems of implementation at national level. However, one potential area of difficulty is the treatment of same-sex relationships. Whilst the EU has competence to prohibit discrimination on grounds of sexual orientation, the regulation of marriage and related matters is left to the Member States.[81] This gives rise to a potential grey area where national law draws a distinction between marriage and same-sex relationships.

In the *Maruko* case, the claimant sought payment of a widower's benefit from his same-sex partner's pension scheme after his partner's death.[82]

---

[78]   Case C–13/94 *P v S and Cornwall County Council* [1996] ECR I–2143.
[79]   Case C–249/96 *Grant v South-West Trains* [1998] ECR I–621.
[80]   Directive 2000/78, Art 1.
[81]   Directive 2000/78, Preamble, recital 22.
[82]   Case C–267/06 *Maruko v Versorgungsanstalt der deutschen Bühnen* [2008] ECR I–1757.

He was refused the payment because it was only afforded to spouses. The Court noted that the regulation of marriage was left to the Member States but held that the widower's benefit was 'pay' within the meaning of the Framework Directive. This meant that the benefit fell within the scope of EU law and the Member States were obliged not to discriminate in the conditions for receipt of the benefit. The Court further held that:

> [i]f the referring court decides that surviving spouses and surviving life partners are in a comparable situation so far as concerns that survivor's benefit, legislation such as that at issue in the main proceedings must, as a consequence, be considered to constitute direct discrimination on grounds of sexual orientation.[83]

There are two interesting features of this ruling. One is the Court's decision to regard the situation as one of direct discrimination (thereby removing any possibility for justification). In some of its previous case-law, the Court had insisted that direct discrimination only occurs where the offending characteristic (in this case, sexual orientation) is a *formal* part of the employer's decision-making process.[84] Strictly speaking, this was not the case in *Maruko*, because the distinction drawn was between marriage and civil partnership. It is therefore significant that the Court took the broader view that distinguishing between marriage and civil partnership could constitute direct discrimination on grounds of sexual orientation, since marriage is only available to heterosexual couples.

The other significant part of the ruling is the requirement that the situation of married couples and civil partners should be 'comparable'. Of course, this flows from the definition of direct discrimination, which focuses on treating individuals who are in comparable situations equally. In *Maruko*, the Court left the decision on comparability to national courts, which had the benefit of respecting the different situations in the Member States in view of their competence to regulate marital status.[85] But it also meant that a claimant's entitlement to a survivor's benefit might vary between the Member States depending on how the comparability question was resolved. The recent decision in *Römer* has continued this approach but has also offered further guidance on the matter by emphasising that the comparability question does not require a general assessment of marriage

---

[83] Ibid, [72].

[84] cf Case C–79/99 *Schnorbus v Land Hessen* [2000] ECR I–10997, and for discussion see C. Tobler and K. Waaldijk, 'Case Comment: Case C–267/06, *Tadao Maruko v Versorgungsanstalt der deutschen Bühnen*' (2009) 46 CMLR 723, 735–41.

[85] For comparison of the laws of different Member States on this point, see Tobler and Waaldijk, ibid, 741–6.

and civil partnership in the Member State in question, but instead a focused enquiry relating to the benefit being sought.[86] This may simplify the task of the national courts and may make it more likely that the comparability requirement will be satisfied. In *Römer* itself, the Court gave a strong hint that the supplementary pension at issue in the case should apply to civil partners as well as married couples because the law imposed the same obligations of financial support on civil partners and on spouses.

PROMOTING EQUALITY

An important feature of the equality literature nowadays is its emphasis on the limits of legislation as a strategy for achieving a more equal society in practice. It is widely recognised that, in addition to prohibiting discrimination, it is also important to take active steps to promote equality. In this section we will examine two examples of this: the EU's adoption of 'mainstreaming', and the role of the Europe 2020 strategy in encouraging the Member States to pursue policies to address inequality.

Before considering these examples in detail, it is worth pausing for a moment to consider the critique of traditional anti-discrimination legislation.[87] This criticism takes as its starting-point the fact that anti-discrimination legislation has been in place for many years now, but examples of inequality persist. The most obvious is the gender pay gap: still clearly in evidence despite the EU's early intervention to prohibit unequal pay.[88] Whilst no-one doubts the importance of individuals being able to seek redress when they are the victims of discrimination, critics of legislation point to the weaknesses of enforcement through individual litigation as one of the main reasons for the persistence of inequality in society. The perceived weaknesses of individual litigation include the commitment of time and money required to bring a claim; the complexities of mounting a challenge that is legally sound (for example, finding an appropriate comparator and discovering what he (or, very occasionally, she) earns); and the fact that a successful claim is unlikely to make a difference outside the claimant's workplace. The alternative techniques for promoting equality all have in common an attempt to tackle discrimination proactively, without waiting for complaints, and on a larger scale.

---

[86] Above n. 54, [43].
[87] S. Fredman, 'European Community Discrimination Law: A Critique' (1992) 21 ILJ 119.
[88] According to Eurostat, women across the EU earned on average 17 per cent less than men in 2009.

Mainstreaming

'Mainstreaming' denotes a particular approach to equality in which bodies
are encouraged to review their policies for their impact on disadvantaged
groups. Mainstreaming is about preventing unequal treatment by identifying and avoiding discriminatory policy choices. Importantly, it need not
be confined to the examination of policies with an obvious potential to
discriminate, like childcare policies (which might treat men and women
unequally). In its most radical and potentially transformative incarnation,
it could be used to examine whether any aspect of government policy, such
as the tax system or research funding, might have an adverse impact on
disadvantaged groups.

The EU has adopted a mainstreaming policy, primarily in relation
to gender, and has encouraged the Member States to do the same. In
this section, we will focus in particular on the mainstreaming of gender
equality by the EU institutions themselves.

The EU's adoption of the policy of mainstreaming can be traced back to
a Commission Communication in 1996.[89] This defined mainstreaming as:

> not restricting efforts to promote equality to the implementation of specific
> measures to help women, but mobilising all general policies and measures spe-
> cifically for the purpose of achieving equality by actively and openly taking into
> account at the planning stage their possible effects on the respective situations
> of men and women (gender perspective).[90]

The Communication proposed more specific action in employment policy
and other areas (such as the EU's external relations) and placed emphasis
on prioritising equality in the allocation of Structural Fund money. In a
candid assessment of progress published in 1998, the Commission noted
that mainstreaming had made a difference in areas with 'solid traditions'
of promoting gender equality, such as women's human rights in external
relations, employment policy and training, but admitted that it has not
made much impact on areas not usually thought of in equality terms, such
as economic policy or enlargement.[91] The Commission therefore proposed
greater use of gender impact assessments throughout the policy process,
and recognised that this would require a programme of training to develop

---

[89]   European Commission, *Incorporating Equal Opportunities for Women and Men into all
Community Policies and Activities* (COM (96) 67 final).

[90]   Ibid, 2.

[91]   Commission, *Progress Report on the Follow-Up to the Communication: Incorporating
Equal Opportunities for Women and Men into all Community Policies and Activities* (COM
(98) 122 final), 3.

the necessary expertise in all Directorates-General. The proposals were reinforced by the Treaty of Amsterdam, then awaiting ratification, which brought gender equality to the forefront of the EU's objectives.[92]

In 2000, a further Communication proposed a Gender Equality Framework Strategy.[93] This continued the policy of mainstreaming but sought to reinforce it in various ways. First, it made explicit the links with the Member States' activities by proposing that the EU would use the EES (discussed below) to encourage the Member States to review various policies for their gender impact.[94] Second, it proposed some more specific actions to mainstream gender issues in policy areas outside the employment sphere. A notable example of this was the proposal to prepare a Commission Communication on social issues in public procurement.[95] And third, the document is noteworthy compared to its predecessors for its greater emphasis on engaging with employers, NGOs and social partners in developing mainstreaming policies.

Since then, the Commission has published a five-yearly strategy for gender equality,[96] so there was a further Communication in 2006 covering the period 2006–10,[97] and another published in 2010 to address the period 2010–15.[98] What is noticeable here is that the 2006 document refers repeatedly to mainstreaming in a wide variety of policy areas, whereas the 2010 document hardly mentions it at all, despite an assertion at the beginning that it is part of the Commission's equality strategy.[99] There are two possible reasons for this. One may be that gender mainstreaming has become well established in EU policy making, to the extent that it is no longer necessary to talk about it. And of course the other may be that mainstreaming is slipping down the list of policy priorities.

Let us conclude this section with three observations. First, although gender mainstreaming in the EU has been supported by a number of committees and bodies, at the time of writing the new European Institute

---

[92] Treaty of Amsterdam, Articles 2 and 3.

[93] Commission, *Towards a Community Framework Strategy on Gender Equality (2001–2005)* (COM (2000) 335 final).

[94] Ibid, 5–6.

[95] Commission, *Interpretative Communication on the Community Law Applicable to Public Procurement and the Possibilities for Integrating Social Considerations into Public Procurement* (COM (2001) 566 final).

[96] For a critical analysis of the EU's activities up to 2006, see F. Beveridge, 'Building Against the Past: the Impact of Mainstreaming on EU Gender Law and Policy' (2007) 32 EL Rev 193.

[97] Commission, *A Roadmap for Equality Between Women and Men 2006–2010* (COM (2006) 92 final).

[98] Commission, *Strategy for Equality Between Women and Men 2010–2015* (COM (2010) 491 final).

[99] Ibid, 4.

for Gender Equality is only just beginning its work.[100] As an independent body, this may prove to be an important means of holding the Commission to account for the effectiveness of its mainstreaming activities. Second, in view of the EU's expanded competence over other grounds of discrimination, there is probably greater scope for mainstreaming equality more generally. For example, some efforts have been made with regard to mainstreaming disability equality,[101] but these do not seem to have attracted the same high profile as gender mainstreaming. Finally, it seems to be the case that the less obvious the connection with equality, the more difficult mainstreaming becomes. So, whilst the Commission has reported successes in the employment field, truly transformative mainstreaming would require the integration of an equality perspective into *all* EU policies. This would require a very considerable commitment on the part of the Commission and the Member States.

Europe 2020

As we saw in Chapter 2, the co-ordination of the Member States' social and employment policies takes place through the Europe 2020 strategy. This involves setting targets at EU level and translating them into national targets for each Member State. Progress towards the targets is monitored through an annual reporting regime. Equality (particularly gender equality, given its longer pedigree in EU law) has always been a theme in the EES, so we will examine the history very briefly first before considering the current Europe 2020 regime.

Evolution
When the 'Luxembourg process' began in 1998, promoting equal opportunities was one of the four 'pillars' or headings under which targets or guidelines were to be developed for the Member States.[102] The guidelines were initially quite vague. The Member States were encouraged to close the gap between the employment rates of men and women, but were not given a specific numerical target; to implement the Parental Leave Directive and the Part-Time Work Directive; and to address the needs of disabled people in the workplace. The 1999 guidelines focused in greater detail on ways of

---

[100]   See http://www.eige.europa.eu (last visited 5 September 2011).

[101]   See Commission, *Equal Opportunities for People with Disabilities: A European Action Plan* (COM (2003) 650 final). For a critique, see D. Mabbett, 'The Development of Rights-Based Social Policy in the European Union: the Example of Disability Rights' (2005) 43 *Journal of Common Market Studies* 97.

[102]   Council Resolution of 15 December 1997 adopting the 1998 Employment Guidelines OJ C 30/98, 28 January 1998.

increasing women's participation and included a reference to the inclusion of ethnic minorities.[103]

The Lisbon Strategy did not include equality as one of its 'headline' goals but it did continue the emphasis on equality within its goal of modernising the European social model.[104] This included the aim of creating 'more and better jobs'. The Lisbon Strategy set a target for the overall employment rate of 70 per cent, but most importantly for our purposes, a target of 60 per cent for women's employment.[105] In its Social Policy Agenda, published in 2000, the Commission set out a series of objectives relating to what it termed the quality of social policy.[106] These included combating social exclusion, promoting gender equality and adopting the Race and Framework Directives. This fed into the EES process so, for example, in 2003 the Member States were encouraged to take steps to close the gender pay gap and were set a numerical target for the provision of childcare places.[107]

As we saw in Chapter 2, the relaunch of the Lisbon Strategy in 2005 aimed to reduce the number of targets that the Member States should pursue and to achieve a better integration of employment and other policies.[108] This resulted in a set of 23 'integrated guidelines'.[109] Equality does not feature as one of these guidelines, though some of the targets and actions for the Member States include equality. The target for women's employment was retained from the original Lisbon Strategy, and guideline 18 on 'promoting a lifecycle approach to work' included references to promoting women's participation and encouraging 'active ageing'.

Current targets

The Europe 2020 agenda contains two headline targets of relevance to equality: the employment target (achieving 75 per cent employment for people aged between 20 and 64) and the social inclusion target (reducing by

---

[103] Council Resolution of 22 February 1999 adopting the 1999 Employment Guidelines, OJ C 69, 12 March 1999.

[104] Presidency Conclusions, Lisbon European Council (23 and 24 March 2000), paras 24–34.

[105] Ibid, para 30.

[106] Commission, *Social Policy Agenda* (COM (2000) 379 final).

[107] Council Decision of 22 July 2003 on guidelines for the employment policies of the Member States (2003/578/EC), guideline 6.

[108] Communication from President Barroso in agreement with Vice-President Verheugen, *Working together for growth and jobs: A new start for the Lisbon Strategy* (COM (2005) 24 final), 5.

[109] Communication from the President, in agreement with Vice-President Verheugen and Commissioners Almunia and Spidla, *Integrated Guidelines for Growth and Jobs* (2005–2008) (COM (2005) 141 final).

20 million the number of people at risk of poverty and social exclusion).[110] The employment target is relevant to equality for the obvious reason that discrimination against people from certain groups may inhibit their ability to participate in the labour market. The social inclusion target is relevant to equality because having a job usually helps to alleviate poverty (though this may not always be the case for some very low-paid workers). It is important to note that, whilst they overlap with our employment concerns, the social inclusion aspects of Europe 2020 also cover many other issues beyond the employment sphere. This reflects the fact that equality is not just an employment matter.

The Commission's main contribution to the employment target is the Communication entitled *Agenda for New Skills and Jobs*.[111] As we saw in Chapter 2, this addresses four priorities: 'flexicurity', skills, job quality and job creation. The flexicurity policy is seen as a way of creating jobs and using them as a stepping-stone to more permanent, legally protected forms of employment.[112] It is relevant to the equality goal because workers on the fringes of the labour market may be more likely to find themselves in atypical jobs (which might or might not be a good thing, a point we will return to below). The 'job quality' target includes within it the Commission's proposed review of the labour law *acquis*.[113] Equality law is not exempt from this and the Commission plans to review the Framework Directive and the Race Directive in 2012.[114]

Perhaps the most interesting feature of the Communication is the emphasis on combating discrimination against migrant workers.[115] The Commission notes that such workers often find it difficult to integrate into Member States' labour markets or to obtain jobs commensurate with their skills. The Commission notes the role of the European Integration Fund in paying for projects in the Member States designed to assist the inclusion of migrants in national society alongside the employment initiatives paid for by the European Social Fund.[116] This focus is in sharp contrast to the problematic legal position we discussed above, in which migrants who

---

[110]   See, generally, http://ec.europa.eu/europe2020/index_en.htm (last visited 31 August 2011).

[111]   European Commission, *Agenda for New Skills and Jobs* (COM (2010) 682 final).

[112]   Ibid, 3–8.

[113]   Ibid, 15.

[114]   Ibid, 16.

[115]   Ibid, 11.

[116]   Ibid, 20. See also Commission Decision 2008/457/EC laying down rules for the implementation of Council Decision 2007/435/EC establishing the European Fund for the Integration of third-country nationals for the period 2007 to 2013, and for the operation of the Fund see http://ec.europa.eu/home-affairs/funding/integration/funding_integration_en.htm (last visited 31 August 2011).

are TCNs do not benefit from the same legal protections as EU citizens. It reflects the Commission's view that migrant labour will be essential to the EU's economic development in the coming years, and in particular, in combating the effects of the ageing EU population. It remains to be seen whether the emphasis on integrating migrants through 'softer' policy initiatives will be enough to make up for the weaknesses in their legal protection.

We saw above that, historically, the EES has placed varying degrees of emphasis on equality between men and women. The Commission's *Agenda for New Skills and Jobs* is relatively quiet on this topic because there is a separate *Strategy for Equality Between Men and Women 2010–2015*.[117] This latter document contains a number of initiatives of relevance to employment. These include assessing the gaps in existing EU legislation on parental leave (considered in Chapter 4),[118] analysing the performance of national equality bodies,[119] reviewing the Member States' provision of childcare,[120] and considering the implications of discrimination on multiple grounds including gender (for example, discrimination against older women).[121]

The problems facing individuals who encounter discrimination on grounds other than gender are largely dealt with through the European Platform Against Poverty and Social Exclusion.[122] This is linked not to the employment OMC, but to the social inclusion OMC.[123] Whilst many of the social inclusion initiatives extend beyond employment, there are some important overlaps with our concerns. For example, the Commission is pursuing separate initiatives relating to the inclusion in the labour market of people with disabilities,[124] migrants,[125] and Roma.[126] The year 2012 has been declared the European Year for Active Ageing, so at the time

---

[117] European Commission, *Strategy for Equality Between Women and Men 2010–2015* (COM (2010) 491 final).

[118] Ibid, 6.

[119] Ibid, 11, and see M. Ammer and others (2010), *Study on Equality Bodies set up under Directives 2000/43/EC, 2004/113/EC and 2006/54/EC* (Brussels: European Commission).

[120] Commission, *Strategy for Equality Between Women and Men 2010–2015*, above n. 118, 6.

[121] Ibid, 11.

[122] European Commission, *The European Platform against Poverty and Social Exclusion: A European Framework for Social and Territorial Cohesion* (COM (2010) 758 final).

[123] On which see Commission, *A Renewed Commitment to Social Europe: Reinforcing the Open Method of Coordination for Social Protection and Social Inclusion* (COM (2008) 418 final).

[124] Ibid, 10, and see also European Commission, *European Disability Strategy 2010–2020: A Renewed Commitment to a Barrier-Free Europe* (COM (2010) 636 final).

[125] Commission, *A Renewed Commitment to Social Europe*, above n. 124, 9.

[126] Ibid, 10.

of writing there is a growing emphasis on encouraging older workers to remain in the labour market for longer.[127] This will help to meet the Europe 2020 employment target though it is worth noting that the target applies only to people up to the age of 64.

Assessment

As we saw in Chapter 2, the practical impact of policy initiatives like Europe 2020 is difficult to discern, largely because it is hard to tell whether there is a cause-and-effect relationship between the EU's initiatives and the Member States' adoption of particular policies. This is highlighted in an important study by Skidmore of German law and policy relating to the employment of older workers. He notes that there is a degree of dissonance between government policies and the way they are presented by governments for OMC purposes, and given the variety of influences on policy makers he is sceptical of the capacity of the OMC to change government policy in a particular direction.[128] By contrast, in relation to gender in particular, Rubery offers a cautiously optimistic assessment.[129] She admits that it can be hard to separate real commitments from rhetorical flourishes in the Member States' reports, and notes that the impact of the EES must be assessed relative to the different starting-points of the Member States in terms of equality policies. Moreover, some of the really intractable problems, like the gender pay gap, have remained largely untouched.[130] However, in terms of positive benefits, she suggests that the EES has encouraged the Member States to reform policies on, for example, access to training and the provision of childcare places.

In terms of the Europe 2020 targets themselves, two criticisms can be made. First, it can be argued that equality (particularly gender equality) appears to have declined in status over time.[131] As we saw above, in 1998 equality was one of the four main targets of the Luxembourg process, whereas now equality does not feature in the 'headline' targets and is not even central to the Commission's main policy document on the employ-

---

[127] European Commission, *Proposal for a Decision of the European Parliament and of the Council on the European Year for Active Ageing (2012)* (COM (2010) 462 final) and see http://ec.europa.eu/social/ey2012.jsp (last visited 31 August 2011).

[128] P. Skidmore, 'The European Employment Strategy and Labour Law: a German Case Study' (2004) 29 EL Rev 52.

[129] J. Rubery, 'Gender Mainstreaming and Gender Equality in the EU: the Impact of the EU Employment Strategy' (2002) 33 *Industrial Relations Journal* 500.

[130] On which see also J. Rubery, D. Grimshaw and H. Figueiredo, 'How to Close the Gender Pay Gap in Europe: Towards the Gender Mainstreaming of Pay Policy' (2005) 36 *Industrial Relations Journal* 184.

[131] See M. Smith and P. Villa, 'The Ever-Declining Role of Gender Equality in the European Employment Strategy' (2010) 41 *Industrial Relations Journal* 526.

ment target. However, it is important not to exaggerate this criticism. The strong early focus on gender equality may have been a reflection of the limitations of EU law: that gender equality was one of the few areas of employment policy in which the EU had made a noticeable impact. It is perhaps inevitable that, as the EU's competence has expanded to include other grounds of discrimination, gender equality should recede from the foreground. And even if the EU's gender strategy has been hived off into a separate policy document, it still contains some significant policy initiatives.

The second criticism is more profound. This is that the emphasis on achieving the employment target may lead to the creation of poor-quality, atypical jobs.[132] This could work to the disadvantage of women and other minorities because it is already the case that they are disproportionately represented in such jobs. Although job quality is another important plank of the Commission's policies, the real worry for most commentators is the emphasis on flexicurity in the job creation target. Flexicurity suggests that part-time or temporary jobs are not to be discouraged. Although they are often presented as stepping-stones to full-time, permanent, well-paid work, critics regard them as a trap for the disadvantaged. The Commission has itself admitted that vulnerable groups suffered dispro-portionately during the recession because they were strongly represented in insecure jobs which soon fell victim to employer cutbacks. Of course, against this, we find the familiar argument that it is better to have a job – even a low-quality, atypical job – than no job at all.

FURTHER READING

As with any 'new' body of legislation, there is a substantial literature on recent developments in EU equality law and there are many different directions you might take in exploring it.

One interesting set of issues relates to the differences between the various grounds of discrimination now addressed in EU law. For a helpful discus-sion of these differences and the possible justifications for them, see M. Bell and L. Waddington, 'Reflecting on Inequalities in European Equality Law' (2003) 28 EL Rev 349. This is a particular problem in relation to race, religion and nationality, on which see B. Hepple, 'Race and Law in Fortress Europe' (2004) 67 MLR 1, and S.B. Lahuerta, 'Race Equality

---

[132] S. Fredman, 'Women at Work: The Broken Promise of Flexicurity' (2004) 33 ILJ 299.

and TCNs, or How to Fight Discrimination with A Discriminatory Law' (2009) 15 ELJ 738.

A related but somewhat separate problem is that as the grounds of prohibited discrimination multiply, so does the potential for conflicts between them. For an overview of this problem see C. O'Cinneide, 'The Uncertain Foundations of Contemporary Anti-Discrimination Law' available at http://papers.ssrn.com/s013/papers.cfm?abstract_id=1769068 (last accessed 5 January 2012). Of course, many individuals experience discrimination on more than one ground, but the mere multiplication of prohibited grounds of discrimination in EU law does not necessarily mean that 'intersectional' discrimination is properly addressed. For discussion, see R. Nielsen, 'Is European Union Equality Law Capable of Addressing Multiple and Intersectional Discrimination Yet? Precautions Against Neglecting Intersectional Cases', in D. Schiek and V. Chege (eds) (2009), *European Union Non-Discrimination Law: Comparative Perspectives on Multidimensional Equality Law* (Abingdon: Routledge-Cavendish).

As we have seen, age discrimination has given rise to the largest body of case-law and for an analysis of this see C. Kilpatrick, 'The Court of Justice and Labour Law in 2010: A New EU Discrimination Law Architecture' (2011) 40 ILJ 280, and D. Schiek, 'Age Discrimination Before the ECJ— Conceptual and Theoretical Issues' (2011) 48 CMLR 777. Both authors are concerned with the various tests adopted by the Court when considering whether or not age discrimination can be justified. This can be linked to a broader set of concerns (explored in Chapter 1) about whether EU equality law is 'constitutionalised', in the sense of being based on fundamental rights, or whether it remains rooted in economic considerations. This issue is explored in relation to disability discrimination by C. O'Brien, 'Equality's False Summits: New Varieties of Disability Discrimination, "Excessive" Equal Treatment and Economically Constricted Horizons' (2011) 36 EL Rev 26, and in the burgeoning literature on *Mangold* and 'general principles' cited in this chapter.

In relation to mainstreaming and the Europe 2020 strategy, there is an emerging literature exploring the effectiveness of these novel techniques. For some good examples of this type of scholarship, see F. Beveridge, 'Building Against the Past: the Impact of Mainstreaming on EU Gender Law and Policy' (2007) 32 EL Rev 193, P. Skidmore, 'The European Employment Strategy and Labour Law: a German Case Study' (2004) 29 EL Rev 52, and J. Rubery, 'Gender Mainstreaming and Gender Equality in the EU: the Impact of the EU Employment Strategy' (2002) 33 *Industrial Relations Journal* 500.

6.   Workers and 'atypical' workers

Most books on domestic labour law would spend a lot of time identifying the subject's 'personal scope': in other words, who are the beneficiaries of labour law? This is because a distinction usually needs to be drawn between labour law and commercial law. Those who are running their own businesses are generally thought not to need the protection of labour law so there is a need to distinguish these people from employees, who do. However, EU labour law has been imposed on existing national systems of labour law which already have mechanisms for solving this problem. Thus, in most instances EU labour law respects the Member States' autonomy on the matter. This chapter will consider that approach and will explore some of the situations in which 'worker' is defined at EU level.

In recent years, labour lawyers in many countries have become concerned with the 'atypical' workforce. These are individuals whose employment arrangements deviate in one or more respects from the norm of full-time work on an indefinite contract with the employer: for example, because they work part-time, on a fixed-term contract, or through an employment agency. Legal systems have reacted to these developments in varying ways. Some have sought to restrict the development, for example by limiting the number of times an individual's contract can be renewed on a fixed-term basis. Other legal systems (including that of the UK) have not sought to regulate atypical work at all, instead adopting the view that it offers employers a flexible source of labour and promotes job creation. After some long political struggles, EU labour law has intervened in some of these issues. This intervention has two interesting features: it has involved the use of the social dialogue, described in Chapter 2, and it has been drawn together by the Commission into the 'flexicurity' policy agenda, examined in Chapter 1. We will explore both of these features in the course of this chapter.

DEFINING 'WORKER'

Most labour law systems make clear *to whom* the rules of labour law apply using a central concept such as 'worker' or 'employee'. In EU labour law, there are two different approaches to this issue. For some purposes, such as free movement of workers under Article 45 TFEU or equal pay under Article 157 TFEU, there is an EU definition of 'worker'. But in most cases, EU labour law allows the Member States to define the 'workers' to whom the relevant legal protections will apply. This reflects the EU's limited role of 'harmonising' labour law rather than creating a uniform system throughout the Member States.

EU Definitions

Where EU law does define 'worker', it is important to consider the context, since the Court of Justice has used slightly different terminology depending on the treaty provisions in question.[1]

In the context of Article 45 TFEU on the free movement of workers, the Court of Justice has held in *Lawrie-Blum* that 'the essential feature of an employment relationship . . . is that for a certain period of time a person performs services for and under the direction of another person in return for which he receives remuneration'.[2] It is clear from *Levin* that the work need not be full-time, nor is it a requirement that the individual should obtain any particular level of income from the work.[3] However, in the same case the Court stated that the free movement rules apply 'only [to] the pursuit of effective and genuine activities, to the exclusion of activities on such a small scale as to be regarded as purely marginal and ancillary'.[4] On this basis, an individual performing work as part of a therapeutic programme for recovering drug addicts was held not to be a worker for the purposes of Article 45.[5] As we saw in Chapter 3, in this context it is more important to distinguish workers from economically inactive people, who only get the rights afforded to citizens, than to distinguish them from the self-employed, who get similar rights.[6]

Another context in which there is an EU-wide definition of worker is for the purposes of equal pay for men and women under Article 157 TFEU.[7] In *Allonby*, the Court cited the *Lawrie-Blum* definition just given, and made it clear that Article 157 does not protect the self-employed: 'it is clear from that definition that the authors of the Treaty did not intend that the

---

[1] Case C–85/96 *Martinez Sala v Freistaat Bayern* [1998] ECR I–2691 [31].
[2] Case 66/85 *Lawrie-Blum v Land Baden-Württemberg* [1986] ECR 2121, [17].
[3] Case 53/81 *Levin v Staatssecretaris van Justitie* [1982] ECR 1035, [16].
[4] Ibid, [17].
[5] Case 344/87 *Bettray v Staatssecretaris van Justitie* [1989] ECR 1621, but see also Case C–456/02 *Trojani v CPAS* [2004] ECR I–7573.
[6] See Directive 2004/38/EC, discussed in detail in Chapter 3.
[7] See Chapters 4 and 5 for a detailed discussion of EU equality law.

term "worker" . . . should include independent providers of services who are not in a relationship of subordination with the person who receives the services'.[8] However, the Court also noted the importance of classifying individuals as workers where they are not genuinely self-employed, regardless of the approach that would be taken in national law.[9] This is an important move given the possibility of 'sham' self-employment in some legal systems.

Fredman has criticised the Court's case-law for its focus on subordination rather than economic dependence, arguing that the latter concept would capture a broader range of 'atypical' workers.[10] Whilst the Court has continued to emphasise subordination in later cases, it has applied the term in a flexible way that suggests that it will not prove much of an obstacle in practice. *Danosa* is a good example of this.[11] In that case, the claimant was a company director who was dismissed from her employment on grounds of her pregnancy. She brought a claim under Directive 92/85.[12] The Court held that the application of the worker definition required a careful assessment of the context by the national court:

> The fact that Ms Danosa was a member of the Board of Directors of a capital company is not enough in itself to rule out the possibility that she was in a relationship of subordination to that company: it is necessary to consider the circumstances in which the Board Member was recruited; the nature of the duties entrusted to that person; the context in which those duties were performed; the scope of the person's powers and the extent to which he or she was supervised within the company; and the circumstances under which the person could be removed.[13]

The Court suggested that it was significant for the purposes of 'subordination' that the claimant had to report on her work to the supervisory board and could be dismissed by the shareholders.[14]

---

[8] Case C–256/01 *Allonby v Accrington & Rossendale College* [2004] ECR I–873, [68].
[9] Ibid, [71].
[10] S. Fredman, 'Marginalising Equal Pay Laws' (2004) 33 ILJ 281, 284–5.
[11] Case C–232/09 *Danosa v LKB Lzings* [2010] nyr.
[12] Council Directive 92/85/EEC of 19 October 1992 on the introduction of measures to encourage improvements in the safety and health at work of pregnant workers and workers who have recently given birth or are breastfeeding. The Court held in *Kiiski* that the term 'pregnant worker' in Art 2 of the Directive should be given an EU meaning: Case C–116/06 *Kiiski v Tampereen kaupunki* [2007] ECR I–07643, [24].
[13] Above n. 11, [47].
[14] Ibid, [49]–[50].

Member States' Definitions

In most areas of EU labour law, the definition of 'worker' is a matter
for the Member States.[15] For example, the Acquired Rights Directive
applies to employees, defined as 'any person who, in the Member State
concerned, is protected as an employee under national employment law'.[16]
Interestingly, this is true even of the Posted Workers Directive which, since
it applies to cross-border situations, might have been expected to use an
EU definition.[17] Instead, the Directive states in Article 2(2): 'For the purposes of this Directive, the definition of a worker is that which applies in
the law of the Member State to whose territory the worker is posted'. This
approach respects the autonomy of the Member States in determining the
personal scope of their own labour law systems.

Having said that, there are two potential inroads into the Member
States' discretion in this area. One possibility is that if a Member State
used a very narrow definition of 'worker' when implementing a directive,
this might be open to challenge as a failure to implement the directive
properly. For example, the UK was found to have failed to implement
the Acquired Rights[18] and Collective Redundancies[19] Directives properly
when it did not provide a mechanism for identifying workplace representatives in non-unionised workplaces.[20] The Court was not impressed
with the UK's reliance on its national traditions given that this left many
workers without the protection envisaged by the two Directives. A similar
argument might be made in relation to the use of a 'worker' definition if it
excluded a substantial proportion of the workforce. This might be an issue
for countries like the UK which have a two-tier approach to the personal
scope of labour law, in which the traditional concept of 'employee' has

---

[15]   It should be noted that Directive 91/533/EEC on an employer's obligation to inform
employees of the conditions applicable to the contract or employment relationship just
obliges the Member States to ensure that employers provide information about essential
terms and conditions of employment, and does not have any impact on the definition of
employee or on national rules surrounding the contract of employment.

[16]   Directive 2001/23/EC of 12 March 2001 on the approximation of the laws of the
Member States relating to the safeguarding of employees' rights in the event of transfers of
undertakings, businesses or parts of undertakings or businesses, Art 2(1)(d), but see also Art
2(2). This Directive is discussed in more detail in Chapter 8.

[17]   Directive 96/71/EC of the European Parliament and of the Council of 16 December
1996 concerning the posting of workers in the framework of the provision of services, considered in more detail in Chapter 3.

[18]   Above n. 16.

[19]   Council Directive 98/59/EC of 20 July 1998 on the approximation of the laws of the
Member States relating to collective redundancies, considered in detail in Chapter 8.

[20]   Cases C–382/92 *Commission v UK* [1994] ECR I–2435; C–383/92 *Commission v UK*
[1994] ECR I–2479.

been supplemented by a (slightly) broader concept of 'worker' in some legislation.[21] It is not clear whether the Court of Justice would expect the more inclusive of the two definitions to be used when implementing directives, or whether this would be seen as too great an infringement of national autonomy.

Another way in which EU law reduces the significance of the Member States' worker definitions is by allocating some employment-related rights to self-employed people. Since national definitions generally exclude the self-employed from the scope of labour law, a requirement to extend protection to the self-employed has the effect of overriding such definitions. The most important example of this is Directive 2010/41/EU on equal treatment for self-employed people.[22] This replaces an earlier directive on the subject,[23] and part of its objective is to update the law in this area by introducing definitions of key concepts such as direct and indirect discrimination, like those found in the EU's other equality measures.[24] The directive requires the Member States to outlaw discrimination based on sex in self-employed activities, such as the conditions for setting up in business,[25] and to provide at least 14 weeks' maternity benefit to self-employed women with a view to enabling them to take maternity leave.[26] However, the application of EU labour law, like national labour law, to self-employed people remains the exception rather than the rule.

Conclusion

The advantage of the EU definition of worker, where it applies, is that it leads to a uniform application of the law across the EU. This seems particularly attractive in areas such as free movement, in which there is a cross-border dimension to the issues. However, there is another aspect of consistency to be considered: consistency within national labour law systems. It would be very strange if individuals who are not normally protected by their national labour law systems should be covered when the rules have an EU source. Allowing the Member States to apply their

---

[21] See the discussion of this in relation to fixed-term work in Fredman, above n. 10, 285.

[22] Directive 2010/41/EU of the European Parliament and of the Council of 7 July 2010 on the application of the principle of equal treatment between men and women engaged in an activity in a self-employed capacity and repealing Council Directive 86/613/EEC.

[23] Directive 86/613/EEC.

[24] Directive 2010/41/EU, Art 3. For discussion of EU equality law, see Chapters 4 and 5.

[25] Directive 2010/41/EU, Art 4.

[26] Ibid, Art 8.

own definitions in most cases helps to respect and preserve their historical traditions of labour law and reflects the EU's limited role of 'harmonisation', not unification.

'ATYPICAL' WORKERS

Although EU labour law has not focused particularly closely on the definition of worker, it has made a considerable contribution to addressing the problem of 'atypical' workers. Atypical workers include those who work on a casual basis, part-time, on fixed-term contracts, through employment agencies or from home. The term 'atypical worker' is problematic in that these workers may be more numerous than typical workers in some sectors. Moreover, individuals may be 'atypical' in more than one respect, for example by working from home on a casual basis or by obtaining part-time work through an agency.

Employers use these workers because of the flexibility they offer: for example, agency workers can be brought in 'as required'. Some workers may also welcome the opportunity to work more flexibly, for example, by moving to part-time work whilst raising a family. However, there are disadvantages associated with atypical work. Some forms of atypical work can be highly insecure from the worker's perspective, with poor terms and conditions and reduced or no entitlement to legal protections enjoyed by typical workers. Moreover, as Fredman has noted, these problems are often exacerbated by the fact that the risk of atypical work falls more heavily on already disadvantaged groups, such as women with childcare responsibilities or recent immigrants.[27] Atypical work has been regarded differently by the Member States, with some seeking to restrict it (France and Belgium, for example) and some allowing it to develop without much regulation (like the UK).

This section will consider the Commission's policy on atypical work, often summed up under the label 'flexicurity', before examining the directives on fixed-term work, part-time work and temporary agency work, and the agreement on 'telework'. The social dialogue procedure has been used for most of the initiatives in this area, so this chapter will provide a good opportunity to explore it more fully, and it is to this that we will turn first.

---

[27]   S. Fredman, 'Women at Work: The Broken Promise of Flexicurity' (2004) 33 ILJ 299.

Social Dialogue

In Chapter 2, we highlighted two themes in relation to the social dialogue: the process of negotiating and reaching an agreement, and the worry about the parties' representativeness.

Unlike 'normal' collective bargaining, the parties' negotiations in the social dialogue are not backed by the usual industrial threats. Instead, there is a political calculation to be made about what will happen if no agreement is reached:[28] will the Member States agree on legislation instead, and will this be better or worse (from the employers' or unions' perspectives) than what is on the table in the social dialogue negotiations? Interestingly, though, the social dialogue agreements in the field of atypical work do not fit this pattern exactly. As Jeffery explains, the Commission had been seeking agreement on a set of directives in this area since the 1970s, without success.[29] So the backdrop to the social partners' negotiations was one of hostility on the part of some Member States (particularly, but not exclusively, the UK) to any legislation on these matters. This may have given the social partners another incentive to agree: to show that the new procedure for social dialogue could succeed where the normal political process had failed, and thus to secure the long-term future of the social dialogue as a regulatory technique. As we shall see, the agreement on part-time work, subsequently enacted as Directive 97/81/EC, involved some very considerable compromises on the part of the ETUC in particular, and these may be explained by the perceived need to reach an agreement even at some cost.[30]

In 1997, the political landscape changed significantly because the UK signed up to the Agreement on Social Policy, and although the UK government continued to oppose many new developments in EU labour law, it is arguable that the climate for new proposals from the Commission improved slightly. The social partners reached another agreement (again containing significant compromises from earlier Commission proposals)[31] on fixed-term work, subsequently enacted as Directive 99/70, but failed to agree on agency work. This topic was eventually regulated by means of a

---

[28] Characterised by Bercusson as 'bargaining in the shadow of the law': B. Bercusson (2009), *European Labour Law* (2nd edn, Cambridge University Press), 573.

[29] M. Jeffery, 'The Commission Proposals on "Atypical Work": Back to the Drawing-Board . . . Again' (1995) 24 ILJ 296.

[30] M. Jeffery 'Not Really Going to Work? Of the Directive on Part-Time Work, "Atypical Work" and Attempts to Regulate It' (1998) 27 ILJ 193, 202.

[31] J. Murray, 'Normalising Temporary Work. The Proposed Directive on Fixed-Term Work' (1999) 28 ILJ 269, 271–3.

Directive enacted through the normal legislative process.[32] Of course, all legislative processes involve some degree of bargaining and compromise, but the social dialogue is a stark example because of the opposing interests of the negotiating parties and the complex political background against which their negotiations take place.

The other concern we examined in Chapter 2 related to the representativeness of the social partners. The agreements resulting from the social dialogue to be considered in this chapter raise the concern about representativeness in a particularly acute form. It is generally the case that atypical workers are less likely to be trade union members than 'standard' employees. Thus, it is not clear that the trade union side can claim to speak for these workers when negotiating agreements to regulate their working lives.[33] This concern is exacerbated by the fact that the political actors' role is limited when a social dialogue agreement is presented for enactment as a directive. The European Parliament has no say at all, and it was decided at an early stage that the Member States would enact social partner agreements as directives without accepting any amendments from the European Commission.[34]

Of course, as we saw in Chapter 2, there is a counter-argument to this. If we view the social dialogue as a 'labour law' matter rather than a political matter, these concerns are less severe.[35] It can be argued that unions generally claim to speak on behalf of working people, not just their members, and that their legitimacy stems not just from their ability to represent people but from their expert knowledge of workplace issues. And the lack of involvement on the part of the political actors can be seen in a positive light as a means of preserving the social partners' autonomy, an important value in collective labour law. What is less clear is why the 'labour law' analysis is appropriate when the outputs of the process are enacted as legislation.[36]

Flexicurity

Since the enactment of the Directive on Fixed-Term Work in particular,[37] the legislative measures on atypical work have been tied up with the

---

[32] Directive 2008/104/EC of the European Parliament and of the Council of 19 November 2008 on temporary agency work.

[33] See J. Kenner (2003), *EU Employment Law: From Rome to Amsterdam and Beyond* (Oxford: Hart), 262.

[34] See Jeffery, above n. 30, 202–3.

[35] B. Bercusson, 'Democratic Legitimacy and European Labour Law' (1999) 28 ILJ 153.

[36] On which see Kenner, above n. 33, 263–66.

[37] See Murray, above n. 31, 272–3.

developing policy of 'flexicurity' in EU labour law, introduced in Chapter 1. The relationship between this policy and the regulation of atypical work is a complex one and we will examine some aspects of it here.

According to the European Commission, 'flexicurity . . . promotes a combination of flexible labour markets and adequate security. Flexicurity can also help provide an answer to the EU's dilemma on how to maintain and improve competitiveness whilst reinforcing the European social model.'[38] We saw in Chapter 1 that this 'dilemma' stems from the need for the EU to compete in global marketplaces despite its relatively high employment costs. The Commission has identified four main components within flexicurity: 'flexible and reliable contractual arrangements', 'comprehensive lifelong learning strategies', 'effective active labour market policies' and 'modern social security systems'.[39] The first of these components is of particular relevance to the regulation of atypical work.

The Commission's view appears to be that atypical work is not a bad thing in itself. Its main contribution is as a 'stepping-stone' to typical work, by providing opportunities for the unemployed to get back into work or for people with other commitments (such as childcare responsibilities) to engage in some economic activity.[40] The Commission is conscious that the use of atypical work opens up a gap between so-called 'insiders' and 'outsiders' in the labour market: in other words, between those with secure jobs and those with insecure, atypical jobs. The aim of regulation should be to reduce this gap.[41] For 'outsiders' or atypical workers, the aim should be to provide better protection without regulating this form of work out of existence. And for 'insiders', although the Commission is reluctant to admit it, the aim should be to reduce protection somewhat, so that the focus is not on keeping a particular job (what labour lawyers traditionally think of as 'job security') but instead on staying employed ('employment security').[42] This is highly controversial because it may undermine existing unfair dismissal laws in some Member States, but it is beyond the scope of the present discussion.

The 'stepping-stone' argument is an attractive one, but it is not clear whether there is any empirical evidence to support the idea of atypical work as a means of enabling workers to move to better jobs. It may equally be the case that individuals become 'trapped' in atypical work.[43]

---

[38] European Commission, *Towards Common Principles of Flexicurity: More and Better Jobs through Flexibility and Security* (COM (2007) 359 final), 7.

[39] Ibid, 12.

[40] Ibid, 20.

[41] Ibid, 28.

[42] Ibid, 7.

[43] A risk the Commission acknowledges: above n. 38, 28.

Indeed, since there is a significant overlap between atypical work and other forms of disadvantage in the labour market, the possibility of getting trapped in atypical work might be more plausible. For example, women (particularly women with children) and migrant workers are disproportionately represented in atypical work.[44] To some extent, the legislation we will discuss below seeks to address this by providing for atypical workers to be informed of better jobs in the user enterprise, but these requirements are sometimes framed in rather aspirational terms.

Another problem with the 'stepping-stone' argument, and with flexicurity more generally, is that it tends to focus on atypical work as a single phenomenon. But we established in the Introduction that there are different forms of atypical work and that they may carry with them different sets of advantages and disadvantages. For example, part-time work can be an attractive way of combining economic activity with other responsibilities, such as study or childcare. But fixed-term work does not carry any obvious benefits for the worker, other than the very basic one that a fixed-term job may be better than no job at all.[45] Fixed-term work is inherently precarious and, given the choice, it is hard to envisage a worker opting for a fixed-term job over a job of indefinite duration (given that it is generally easy to resign if a better opportunity comes along).

Once we start distinguishing between forms of atypical work, there are two important consequences for regulation. First, it might be the case that we want to encourage some forms of atypical work but not others: part-time but not fixed-term, for example. And second, we might want to adopt different regulatory techniques to address the specific problems faced by different groups of workers. For example, a particular concern for part-time workers might be to have some control over the hours they work or over the amount of notice they are given about a change to their hours, so that they can juggle their work with their other commitments.[46] And for fixed-term workers, a big issue is the use of successive fixed-term contracts which leave the worker in a precarious position when the reality is that they are likely to keep their job over the longer term.[47] As we shall see, EU law has had varying degrees of success in identifying and addressing these more specific problems.

This leads to a final point about the underlying policy of regulation in

---

[44]   Fredman, above n. 27.

[45]   See Murray, above n. 31, 274.

[46]   See Jeffery, above n. 30, 199, for a critique of the Directive's failure to address this point.

[47]   This is addressed in clause 5 of the Agreement annexed to Directive 99/70, and will be discussed in more detail below.

this area. The flexicurity agenda, as we saw above, aims to reduce the differences between typical and atypical workers. In part for this reason, a significant focus in all the directives we are about to consider is the principle of equal treatment: atypical workers are given a right to seek equality with full-time, or indefinite, or directly hired workers, as the case may be. Moreover, since equal treatment is a generally well-accepted principle, it may be easier to reach agreement on legislation incorporating it. The equal treatment principle may be an important source of protection for atypical workers: for example, it was common in the past for employers to pay part-timers less per hour than full-timers.[48] But there are two worries. First, the equal treatment principle does not address the specific problems faced by atypical workers, discussed above, so it may create the impression that 'something is being done' when in fact very little is being done. And second, as the case-law develops, the regulation of atypical work may end up as just another branch of EU equality law (to be considered in the next two chapters). As Bercusson points out, this may distort the social dialogue.[49]

With this policy background in mind, we are now in a position to examine the EU's legislative initiatives on atypical work.

Part-time Work

Although our primary focus in this section will be on Directive 97/81/EC on part-time work,[50] it is important to be aware of the broader context of the regulation of part-time work in EU law. Long before the directive was enacted, the Court of Justice had been active in developing rights for part-time workers through sex equality law. We will consider some of this jurisprudence (which is not affected by the enactment of the directive) before examining the directive itself.

Part-time work and equality law

Since most part-time workers are women, it is possible to argue that inferior treatment of part-time workers constitutes indirect discrimination on grounds of sex. This is unlawful unless it can be justified as the proportionate pursuit of a legitimate aim unrelated to sex. The Court has used sex discrimination law to tackle various problems facing part-timers, including unequal pay, unequal access to pension schemes and unequal access to

---

[48] As we shall see below, this was usually open to challenge as a breach of the principle of equal pay for men and women (now Art 157 TFEU) prior to the regulation of part-time work per se.

[49] Bercusson, above n. 28, 631.

[50] Extended to the UK by Directive 98/23/EC.

opportunities for training and promotion. As is so often the case, the Court of Justice's initial approach was relatively cautious but over time it has become more willing to scrutinise employers' claims in these cases.[51]

A large chunk of the case-law is concerned with occupational pension schemes. Indeed, it is often forgotten that one of the best-known sex discrimination cases, *Bilka-Kaufhaus*, is in fact a case about the employer's refusal to allow part-time workers to join the company pension scheme.[52] The Court of Justice held that the employer's aim – to discourage part-time work – was legitimate, but that the means used had to be examined by the national court using a proportionality test. Although this does not seem particularly encouraging, over time the effect of *Bilka* (coupled with legislative developments)[53] has been to dismantle rules excluding part-timers from pension schemes. This has generated a further body of case-law in which the Court has tried to figure out the exact implications of allowing part-timers to have retrospective access to pension schemes.[54]

In relation to pay, the early case of *Jenkins v Kingsgate* was relatively restrictive.[55] In that case, the employer paid part-timers 10 per cent less per hour than full-timers. Although this appeared to be a clear-cut case of sex discrimination given that the majority of the part-timers were female, the Court held that the onus remained on the claimants to show that sex was the reason for the difference in treatment. In later cases, the Court was much more assertive, holding that part-timers' lack of access to sick pay (in *Rinner-Kühn*)[56] and severance pay (in *Kowalska*)[57] were clear instances of sex discrimination.

---

[51]   For a detailed discussion, see E. Traversa, 'Protection of Part-Time Workers in the Case Law of the Court of Justice of the European Communities' (2003) 19 *International Journal of Comparative Labour Law and Industrial Relations* 219.

[52]   Case 170/84 *Bilka-Kaufhaus v Weber von Hartz* [1986] ECR 1607.

[53]   The starting point was Council Directive 86/378/EEC of 24 July 1986 on the implementation of the principle of equal treatment for men and women in occupational social security schemes, but this had to be amended to accommodate the Court's case-law, which removed significant derogations agreed by the Member States: Council Directive 96/97/EC of 20 December 1996 amending Directive 86/378/EEC on the implementation of the principle of equal treatment for men and women in occupational social security schemes. The current provisions are in the Recast Directive, Directive 2006/54/EC of the European Parliament and of the Council of 5 July 2006 on the implementation of the principle of equal opportunities and equal treatment of men and women in matters of employment and occupation.

[54]   This has been complicated by the fact that the Court limited the temporal effect of its judgment in Case C–262/88 *Barber v Guardian Royal Exchange Assurance Group* [1990] ECR I–1889 on equal treatment in pension benefits, but not its judgment in *Bilka* on access to pension schemes. See Directive 2006/54/EC, Art 12, and Case C–246/96 *Magorrian v Eastern Health and Social Services Board* [1997] ECR I–7153, [20]–[35].

[55]   Case 96/80 *Jenkins v Kingsgate* [1981] ECR 911, [14]–[15].

[56]   Case 171/88 *Rinner-Kühn v FWW Spezial-Gebäudereinigung* [1989] ECR 2743.

[57]   Case C–33/89 *Kowalska v Freie und Hansestadt Hamburg* [1990] ECR I–2591.

A similar pattern of initial caution followed by more radical approaches is evident from the Court's decisions on overtime pay for part-time workers. In *Helmig*, part-timers were only paid overtime premiums where they worked additional hours over and above those normally worked by full-timers.[58] The Court held that this was not discriminatory because it amounted to equal treatment with full-timers. However, the opposite is also arguable: if the overtime premium is designed to reward a person who works more than his or her normal hours, equal treatment for part-time workers would require payment of the premium whenever the normal *part-time* hours were exceeded. In two later cases, the Court adopted approaches that were more favourable towards part-timers. The *Elsner-Lakeberg* case concerned a rule that workers (part-time or full-time) would only be paid for overtime if it was in excess of three hours per week.[59] The Court held that this was unequal treatment, because the impact of working an extra two hours per week was greater on a part-timer than on a full-timer. And in *Voß*, the Court found that a rule applying lower pay to part-time and full-time workers who worked in excess of their normal (part-time or full-time) hours was discriminatory, because a part-timer who happened to work full-time hours because of overtime would be paid less than a full-timer who worked those hours as normal.[60]

The Court of Justice has also considered employers' practices of restricting part-timers' ability to secure promotion. In *Nimz* and *Gerster*,[61] public sector employers required employees to accumulate a certain number of years' experience before they could be considered for promotion. Part-timers accumulated this experience more slowly than full-timers. The Court was sceptical about the employers' strategies, holding that it might well be possible to acquire sufficient experience to do a particular job without having to work a stated number of years. The 'automatic' nature of the rules was called into question.

These and other decisions on part-time work have led some to conclude that it was not necessary for the EU to legislate on the subject because many of the disadvantages faced by part-time workers had already been removed by the Court. However, there are two obvious problems with examining part-time work through a sex discrimination lens. First, the sex discrimination element of the claim must be proved, so the claimant must be able to demonstrate that rules which disadvantage part-time workers

[58]   Case C–399/92 *Stadt Lengerich v Helmig* [1994] ECR I–5727.
[59]   Case C– 285/02 *Elsner-Lakeberg v Land Nordrhein-Westfalen* [2004] ECR I–5861.
[60]   Case C–300/06 *Voß v Land Berlin* [2007] ECR I–10573.
[61]   Case C–184/89 *Nimz v Freie und Hansestadt Hamburg* [1991] ECR I–297, [14]. Case C–1/95 *Gerster v Freistaat Bayern* [1997] ECR I–5253, [39]–[41].

do indeed have a disproportionate impact on one sex. This may be difficult where the relevant statistics are not available. Second, male part-time workers cannot bring a claim unless the usual circumstances are reversed: in other words, that the full-timers in their firm are mostly female and the disadvantaged part-timers are mostly male. This seems unlikely to occur in practice.

The Directive on Part-Time Work

Directive 97/81/EC implements the social partners' framework agreement on part-time work, concluded in 1997.[62] Clause 1 of the Agreement (which is annexed to the Directive) sets out its purpose:

> The purpose of this Framework Agreement is:
> (a) to provide for the removal of discrimination against part-time workers and to improve the quality of part-time work;
> (b) to facilitate the development of part-time work on a voluntary basis and to contribute to the flexible organization of working time in a manner which takes into account the needs of employers and workers.

This is significant because it highlights the link between legislation of this type and the Commission's flexicurity agenda. The purpose of the Agreement is not just a worker-protective one, although this element is evident from paragraph (a). As paragraph (b) makes clear, encouraging part-time work is also a significant concern.

The most important worker-protective right in the Agreement is the right not to be discriminated against by reason of working part-time.[63] A part-time worker is defined as 'an employee whose normal hours of work, calculated on a weekly basis or on average over a period of employment of up to one year, are less than the normal hours of work of a comparable full-time worker'.[64] A comparable full-time worker is defined as someone 'in the same establishment having the same type of employment contract or relationship, who is engaged in the same or a similar work/occupation, due regard being given to other considerations which may include seniority and qualification/skills'.[65] The Agreement also provides for a broader range of comparison where there is no comparable full-time worker in the 'same establishment', using either a collective agreement (where relevant) or other approaches provided for in national law or practice.[66] Clause 4(1)

---

[62] See, generally, Jeffery, above n. 30.
[63] Directive 97/81/EC, Annex, cl 4.
[64] Ibid, cl 3(1).
[65] Ibid, cl 3(2).
[66] Ibid.

of the Agreement lays down the right not to be discriminated against: 'in respect of employment conditions, part-time workers shall not be treated in a less favourable manner than comparable full-time workers solely because they work part time unless different treatment is justified on objective grounds'. There is no distinction here between direct and indirect discrimination, so in contrast to most other areas of discrimination law, it is theoretically possible to justify direct discrimination against part-time workers.

The Court of Justice has held that clause 4 of the Agreement is directly effective,[67] by analogy to the equivalent clause in the Agreement on Fixed-Term Work, to be discussed further below.[68] It has also held, consistently with earlier case law in the area of equal pay for men and women, that the term 'employment conditions' in clause 4 extends to pensions where they are provided by the employer.[69] So the Court found discrimination where 'vertical' part-timers, people who work full-time hours but only for part of the month, would take longer to accumulate pension entitlement than full-timers (or 'horizontal' part-timers, who work a little bit every week).

Clause 5 of the Agreement contains various measures designed to promote the availability of part-time work. Clause 5(1) of the Agreement states that the Member States and the social partners should 'identify and review obstacles of a legal or administrative nature which may limit the opportunities for part-time work and, where appropriate, eliminate them'. Although this might seem to be a relatively softly worded provision, the Court gave effect to it in *Michaeler*.[70] That case concerned an Italian rule that required employers to provide the authorities with a copy of the contract of employment of any part-time workers within 30 days of hiring them, or face a fine. The Court held that this would act as a deterrent to the use of part-time work, particularly by small and medium-sized enterprises.

Clause 5(2) makes clear that a worker's refusal to transfer from full- to part-time or vice versa should not constitute a valid reason for dismissal. Clause 5(3) addresses the opportunities for workers to change their

---

[67] Case C–486/08 *Zentralbetriebsrat der Landeskrankenhäuser Tirols v Land Tirol* [2010] ECR I–3527, [25].
[68] See Case C–268/06 *Impact v Minister for Agriculture and Food* [2008] ECR I–2483, [59]–[68].
[69] Case C–395/08 *INPS v Bruno* [2010] ECR I–5119. The Agreement does not apply to social security, an exclusion that has been criticised on the ground that it waters down the Commission's earlier proposals. But it is arguable that a social partner agreement relating to social security (which is a state responsibility) would have been highly controversial in other ways. See Jeffery, above n. 30, 195.
[70] Case C–55/07 *Michaeler v Amt für sozialen Arbeitsschutz and Autonome Provinz Bozen* [2008] ECR I–3135.

working hours, though this is expressed largely in aspirational terms: 'as far as possible, employers should give consideration to' requests to transfer from full-time to part-time work and vice versa. Interestingly, there is some intersection between clause 5 and the obligation not to discriminate under clause 4 in this regard. In *Zentralbetriebsrat der Landeskrankenhäuser Tirols*, the Court considered a rule that disadvantaged individuals who transferred from full-time to part-time work.[71] The rule provided that if they had not used up the paid holiday entitlement they had accrued while they were full-time, they would only be able to take it on less advantageous terms once they were working part-time. The Court held that this was discrimination contrary to clause 4. Whilst this removes a deterrent to transferring status, though, it is still not the same as providing a right to transfer.

The Agreement's failure to provide any clear-cut rights to transfer from one status to another is open to criticism from the perspectives of both worker protection and encouraging part-time work. Arguably, it is weaker than the (still quite vague) obligation in the ILO Convention on Part-Time Work: 'Where appropriate, measures shall be taken to ensure that transfer from full-time to part-time work or vice versa is voluntary, in accordance with national law and practice'.[72] Of course, it is problematic to provide a right to transfer to full-time status when the employer does not have enough work available, though a lesser obligation, such as giving priority to part-timers when full-time vacancies arise, might be feasible. But if part-time work is regarded as desirable, it might have been appropriate to provide a right to do any particular job on a part-time basis unless the employer could justify a requirement for full-time working. There is evidence to suggest that people who want to combine work with raising a family often have to settle for jobs for which they are over-qualified, because employers are reluctant to allow more senior roles to be performed on a part-time basis.

Another potential area of concern for part-time workers, on which the Agreement is silent, is control over their hours of work. Part-timers might want predictable hours either to balance work with other commitments, or to achieve a reliable income. But in the *Wippel* case, the Court rejected a creative argument which sought to use the Agreement to tackle these problems.[73] The claimant in that case had a casual work arrangement

---

[71]   Above n. 67, [32]–[5].

[72]   ILO, Convention 175, Part-Time Work Convention, 1994, Art 10. Although this is often treated as a benchmark for the regulation of part-time work, it should be noted that it has not been ratified by many states.

[73]   Case C–313/02 *Wippel v Peek & Cloppenburg* [2004] ECR I–9483.

with her employer. She could be called in to work when needed and had the right to refuse particular assignments. She argued that she was being discriminated against on grounds of part-time work (and on grounds of sex) because, unlike full-time workers (and other, non-casual, part-time workers) who had fixed weekly hours, her earnings were unpredictable. The Court rejected this argument on the basis that there was no 'comparable full-time worker' within the meaning of the Agreement, because all the full-time workers had fixed hours. Whilst this is probably correct on a strict reading of the Agreement, it ignores the possibility that there might be a strong link in practice between part-time work and the casual contract at issue in the case.

Ultimately, as one would expect from a social dialogue measure, the directive on part-time work is a compromise. It achieves some protection for part-time workers, and promotes the availability of part-time work, but not to the extent that campaigners or unions might have wished. As we saw above, it has been suggested that since this was the first example of social dialogue being used in this way, it was more important to reach an agreement which could be enacted as a directive than to reach an agreement that would provide optimal protection for part-time workers. However, now that the directive is in place, it is difficult to imagine the political will emerging to enact a more worker-protective measure.

Fixed-term Work

The social partners reached an agreement on fixed-term work in 1999 which was given legal effect in Directive 99/70.[74] Before we consider this in detail, it should be noted that it is not the only EU legislation on fixed-term work. In 1991, the European Commission did succeed in one of its early attempts to get legislation on atypical work, in the form of Directive 91/383/EEC on the health and safety of fixed-term and agency workers. This Directive seeks to ensure that workers with these types of contract have the same health and safety protection at work as other workers covered by the body of EU health and safety legislation.[75] As a health and safety measure, this proved less controversial than the Commission's other (unsuccessful) proposals at that time.[76] Since health and safety is beyond the scope of this book, we will focus on Directive 99/70.

A fixed-term worker is defined as 'a person having an employment contract or relationship entered into directly between an employer and

---

[74] See, generally, Murray, above n. 31.
[75] Directive 91/383/EEC, Art 1.
[76] See Jeffery, above n. 29.

a worker where the end of the employment contract or relationship is determined by objective conditions such as reaching a specific date, completing a specific task, or the occurrence of a specific event'.[77] Like the Agreement on Part-Time Work, the Agreement on Fixed-Term Work contains a clause (clause 4) protecting fixed-term workers against discrimination, though in this case the comparators are the employer's permanent workers.[78] This clause has direct effect.[79]

As with part-time work, the Court of Justice has held that the term 'employment conditions' in clause 4 covers pay and pensions (where the latter are provided by the employer).[80] The clause has been used to combat various forms of discrimination against fixed-term workers, such as a rule precluding them from obtaining pay increments for length of service afforded to permanent workers,[81] and a rule that previous experience as a fixed-term worker did not count in a competition for civil service jobs.[82]

Another important worker-protective provision in the Agreement addresses a problem specific to fixed-term workers: the possibility that they might be employed by the same employer on a series of fixed-term contracts, so that the employer gets the benefit of their labour over the longer term, but leaves them in a precarious legal and financial position. Clause 5 of the Agreement requires the Member States to take steps to prevent the 'abuse' of successive fixed-term contracts, but gives them the choice of requiring the employer to have objective reasons for renewing a fixed-term contract, limiting the maximum total duration of successive fixed-term contracts, or limiting the number of renewals, or some combination of these measures. Because this clause gives the Member States a discretion, it has been found to be insufficiently precise for the purposes of direct effect.[83]

Despite the discretion, national governments remain obliged to secure effective implementation of the directive. This has generated quite a lot of litigation. Thus, the Court of Justice found that Greece failed to implement the directive properly because it provided that contracts were not

---

[77] Directive 99/70, Annex, cl 3(1). This excludes agency workers: see below.
[78] Directive 99/70, Annex, cl 4.
[79] *Impact*, above n. 68, [59]–[68].
[80] Ibid, [105]–[34].
[81] Case C–444/09 *Gavieiro Gavieiro v Consellería de Educación e Ordenación Universitaria de la Xunta de Galicia* [2010] nyr.
[82] Case C–177/10 *Santana v Consejería de Justicia y Administración Pública de la Junta de Andalucía* [2011] nyr, [63]–[84], though it was for the national court to determine whether experience as an interim civil servant was comparable to experience gained as a permanent civil servant.
[83] *Impact*, above n. 68, [69]–[80].

'successive' where there was a gap of more than 20 days between them.[84] It was held that this provision lent itself to abuse by employers, who could simply re-employ people on fixed-term contracts after short breaks. Another issue that has arisen in a number of cases relates to the reasons for using successive fixed-term contracts. Here, the Court has held that these reasons must involve 'objective factors relating to the particular features of the activity concerned and to the conditions under which it is carried out'.[85] General legislation permitting the use of successive fixed-term contracts is not sufficient for these purposes. Finally, national law must provide an effective deterrent to the abuse of successive fixed-term contracts by employers, but this need not necessarily involve making the individuals in question permanent employees.[86]

Despite these positive developments, some commentators regard the Agreement as lacking one very important provision: it does not require Member States to place any restrictions on the employer's *first* use of a fixed-term contract. We saw above that, whereas part-time work can have positive benefits for workers, fixed-term work can be regarded as inherently precarious. The Agreement acknowledges this to some extent: in contrast to the Agreement on Part-Time Work, there is no particular emphasis on promoting or encouraging this form of work. The Court has also held that indefinite employment should be regarded as the norm.[87] But – in line with the flexicurity agenda – there is no attempt to limit the creation of jobs on a fixed-term basis. As we saw in Chapter 2, this has given rise to difficult questions for those Member States which already restrict the initial use of fixed-term contracts. The Agreement contains a 'non-regression' clause, which states that its implementation should not be used as an excuse to reduce the level of protection already in place in national law.[88] The Court has held that this applies to legislation requiring employers to justify the initial use of a fixed-term contract, even though the Agreement does not cover this situation.[89] But the effect of this was

---

[84] Case C–212/04 *Adeneler v ELOG* [2006] ECR I–6057, [84]–[6]. The Court indicated that a three-month break might be sufficient in Case C–378/07 *Angelidaki v Organismos Nomarchiakis Autodioikisis Rethymnis* [2009] ECR I–3071, [157].

[85] *Adeneler*, ibid, [72].

[86] See, for example, Case C–180/04 *Vassallo v Azienda Ospedaliera Ospedale San Martino di Genova* [2006] ECR I–7251, [38]–[42]. This is important for those Member States which cannot easily convert fixed-term jobs to permanent ones in the public sector, because this would breach constitutional requirements to award public sector positions only after competition.

[87] *Adeneler*, above n. 84, [73].

[88] Directive 99/70, Annex, cl 8(3).

[89] *Angelidaki*, above n. 84.

undermined by the adoption of a strict test for 'regression'.[90] A change in national law will only fall foul of the non-regression clause where it is connected to the implementation of the relevant directive,[91] and significantly reduces the overall level of protection afforded to workers in the relevant Member State.[92] As a result, restrictions on the initial use of fixed-term contracts in some Member States may be vulnerable to repeal or amendment.

The third main worker-protective element of the Agreement is the requirement to 'count' fixed-term workers for the purpose of determining the size of firms for the purposes of EU or national provisions on worker representation.[93] This is an important move because it begins to acknowledge the importance of ensuring that the use of atypical work does not undermine existing laws on collective representation. Clause 7(3) states that 'as far as possible, employers should give consideration to the provision of appropriate information to existing workers' representative bodies about fixed-term work in the undertaking'.[94] This could be an important support for collective bargaining over fixed-term workers' terms and conditions of employment, but it is phrased in very soft terms.

Finally, in line with the theory that atypical work should be seen as a 'stepping-stone' to a permanent position, the Agreement provides in clause 6 for employers to inform fixed-term workers about vacancies, and 'as far as possible' to 'facilitate' their access to training. This latter obligation could have been phrased in stronger terms.

Like the Agreement on Part-Time Work, the Agreement on Fixed-Term Work is the result of a set of compromises and does not achieve everything that might have been hoped for from the perspective of worker protection or even flexicurity. In the provisions on abuse of successive fixed-term contracts, it does acknowledge the particular problems faced by fixed-term workers, but it remains ambivalent about the desirability of fixed-term work more generally. Perhaps most worrying is the possibility that Member States with existing legislation discouraging this form of work might be able to dismantle it, despite the non-regression clause.

---

[90] For discussion, see L. Corazza, 'Hard Times for Hard Bans: Fixed-Term Work and So-Called Non-Regression Clauses in the Era of Flexicurity' (2011) 17 ELJ 385; and C. Kilpatrick, 'The European Court of Justice and Labour Law in 2009' (2010) 39 ILJ 287, 292–4.

[91] Case C–144/04 *Mangold v Helm* [2005] ECR I–9981, [51]–[3].

[92] *Angelidaki*, above n. 84, [140]–[42].

[93] Directive 99/70, Annex, cl 7(1).

[94] There is a similar provision in cl 5(3)(e) of the Agreement on Part-Time Work, above n. 63.

Telework

The Framework Agreement on Telework (2002) is also a product of the social dialogue, but unlike the agreements on part-time and fixed-term work, it was not enacted as a directive by the Member States.[95] Instead, it is one of four so-called 'autonomous agreements' reached by the social partners.[96] The idea is that such agreements should be implemented by the social partners themselves rather than through EU law. 'Telework' denotes work which is performed using information technology away from the employer's premises: what we might call 'working from home'. This is not to be confused with 'homework': a long-established form of low-paid manual work done at home, often by women, which the EU has not sought to regulate.

In practice, the agreement has been implemented in a variety of different ways in different Member States.[97] Most have chosen to implement it through social dialogue or collective bargaining, either at the national or sectoral levels.[98] In the UK, where most collective bargaining takes place at workplace level, the agreement has been implemented through a code of practice agreed by the CBI and the TUC at national level, with support from the government.[99] In countries with a strong tradition of collective bargaining, these methods of implementation may be very effective, though there is as yet no data on the issue. However, much is likely to depend on the priority given to the issue by the social partners. In some countries, such as the Czech Republic, Hungary and Portugal, the agreement has been implemented through legislation.[100] This is significant because it illustrates the complex interface between EU law and national law. A 'soft' measure at EU level may have legal effects at national level.

The framework agreement contains as one of its key provisions the familiar requirement that teleworkers should not experience worse terms and conditions than comparable workers who are based at the employer's premises.[101] Nor should they be excluded from collective activities.[102] The agreement also emphasises the voluntary nature of telework, suggesting

---

[95] The text is available at http://ec.europa.eu/employment_social/dsw/public/actRetrieveText.do?id=10418 last accessed 27 July 2011.

[96] The other three are on work-related stress (2004), harassment and violence at work (2007) and inclusive labour markets (2010).

[97] European Social Partners, *Implementation of the European Framework Agreement on Telework* (September 2006).

[98] Ibid, 8–11.

[99] Ibid, 12. Worryingly, it is now very difficult to find the text of the agreement online.

[100] Ibid, 12–13.

[101] Agreement on Telework, cl 4.

[102] Ibid, cl 11.

in particular that where the individual is initially employed to work at the employer's premises, both sides must agree before he or she can be transferred to teleworking.[103] Importantly, the agreement addresses some problems specific to teleworking such as responsibility for provision and maintenance of equipment and payment of bills.[104]

On one hand, it might be argued that if these issues are important enough to regulate at all, a directive would be the most effective EU instrument. On the other hand, it could be argued that active involvement of the social partners is more likely to secure change on the ground than a directive, which would lead to legislative change but might be ignored by employers and workers. Without detailed empirical evidence, it is difficult to choose between these views.[105]

Temporary Agency Work

Temporary agency work is the topic on which it has proved most difficult to reach agreement at EU level. The European Commission's first attempt to regulate this form of work was a proposed directive covering fixed-term and agency work in 1982. Further proposals were put forward at various points in the early 1990s. As we saw above, only one of these proposals was agreed, concerning the health and safety of fixed-term and agency workers.[106] Eventually, the Commission decided to try using the social dialogue. As we have seen, this resulted in agreements on fixed-term and part-time work. However, the social partners did not begin negotiations on temporary agency work until 2000, despite a statement in the fixed-term work agreement that they would pursue this topic.[107] In 2001, the negotiations broke down because the employers' side was unwilling to agree that agency workers should be treated equally with the end user's permanent workers.[108] The Commission again took up the challenge but (in part because of opposition from the UK) no agreement could be reached until 2008.[109]

---

[103]   Ibid, cl 3.

[104]   Ibid, cl 7.

[105]   For an early assessment, concluding that much depends on the strength of national trade unions, see C. Niforou, 'The Role of Trade Unions in the Implementation of Autonomous Framework Agreements', *Warwick Papers in Industrial Relations*, No 87, April 2008.

[106]   Above n. 75.

[107]   Directive 99/70, Preamble.

[108]   E.L. Jones, 'Temporary Agency Labour: Back to Square One?' (2002) 31 ILJ 183.

[109]   Directive 2008/104/EC of the European Parliament and of the Council of 19 November 2008 on temporary agency work. For a history of the negotiations, see L. Zappala, 'The Temporary Agency Workers' Directive: An Impossible Political Agreement?'

The directive's aims are expressed in terms of the flexicurity agenda. Article 2 refers to the 'protection of temporary agency workers' but also to job creation and 'the development of flexible forms of working'. Like the other measures we have considered in this chapter, the directive offers protection for agency workers, primarily in the familiar form of a right to equal treatment, but unlike those other measures, this right is subject to the possibility of derogation. The directive also contains a controversial requirement for Member States to review any restrictions their law places on the use of agency workers by firms.

A temporary agency worker is defined in Article 3 as 'a worker with a contract of employment or an employment relationship with a temporary-work agency with a view to being assigned to a user undertaking to work temporarily under its supervision and direction'. An immediate difficulty with this definition is that in some legal systems, notably that of the UK, an agency worker's relationship with the agency may not constitute a 'contract of employment or an employment relationship', for example because the agency worker is self-employed. These key concepts are expressly left to national law to define.[110] This may mean that some agency workers are left unprotected by the directive.

The main worker-protective element of the directive is Article 5(1), establishing the principle of equal treatment for agency workers. As noted above, this proved to be a significant sticking point when the social partners sought to negotiate an agreement on temporary agency work, so it is of some importance that the Member States themselves finally agreed to implement the principle. It applies to 'basic working and employment conditions' defined in Article 3(1)(f) to cover 'working time, overtime, breaks, rest periods, night work, holidays and public holidays' and pay. In these various respects, temporary agency workers must be given the same treatment as if they had been recruited to a permanent position in the user enterprise. A key practical issue here will be how to figure out what that treatment would have been. If a user undertaking only employs agency workers to do particular jobs, it may be impossible for them to identify the relevant 'permanent terms'. Importantly, though, there is no 'objective justification' exception to these requirements so it is not possible for Member States to give employers the possibility of defending different treatment of agency workers. In that respect, the agency work directive is stronger than the part-time work directive, for example.

However, Article 5 permits various derogations. Article 5(3) allows the

---

(2003) 32 ILJ 310, and on the Directive generally, see N. Countouris and R. Horton, 'The Temporary Agency Work Directive: Another Broken Promise?' (2009) 38 ILJ 329.
[110]   Directive 2008/104/EC, Art 3(2).

Member States to choose to implement the directive through collective bargaining at national level. Whilst this is uncontroversial in itself, the Member States may allow the social partners to derogate from the equal treatment principle: 'while respecting the overall protection of temporary agency workers, [the social partners] may establish arrangements concerning the working and employment conditions of temporary agency workers which may differ from those referred to in [Article 5(1)]'. Moreover, Article 5(4) allows a Member State in which there is no system for extending the results of collective bargaining to all workers to create different arrangements for the regulation of agency work based on an agreement between the social partners at national level. This provision was introduced to accommodate the UK, which had long held out against the directive. It allows the UK government to implement an agreement between the national social partners in place of the directive's provisions.[111] Significantly, this agreement provides that the principle of equal treatment only applies after the worker has worked for the end user for a qualifying period of 12 weeks. Article 5(4) makes clear that this is acceptable. Thus, although the right to equal treatment has hitherto been regarded as a relatively uncontroversial and basic right for atypical workers, the agency work directive opens up the possibility of derogations.

The directive also includes some other worker-protective provisions. For example, under Article 6(4), agency workers are entitled to equal access to facilities such as childcare and canteen services at the user enterprise, though this is subject to an objective justification defence. Under Article 7, the Member States must ensure that agency workers 'count' towards thresholds for determining the size of firms for the purposes of collective representation arrangements (though the Member States may choose whether to apply this against the agency or the end user), and under Article 8, obligations to provide information to workers' representatives must be amended to include 'information on the use of temporary agency workers'.

The directive has two main features which fit the 'flexicurity' agenda: some 'stepping-stone' provisions, and a requirement to remove obstacles to agency work. The 'stepping-stone' provisions are designed to help agency workers to move into permanent employment. Article 6(1) provides for agency workers to be informed about vacancies in the user undertaking. Article 6(2) and (3) require the Member States to prohibit, respectively, clauses that bar agency workers from taking up permanent

---

[111]   Details are available at http://www.bis.gov.uk/policies/employment-matters/strategies/awd, last accessed 27 July 2011.

employment with the end user, and requirements to pay a fee to the agency on taking up such employment.

More controversially, Article 4(1) of the directive requires the Member States to justify any provisions limiting the use of agency work:

> Prohibitions or restrictions on the use of temporary agency work shall be justified only on grounds of general interest relating in particular to the protection of temporary agency workers, the requirements of health and safety at work or the need to ensure that the labour market functions properly and abuses are prevented.

This is coupled with an obligation to review such restrictions and to report to the Commission by December 2011.[112] This will have a particular impact in those Member States, such as France and Belgium, which have traditionally insisted that the end user may only have recourse to agency work if certain conditions are met. Of course, restrictive legislation may be justifiable in accordance with Article 4(1), but it may be difficult to sustain the more general proposition that permanent work should be regarded as the norm. Moreover, the Court may subject restrictions to review, by analogy with *Michaeler*, considered above.[113] But whereas part-time work can bring clear benefits for the worker, some commentators would question whether agency work is something to be encouraged.

In some respects, the agency work directive is a significant triumph for the Commission after many years of failed attempts to legislate on the issue. It helps to complete the picture of atypical work regulation in the EU when viewed alongside the social dialogue directives. However, it is clear that the worker protections in the directive have come at a price with significant possibilities for derogation and with a clear emphasis on increasing the availability of agency work in those Member States which, historically, have sought to restrict it. Once again, there appears to be a lot of flexibility in flexicurity.

FURTHER READING

As we have seen, the regulation of atypical work in EU law is wrapped up in the flexicurity agenda (European Commission, *Towards Common Principles of Flexicurity: More and Better Jobs through Flexibility and Security* (COM (2007) 359 final)). The aim is to improve job creation (and

---

[112]   Directive 2008/104/EC, Art 4(2) and (3).
[113]   Above n. 70.

to meet the Europe 2020 goals) by making labour markets more flexible, whilst at the same time tackling the emergence of a two-tier labour market by offering some protection to atypical workers. For a powerful criticism of flexicurity, see S. Fredman, 'Women at Work: The Broken Promise of Flexicurity' (2004) 33 ILJ 299.

The directives we have been considering in this chapter have generated a considerable critical literature from a worker-protective perspective. See, for example, M. Jeffery, 'Not Really Going to Work? Of the Directive on Part-Time Work, "Atypical Work" and Attempts to Regulate It' (1998) 27 ILJ 193; J. Murray, 'Normalising Temporary Work: The Proposed Directive on Fixed-Term Work' (1999) 28 ILJ 269; N. Countouris and R. Horton, 'The Temporary Agency Work Directive: Another Broken Promise?' (2009) 38 ILJ 329.

As we noted earlier, part-time work deserves special consideration because it is arguable that (unlike fixed-term or agency work) it has significant attractions for workers themselves, because it enables them to balance work with other commitments such as family responsibilities. A persistent problem is ensuring that part-time work is available in all levels and sectors of the economy. For a fascinating discussion of this from a UK perspective, see M. Bell, 'Achieving the Objectives of the Part-Time Work Directive? Revisiting the Part-Time Workers Regulations' (2011) 40 ILJ 254. Another way of tackling the problem is to provide workers with a right to work part-time, but as Schmidt explains, much depends on how this right is implemented in practice and what grounds employers are given for a refusal: M. Schmidt, 'The Right to Part-Time Work under German Law: Progress in or a Boomerang for Equal Employment Opportunities?' (2001) 30 ILJ 335. There are important links between part-time work and so-called 'family-friendly policies', so you may find it helpful to revisit the material on parental and other forms of leave in Chapter 4.

7. Working time

Our main focus in this chapter is on the Working Time Directive.[1] This lays down a series of rights for workers in respect of their working hours, such as the right to work no more than 48 hours in a week, on average,[2] and the right to four weeks' paid annual leave.[3] The Directive has been controversial from the outset and has given rise to considerable litigation, as well as a series of attempts at reform.

Our discussion will pick out three main themes. First, we will consider the emergence of the regulation of working time at EU level. Although this might be explained in terms of preventing undercutting, because some countries had working time regulation and some did not, in fact the explanation is more political than economic and reflects the desire to advance the European Social Model (ESM) at EU level. Second, we will consider the role a rights analysis has played in the Court of Justice's interpretation of the Directive, picking up on our 'constitutionalisation' theme. Third, we will revisit the idea of reflexive law – adapting the law to the needs of workers and employers – because there is a long-running debate about whether the Directive is too rigid or too flexible.

THE ENACTMENT OF THE WORKING TIME DIRECTIVE

The regulation of working time is a surprisingly complex issue. On one hand, there are powerful arguments for not regulating working time at all. Employees may be happy to work long hours, particularly where this enables them to earn extra money (often in the form of overtime paid at higher rates); and employers may value the flexibility of being able to get their regular workers to work extra hours when the firm is busy. On the other hand, there are a range of reasons that might possibly be advanced

---

[1] Originally Directive 93/104/EC concerning certain aspects of the organisation of working time, amended by Directive 2000/34/EC. The current Directive is Directive 2003/88/EC.

[2] Directive 2003/88, Art 6.

[3] Ibid, Art 7.

for limiting the hours people can work. One possibility is health and safety: long hours may make workers tired and more prone to accidents. Another possibility is what we might term work/life balance: the idea that it is not healthy (in a broader, social sense) to work very long hours and that workers should have time for other activities. Of course, these arguments all involve overriding some workers' preference for working longer hours. This might be justified either on the basis that (in some cases at least) workers' agreement to work longer hours might not be genuine, because of the employer's superior bargaining power, or that workers themselves may not know what is in their own best interests (a paternalistic approach).

But of course none of this particularly helps to explain why one might regard working time as a proper subject of regulation at EU level, as opposed to the national level. Prior to the introduction of the Working Time Directive, most Member States had some form of regulation, with the UK being a notable exception. So one justification for regulation might be to prevent distortions of competition based on different limits on working time in different Member States. This would fit with the worry we identified in Chapter 1 that the creation of the internal market might prompt a 'race to the bottom' as states gravitate towards lower levels of regulation in order to attract investment.

However, looking at the political context of the Working Time Directive, this does not appear to have been the main motivating factor. When it was enacted, most Member States were keen to develop the social dimension of the EU.[4] They regarded the ESM as a good thing in itself and they wanted to have more EU labour legislation. This becomes apparent when we examine the Treaty basis for the Directive.

The Working Time Directive was based on then Article 118a, on health and safety.[5] As we saw above, health and safety is one of the many possible justifications for regulating working time. But the choice of Treaty basis in this instance had a broader political significance. At the time, the UK government (in Conservative hands) resisted all attempts by the EU to enact new employment legislation. This meant that whenever a Treaty Article required unanimity in the Council, the UK simply voted against, effectively vetoing the proposal in question. From the Commission's perspective, the advantage of Article 118a was that it provided for directives to be enacted after a qualified majority vote in the Council, so that new

---

⁴   For discussion, see B. Bercusson (2009), *European Labour Law* (2nd edn, Cambridge University Press), 120–25.

⁵   Art 118a was inserted in the Treaty of Rome by the Single European Act in 1986. The relevant provision is now Art 153 TFEU.

initiatives could not be vetoed by the UK. The UK's challenge to the validity of health and safety as a legal basis for the Directive was rejected by the Court, in a decision to be discussed further below.[6]

This leaves us in the interesting situation of having a formal health and safety basis for the Directive, but with the knowledge that this was a pragmatic choice. As we shall see in the next section, the Court has played an instrumental role in ensuring that the choice of Treaty basis has not resulted in a narrow interpretation of the Directive. It is to this that we will now turn.

CONSTITUTIONALISATION

The Court's interpretation of the Directive can be regarded as an example of 'constitutionalisation' in two respects. First, the Court adopted a broad, dignitarian understanding of health and safety, and second, the Court has indicated that some aspects of the Directive are concerned with the protection of social rights.

In *UK v Council*, the UK government's challenge to the Treaty basis of the Directive, the UK argued for a traditional, narrow interpretation of health and safety focused on the avoidance of accidents and the prevention of disease.[7] The claim was that the Directive went beyond what could legitimately be regarded as a concern for health and safety so defined. However, unsurprisingly, the Court upheld the Directive.[8] The key passage in the Court's judgment adopts a much broader understanding of health and safety:

> There is nothing in the wording of Article 118a to indicate that the concepts of 'working environment', 'safety' and 'health' as used in that provision should, in the absence of other indications, be interpreted restrictively, and not as embracing all factors, physical or otherwise, capable of affecting the health and safety of the worker in his working environment, including in particular certain aspects of the organization of working time. On the contrary, the words 'especially in the working environment' militate in favour of a broad interpretation of the powers which Article 118a confers upon the Council for the protection of the health and safety of workers. Moreover, such an interpretation of the words 'safety' and 'health' derives support in particular from the preamble to the Constitution of the World Health Organization to which all the Member States

[6]   Case C–84/94 *UK v Council* [1996] ECR I–5755.
[7]   Ibid, [13].
[8]   With one exception: the Court was persuaded that the designation of Sunday as the normal day of rest could not be justified on a health and safety basis: ibid, [37].

belong. Health is there defined as a state of complete physical, mental and social well-being that does not consist only in the absence of illness or infirmity.[9]

This treats all aspects of workers' general wellbeing as part of the notion of health and safety. Interestingly, the EU Charter of Fundamental Rights, proclaimed in 2000, links health and safety with workers' dignity, an approach which is very much in line with that of the Court in this case.[10] The Court's decision also renders less stark the choice between the different reasons for regulating working time considered in the previous section. Its broad view seems to incorporate 'work/life balance' justifications, in the sense that a good relationship between work, leisure and family time may reduce stress and contribute to workers' overall wellbeing.

In the *BECTU* case, the Court linked working time regulation to the social rights of workers.[11] That case concerned the UK's implementation of the entitlement to paid annual leave under the Directive. The legislation stated that workers would only become entitled to paid annual leave after they had completed a qualifying period of service with the employer. This was not provided for in the Directive and had the effect that workers on successive short-term contracts might never accrue an entitlement to paid time off. In deciding that the UK had failed to implement the Directive correctly, the Court expressly referred to the citation, in the Directive's Preamble, of the Community Charter of the Fundamental Social Rights of Workers (1989).[12] Interestingly, this refers to annual leave (point 8) and health and safety (point 19) but does not connect the two. Nevertheless, the Court went on to describe the right to paid annual leave as a 'social right'.[13] Furthermore, although the Court did not cite the EU Charter of Fundamental Rights (which was agreed shortly before *BECTU*),[14] the Advocate General did cite it, as part of the justification for his view that paid leave was a fundamental right.[15]

Taken together, the broad understanding of health and safety coupled with references to social rights suggests that we can expect a strongly worker-protective interpretation of the Directive from the Court. However, it is worth noting two criticisms of the Court's approach in some of the working time literature before we examine the case-law. First, for

---

9   Ibid, [15].
10   EU Charter of Fundamental Rights, Art 31(1).
11   Case C–173/99 *R v Secretary of State for Trade and Industry, ex p BECTU* [2001] ECR I–4881.
12   See Directive 93/104, Preamble.
13   Above n. 11, [47].
14   EU Charter of Fundamental Rights, Art 31(2).
15   Opinion of Mr Advocate General Tizzano in *BECTU*, above n. 11, [22]–[8].

some commentators the Court has not gone far enough. Article 13 of the Directive incorporates the principle of the 'humanisation' of work: that working patterns should be adapted to the worker. It states:

> Member States shall take the measures necessary to ensure that an employer who intends to organise work according to a certain pattern takes account of the general principle of adapting work to the worker, with a view, in particular, to alleviating monotonous work and work at a predetermined workrate . . .

This might have resulted in radical transformations of certain types of work in order to fit them around workers' needs but, as we shall see, it has had virtually no impact at all.[16] Second, a rather different criticism is that the Court has gone too far. By treating paid annual leave as a social right, it has made it more difficult to adapt the right through collective bargaining, even though (as we shall see) the Directive generally allows for a high degree of adaptation by this means.[17]

REFLEXIVITY

We saw in Chapter 2 that the idea of 'reflexive regulation' is often used in thinking about EU labour law.[18] This is the idea that dictating solutions through law may not be an effective way of changing people's behaviour. Instead, legislation should focus on setting goals and creating procedures through which people can pursue those goals in ways that fit their particular circumstances. The reflexive analysis can be applied at the macro level (to the freedoms EU law creates for Member States) and at the micro level (to the freedoms EU law allows the Member States to grant to workers, unions and employers). There is a considerable debate about the extent to which the Working Time Directive fulfils the principles of reflexive law.

This debate has manifested itself in the literature as a dispute about whether the Directive is too rigid or too flexible in the standards it lays down. On one hand, the Directive seeks to regulate the working time of virtually all workers in the EU, regardless of the job they do or the sector in which they work (with the exception of transport, which is governed by separate measures). This has led to criticism of its 'one size fits all'

---

[16] See A. Bogg, 'Of Holidays, Work and Humanisation: a Missed Opportunity?' (2009) 34 EL Rev 738.

[17] See A.L. Bogg, 'The Right to Paid Annual Leave in the Court of Justice: the Eclipse of Functionalism' (2006) 31 EL Rev 892.

[18] See, generally, G. Teubner, 'Substantive and Reflexive Elements in Modern Law' (1983) 17 *Law and Society Review* 239, and the discussion in Chapter 2.

approach.[19] On the other hand, the Directive also contains elements of flexibility. As we shall see, a Member State may choose to give individual workers the possibility to opt out of the 48-hour working week. Some rights in the Directive may be varied or even defined by collective agreements.[20] And there are exceptions to the rights for particular types of worker or particular situations (emergencies, surges in activity and so on). This has led some commentators to argue that the Directive does not afford workers enough protection because their rights are too easily altered or bargained away.[21]

So what explains the rigidity/flexibility dilemma? Flexibility is a good thing where it enables the Directive to adapt to conditions in a particular sector or where it enables workers' preferences to be reflected in their working arrangements. But it is a bad thing when – as Supiot puts it – rights are given with one hand and taken away with the other.[22] So the key question to examine is the balance between flexibility and safeguards for workers. Reflexive regulation is about being reflexive – providing flexibility – but it is also about regulation – achieving particular policy goals, in this case the protection of workers' health and safety, broadly understood. Of course, views may differ on how exactly the balance should be struck. We will now turn to a detailed examination of the Directive's main provisions in the light of this question.

The 'Opt-out'

A central right in the Working Time Directive is the limitation of the working week to 48 hours.[23] Member States may provide for this to be achieved on average over a reference period of not more than four months,[24] a provision which may be further varied by collective agree-

---

[19]   See C. Barnard, 'EC "Social" Policy', in P.P. Craig and G. de Búrca (eds) (1999), *The Evolution of EU Law* (Oxford University Press), 488–92.

[20]   Although we will use the term 'collective agreement' as a convenient shorthand, it is important to note that the Member States are given flexibility to adapt this to their national situation so, for example, bargaining might take place at different levels (national, sectoral or workplace) and need not necessarily involve trade unions or 'collective agreements' strictly so called.

[21]   See, for example, J. Kenner (2003), *EU Employment Law* (Oxford: Hart), 173.

[22]   A. Supiot, 'On the Job: Time for Agreement' (1996) 12 *International Journal of Comparative Labour Law and Industrial Relations* 195.

[23]   Directive 2003/88, Art 6. This is capable of having direct effect, but of course, in accordance with the Court's general case-law on directives, this effect is vertical only: Case C–397/01 *Pfeiffer v Deutsches Rotes Kreuz* [2004] ECR I–8835, [104] and [109]. For discussion see the case-note by S. Prechal, (2005) 42 CMLR 1445.

[24]   Directive 2003/88, Art 16.

ment.[25] The UK government – which opposed the Directive generally – secured a very significant concession in relation to the 48-hour limit, which has come to be known as the 'opt-out' (both in the sense of an opt-out for the UK and an opt-out for workers). This is contained in Article 22 of the current Directive, which gives Member States the option of allowing individual workers to agree to work beyond the 48-hour limit.

One view of the opt-out is that it compensates for the rigidity of setting a single weekly working time limit for (virtually) all workers. There are certain jobs for which a 48-hour working week might be quite dangerous, and others where a longer working week might be perfectly safe.[26] And of course, workers themselves may have different preferences. The opt-out allows for adjustment to fit the job or the worker. The safeguard for the worker is that he or she has the right not to work more than 48 hours per week *unless* he or she chooses to give it up. In theory, the rational worker will only give the right up if he or she wants to or if the employer offers a benefit in return.

Against this, it can be argued that workers are in a weak bargaining position relative to employers and may find themselves pressured into exercising their so-called choice in accordance with their employer's wishes. This is particularly likely to be the case because the opt-out is a matter for the individual and not for collective bargaining.[27] Of course, this means that the individual can make his or her own decision and need not do what the majority in the union or workplace want to do. But if the opt-out could only be invoked by collective agreement, there would be more of an opportunity for workers to use their collective strength to bargain with the employer on the matter.

The opt-out was subject to a review by the European Commission in 2003.[28] Whilst, in principle, the Commission is keen to get the opt-out removed altogether, it also suggested a middle position as an alternative. This would involve keeping the opt-out but with additional safeguards for workers.[29] First, the Commission noted that there were no safeguards to ensure that workers' consent is genuine. It suggested that employers should be barred from asking workers to sign the opt-out prior to taking

---

[25] Ibid, Art 18.

[26] Barnard, above n. 19, 491.

[27] Case C–303/98 *SIMAP v Conselleria de Sanidad y Consumo de la Generalidad Valenciana* [2000] ECR I–7963, [71]–[4]; *Pfeiffer*, above n. 23, [80].

[28] European Commission, *Communication Concerning the Re-Exam of Directive 93/104/EC Concerning Certain Aspects of the Organization of Working Time* (COM (2003) 843).

[29] Commission, *Proposal for a Directive of the European Parliament and of the Council amending Directive 2003/88/EC concerning certain aspects of the organisation of working time* (COM (2004) 607 final), 5–6.

up their employment, so that they were not made to feel that signing the opt-out was a condition of getting the job. Second, the Commission was concerned that, once workers have opted out, there are no limits on their weekly working time except the outer limits put in place by the rules on daily and weekly rest breaks. It proposed an upper maximum of 65 hours per week which would not be subject to the opt-out. Finally, the Commission suggested that greater effort should be made to monitor the hours actually worked by opted-out workers. This would help to ensure that the other provisions of the Directive which remain applicable to these workers (such as daily or weekly rest breaks) were respected by employers.

So far, the Commission has failed to obtain an agreement either to abolish the opt-out altogether or to place additional conditions on its use. Part of the explanation for this may be the UK's determination to resist and its ability to use other 'bargaining chips' to preserve its position. For example, it has been suggested that the UK's agreement to the Directive on Temporary Agency Work (discussed in Chapter 4) was part of the 'price' for the retention of the opt-out.[30] Another factor is that, although initially only the UK and Ireland made use of the opt-out (with Ireland subsequently abandoning it), other Member States have come to see its value.[31] One reason for this is the Court's strict interpretation of the provisions on 'on-call' time in the *SIMAP* case, to be discussed further below.[32] In that case, the Court reduced employers' flexibility by ruling that time spent on the employer's premises on call but asleep counted as working time. Some Member States responded by invoking the opt-out in sectors particularly hard hit by this ruling, such as healthcare.

At the time of writing, the Commission is continuing its efforts to reform the Directive but by negotiating with the social partners.[33] This offers a way of getting round the Member States' objections either by agreeing a new directive through the social dialogue under Article 155 TFEU or by using social partner support to persuade the Member States to reach an agreement through the legislative process. However, it appears from the Commission's consultation documents that the social partners are themselves deeply divided on the matter, making progress seem unlikely.

---

[30]   P. Wintour, 'Agency and temporary workers win rights deal', *The Guardian*, 21 May 2008.

[31]   Above n. 28, 15, and more recently, Commission, *Reviewing the Working Time Directive (first-phase consultation) of the social partners at European level* (COM (2010) 106), 7.

[32]   Above n. 27.

[33]   Commission, above n. 31 and *Reviewing the Working Time Directive (second-phase consultation) of the social partners at European level* (COM (2010) 801).

Rest Breaks

The Working Time Directive requires the Member States to ensure that workers benefit from three types of rest time. These are:

- a 'rest break' where 'the working day is longer than six hours';[34]
- 'a minimum daily rest period of 11 consecutive hours per 24-hour period';[35]
- 'a minimum uninterrupted rest period of 24 hours plus the 11 hours' daily rest' referred to above, in every 7-day period.[36]

Flexibility is built into these rights at various different levels, reflecting the less than clear drafting of the Directive.

One form of flexibility features in the way that the rights themselves are defined. The precise details of the Article 4 rest break are to be determined by collective bargaining or, if that is not successful, by national legislation.[37] The weekly rest break in Article 5 may be reduced from 35 to 24 hours 'if objective, technical or work organisation conditions so justify'. Only the daily rest period in Article 3 is unqualified as drafted.

A second form of flexibility can be found in Article 16. This allows a Member State the option of laying down a reference period of 14 days for Article 5, the weekly rest break. In other words, the requirement to give a 24-hour break every week could be satisfied by giving a 48-hour break every fortnight, if the Member State so chose.

A third form of flexibility can be found in Article 17. This provides Member States with a variety of grounds for derogation for various different types of work or work situations. Article 17(1) allows Member States to derogate from various provisions, including all three types of rest break, in the case of workers whose working time is 'not measured'. This allows for the exclusion of workers whose hours are not fixed or who have discretion over their own working time. Article 17(3) allows for derogation from all three rest break provisions in a variety of different fact situations where it might be difficult for the employer to provide breaks. These are too numerous to list here but include cases where a continuous service is required, where there is a 'foreseeable surge in activity' and where there

---

[34]   Directive 2003/88, Art 4.
[35]   Ibid, Art 3.
[36]   Ibid, Art 5.
[37]   As Bercusson notes, this provision is unusual in that it gives priority to collective bargaining as a method of standard setting, not just derogating from established standards: see Bercusson, above n. 4, 349–54.

has been an accident. Article 17(4) allows for derogation from the daily and weekly rest breaks in Articles 3 and 5 in the case of shift workers and workers whose hours are split over the day. The derogations in Article 17(3) and (4) are subject to Article 17(2), which provides that they may be made by legislation or collective agreement, but must normally ensure that the affected workers receive 'equivalent periods of compensatory rest'.

These various forms of flexibility are supplemented by a further option in Article 18.[38] This allows the Member States to permit derogation from all three rest break provisions by means of collective agreements. Again, these collectively agreed derogations should normally ensure that the affected workers are granted compensatory rest periods.

So, do these forms of flexibility allow working hours to be adapted to workers and sectors? Or do they undermine the rights provided by the Directive? Of course, to some extent, this depends on the use made of them by the Member States. Directives as a form of legislation are supposed to give the Member States a degree of discretion, so we should not be critical on that score. Another imponderable is the role of collective bargaining. This varies enormously from state to state. In the 'Nordic' countries, it is regarded as the main method for setting terms and conditions of employment, taking the place of legislation, whereas in the UK its role is nowadays much more limited. Thus, the impact of collective derogations is hard to assess. In theory, they should provide a way of balancing employers' and workers' interests, but in some Member States they may provide employers with a way of forcing workers to accept unwanted arrangements.

More specifically, some of the derogations might have a harmful effect on particular categories of worker. For example, workers whose working time is unmeasured end up with very few rights under the Directive. On one hand, this might be justified because they are able to protect their own health and safety through the way in which they organise their working lives. On the other hand, it might mean that certain workers (either because of employer pressure or because of their own choices or ambitions) end up working unhealthily long hours without any real check at all. Another specific concern relates to the Article 17(4) derogation for shift workers and workers with interrupted days. One of the underlying principles of the Directive, enshrined in Article 13, is the 'general principle of adapting work to the worker'. This is the idea that working time should be organised around the needs of workers, not just those of

---

[38]   The general nature of this provision was recently confirmed in Case C–227/09 *Accardo v Comune di Torino* [2010] nyr, [35]–[6].

employers. The derogation for shift work is an obvious example of where the Directive might have encouraged employers to think more creatively about work patterns but instead the derogation allows existing practices to continue.

Night Work

It is generally thought that night work poses greater risks to workers' health and safety than daytime working. The Directive reflects this in Article 8, which requires Member States to ensure that:

(a) normal hours of work for night workers do not exceed an average of eight hours in any 24-hour period;
(b) night workers whose work involves special hazards or heavy physical or mental strain do not work more than eight hours in any period of 24 hours during which they perform night work.

This places an absolute limit of eight hours on hazardous night work and an average limit of eight hours on other forms of night work. Article 16(c) requires the Member States to lay down a reference period for this latter right (either after consultation with the social partners or through collective agreement) but it does not place any upper limit on how long that reference period might be. Article 8 is also subject to derogations. These include the derogation for unmeasured work in Article 17(1), the derogations for continuity, surges and accidents contained in Article 17(3), and the collective derogation in Article 18.

However, it may be that night workers' health and safety is better protected by a series of more general obligations contained in the Directive. These include regular health assessments for night workers,[39] the opportunity to transfer to daytime working if night work causes health problems,[40] and the provision of appropriate health and safety protections.[41]

This suggests a slightly different approach to the rigidity/flexibility debate. Instead of trying to create fixed limits on working time, perhaps the EU should focus instead on laying down general principles to guide the treatment of workers. Such an approach is less open to the objection that it does not fit with particular jobs or sectors and therefore less likely to lead to demands for exceptions or derogations. However, the downside is that, without any fixed limits at all, it would be difficult for workers to

---

[39] Directive 2003/88, Art 9.
[40] Ibid.
[41] Ibid, Art 12.

know their rights and the interpretation of what constitutes 'safe' working hours might vary considerably between different Member States.

Annual Leave

The Directive provides in Article 7 that workers should be entitled to a minimum of four weeks' paid annual leave.[42] This must be paid at a rate which allows the worker 'to enjoy, during his period of rest and relaxation, economic conditions which are comparable to those relating to the exercise of his employment'.[43] Importantly, Article 7 further specifies that pay can only be given in lieu of leave when the worker's employment comes to an end. Although this Article was subject to an initial transitional phase, in which the Member States had the option to grant three weeks' paid annual leave,[44] it is not subject to the derogations laid down in Articles 17 and 18 discussed above.

In terms of drafting, the right to paid annual leave can be seen as much less flexible than the other rights we have been considering. Perhaps this is because it is easier to say that all workers should be entitled to a certain amount of time away from the workplace, regardless of the particular job they are doing or the circumstances faced by their employer. Moreover, although the right is to be exercised 'in accordance with the conditions for entitlement to, and granting of, . . . leave laid down by national legislation and/or practice',[45] the Court has sought to ensure that national law does not have the effect of depriving workers of the right. For example, in the *BECTU* case, a trade union challenged the UK's use of a 13-week qualifying period before workers became entitled to the right to annual leave.[46] The trade union argued that many of its members worked on successive short-term contracts and would therefore rarely, if ever, become entitled to annual leave. The Court accepted this argument and the UK has since amended the law so that workers become entitled to the leave on a *pro rata* basis during their first year of employment.[47] Similarly, in *Stringer* the Court held that workers who are on sick leave should not lose their entitle-

---

[42]   This is directly effective but (in accordance with general principles) not in a horizontal case. For an interesting discussion of this point see the Advocate General's Opinion in Case C–282/10 *Dominguez v Centre informatique du centre Ouest Atlantique* [2011]. At the time of writing, the Court had not handed down its judgment in the case.

[43]   Case C–155/10 *Williams v British Airways plc* [2011] nyr, [23], holding that airline pilots' holiday pay should include a sum in respect of their flying allowance, a supplement added to their basic pay for time spent in the air.

[44]   Directive 2003/88, Art 22(2).

[45]   Ibid, Art 7(1).

[46]   Above n. 11.

[47]   Working Time Regulations 1998 (SI 1998/1833), r. 15A.

ment to paid annual leave, although it left some flexibility to the Member States on matters of detail.[48]

However, some commentators have criticised the lack of flexibility in relation to annual leave. A number of UK cases before the Court have concerned the practice of 'rolled-up' holiday pay. This is where the employer does not pay workers when they take holiday, but instead pays them an additional sum within their hourly rate of pay in order to cover their holiday time. As Bogg points out, this arrangement has advantages and disadvantages.[49] It may be simpler for employers to administer (particularly when workers have complex working patterns, making the appropriate holiday pay difficult to calculate) and attractive to workers themselves (because it generates extra income). But the downside is that workers might feel discouraged from taking holiday because they will not receive any money during that time and, particularly if they are low-paid, it might not be realistic to expect them to save up the 'holiday' element of their normal pay for the purpose.

In *Robinson-Steele*, the Court held that rolled-up holiday pay should not be permitted because it might discourage workers from taking annual leave.[50] The Court read Article 7 of the Directive to require that pay should be provided contemporaneously with the leave. Bogg argues that this approach is unduly strict.[51] He prefers instead a version of the Advocate General's approach in which rolled-up holiday pay may be permitted where certain conditions are met.[52] In particular, he argues that, where the rolled-up holiday pay forms part of a collective agreement, the courts should be more inclined to permit rolling up because the union's involvement can be expected to safeguard the workers' interests. Indeed, from this perspective, the Court's emphasis on annual leave as a 'social right' may be problematic because it is too rigid and denies the workers the flexibility to achieve a better deal for themselves by collective bargaining.

A final point to note in respect of paid annual leave is that it is an entitlement, not a requirement. Although the Court criticised the UK government for issuing guidance which indicated to employers that leave did

---

[48]   Case C–520/06 *Stringer v Revenue and Customs Commissioners* [2009] ECR I–179. For a critique of *Stringer*, see Bogg, above n. 16. There is ongoing litigation on the relationship between sick leave and annual leave. See also Case C–277/08 *Pereda v Madrid Movilidad SA* [2009] ECR I–8405, Case C–214/10 *KHS AG v Schulte* [2011] nyr, and the Advocate General's Opinion in *Dominguez*, above n. 42.

[49]   Bogg, above n. 17, 893.

[50]   Case C–131/04 *Robinson-Steele v RD Retail Services Ltd* [2006] ECR I–2531.

[51]   Bogg, above n. 17, 904–5.

[52]   See Opinion of Advocate General Stix-Hackl in *Robinson-Steele*, above n. 50.

not have to be taken, it remains the case that workers are not obliged to have time off.[53] Again, this could be seen as a problem (employers might pressure workers into taking less holiday than their due) or as an element of flexibility (allowing workers to continue working if this is what they prefer).

On-call Time

The final area of the Directive to be considered in this section is 'on-call' time.[54] On-call time is not free time: to a greater or lesser extent, the worker is required to make him- or herself available for work. But equally it may not be working time: the worker might be able to stay at home and do other things provided that he or she can be contacted by the employer if required. The key question is whether the whole of the time 'on call' should count as working time (and should attract pay at normal rates).

German case-law provides a sophisticated treatment of the problem, dividing on-call time into three categories: *Arbeitsbereitschaft*, during which the worker is required to be in the workplace and ready to work; *Bereitschaftsdienst*, during which the worker is required to be in a place specified by the employer but may sleep or do other things unless called upon to work; and *Rufbereitschaft*, during which the worker may be in any location provided that he or she can be contacted by the employer if needed.[55] Only the first of these options counts as working time (and attracts normal pay for the full period).

The Working Time Directive contains no definition of 'on-call time'. Instead, it defines working time as:

> any period during which the worker is working, at the employer's disposal and carrying out his activity or duties, in accordance with national laws and/ or practice

and rest periods as 'any period which is not working time'.[56] Thus, the task of applying this regime to time on call fell to the Court. In *SIMAP*, a case concerning doctors on call, the Court held that time spent on call counted as working time if the worker was obliged to remain at

---

[53] Case C–484/04 *Commission v UK* [2006] ECR I–7471, [42]–[4].

[54] For an overview of the case-law in the context of negotiations to amend the Directive, see T. Nowak, 'The Working Time Directive and the European Court of Justice' (2008) 15 *Maastricht Journal of European and Comparative Law* 447.

[55] Case C–151/02 *Landeshauptstadt Kiel v Jaeger* [2003] ECR I–8389, [12]–[17].

[56] Directive 2003/88, Art 2.

the employer's premises, whereas if he or she was merely required to be contactable, only time spent actually working would count as working time.[57] This meant that – using the German classifications above – both *Arbeitsbereitschaft* and *Bereitschaftsdienst* counted as working time whereas *Rufbereitschaft* did not. In *Jaeger*, a case concerning the German regime, the Court followed its earlier ruling in *SIMAP* even though the doctor in *Jaeger* was provided with a room to sleep in when his services were not required.[58]

In its review of the Working Time Directive, the Commission noted that the impact of these decisions, particularly in the healthcare sector, was substantial.[59] If on-call time counts as working time, it would be virtually impossible for Member States to ensure that doctors work no more than 48 hours in a week. As we noted above, some Member States responded by making use of the opt-out, particularly in the healthcare sector, as a means of giving employers greater flexibility. Of course, it is arguable that in healthcare in particular, shorter working hours should be a priority, but – given the money and time required to train and employ additional staff – it is not a sector in which current practices can easily or quickly be altered. The Commission then sought to reform the Directive to define 'on-call time' so that only time spent working would count as working time (unless national law or collective agreements provided otherwise),[60] but as we saw above no agreement was reached.

The Court's approach to the Directive can be praised for its attempt to protect workers' rights. As the Court itself noted, time on call is not the same as rest time, even when the worker is not working, because he or she must always be ready to work and may be required to stay at the employer's premises.[61] However, in practice the decision has been counter-productive: Member States have found ways to avoid its application. Indeed, it is possible that the increased use of the opt-out has been harmful to workers because it makes it harder to ensure that they receive the Directive's other benefits. Of course, it would not be appropriate to 'blame' the Court for these consequences. Perhaps the Member States thought it would be obvious that on-call time would not be treated as

---

[57] Above n. 27. For discussion, see J. Fairhurst, '*SIMAP* – Interpreting the Working Time Directive' (2001) 30 ILJ 236.

[58] Above n. 55; and see also Case C–14/04 *Dellas v Premier ministre* [2005] ECR I–10253.

[59] Commission, *Communication on the re-examination of Directive 93/104/EC*, above n. 28, 19–20.

[60] Commission, *Proposal for a Directive*, above n. 29.

[61] *SIMAP*, above n. 27, [48].

working time, but this could have been made clearer in the Directive's drafting.

Conclusion

The reflexive law analysis of the Working Time Directive is interesting but does not generate straightforward conclusions. It is very much a matter of opinion whether the balance between workers' rights and flexibility has been struck in the right place. We will conclude by drawing out three broader points from the discussion.

First, one of the problems with the Directive is the way in which it presents stark choices: once an element of flexibility has been exercised, a considerable chunk of protection seems to be lost. This is true of the individual opt-out from the 48-hour limit on the working week,[62] and the broad Article 18 derogation for rest breaks.[63] An alternative approach would be to have some 'back-stop' provisions in these situations. For example, opted-out workers could be subject to a higher but binding limit on their weekly hours,[64] and there could be some minimum standards for rest breaks which would not be subject to collective bargaining. On this approach, there would be upper and lower limits within which people could negotiate, individually or collectively. This might offer a better combination of flexibility and protection.

Second, there is a tension surrounding collective and individual flexibility. In general terms, collective bargaining should protect workers' interests better because by grouping together workers can increase their bargaining power. However, collective bargaining necessarily reflects the majority view and may not be able to accommodate each worker's individual preferences. As we have seen, the Directive combines both and the Court (perhaps reflecting its individual rights focus) has not always been sympathetic to collective compromises.

Third, the Directive is breathtaking in its ambition. It proceeds on the assumption that it is possible to lay down a single working-time regime for all sectors and workplaces that will guarantee the health and safety, broadly defined, of all workers. Barnard suggests that a better approach might have been to adopt a framework directive setting out general principles and then to regulate different sectors of activity through the sectoral social dialogue (explained in Chapter 2).[65] For example, the sectoral social

---

[62] Subject to the provisions on rest breaks.
[63] Though this is subject to a requirement to provide compensatory rest.
[64] As proposed by the Commission, above n. 29.
[65] Barnard, above n. 19, 491.

dialogue has been used to regulate the air and rail sectors, which were excluded from the Working Time Directive.[66] A sectoral approach might have resulted in more nuanced legislation and – perhaps – in less of a need to provide extra flexibility at the workplace or individual level.

POSTSCRIPT

As other chapters of this book have illustrated, the Working Time Directive is not the only aspect of EU law dealing with workers' hours of work. In Chapter 4 we considered the Part-time Work Directive,[67] and in Chapter 6 we examined provisions on maternity and parental leave.[68] One option would have been to group these various matters together into a single comprehensive chapter on working hours; but this would not have been an accurate reflection of the shape of EU law in this area. The Part-time Work Directive 'fits' with the other directives on atypical work, and there is an obvious development of the law from sex discrimination to pregnancy discrimination to a broader set of rights for parents. The Working Time Directive is a rather lonely measure.

As we have seen, the Commission remains committed to a reform of the Directive and it is clearly conscious of the relevance of these other measures. In turn, this gives rise to a difficulty about the Directive's legal basis as a piece of health and safety legislation, even broadly defined. The problem is neatly summed up by the Commission in the following passage:

> The regulation of working time has traditionally pursued health and safety objectives, and reforms have often assumed that technical progress would inevitably lead to more time for leisure. The usual justification for working time regulation is the need to offset the negative effects of the overwork that might result from unregulated individual transactions.
>
> More recently however, the focus of the debate has changed, and the organisation of working time has increasingly been perceived as crucially important

---

[66] Directive 93/104, Art 1(3), and see Case C–133/00 *Bowden v Tuffnells Parcels Express Ltd* [2001] ECR I–7031. For examples of sectoral directives see Directive 2000/79/EC concerning the European Agreement on the Organisation of Working Time of Mobile Workers in Civil Aviation concluded by European Airlines (AEA), the European Transport Workers' Federation (ETF), the European Cockpit Association (ECA), the European Regions Airline Association (ERA) and the International Air Carriers Association (IACA); Directive 2005/47/EC on the agreement between the Community of European Railways (CER) and the European Transport Workers' Federation (ETF) on certain aspects of the working conditions of mobile workers engaged in interoperable cross-border services in the railway sector.

[67] Directive 97/81/EC.

[68] Pregnant Workers Directive, Directive 92/85/EC; Directive 2010/18/EU implementing the revised Framework Agreement on Parental Leave.

for improving productivity, enhancing competitiveness, supporting work–life balance, and confronting the growing diversity of preferences and working patterns. So the question arises: has regulation of working time kept pace with these developments? Or are reforms needed to adapt the current rules to the needs of companies, workers and consumers in the 21st century?[69]

This reflects the (controversial) shift from traditional worker-protective objectives for EU labour law to the policy of flexicurity: encouraging diverse arrangements and justifying them in terms of business competitiveness. It remains to be seen whether any reforms can be agreed.

FURTHER READING

The topic of working time has not generated an enormous literature. For a discussion of the emergence of the Working Time Directive in its historical context, see J. Kenner (2003), *EU Employment Law: From Rome to Amsterdam and Beyond* (Oxford: Hart), Chapter 5, or B. Bercusson (2009), *European Labour Law* (2nd edn, Cambridge University Press), Chapter 4.

We noted in this chapter that the Directive has elements of rigidity and flexibility and has been the subject of some debate on this account. For a critique of the rigidity of the Directive, see C. Barnard, 'EC "Social" Policy', in P.P. Craig and G. de Búrca (eds) (1999), *The Evolution of EU Law* (Oxford University Press), 488–92, and for praise of its flexibility, see Bercusson, above, 349–54.

Another area of discussion is the relationship between individual rights and collective bargaining. For critique from the latter perspective, see A.L. Bogg, 'The Right to Paid Annual Leave in the Court of Justice: the Eclipse of Functionalism' (2006) 31 EL Rev 892.

At the time of writing, the Commission continues to seek amendments to the Directive. For up-to-date information on this, see the website of DG Employment at http://ec.europa.eu/social/main.jsp?catId=706&langId=en&intPageId=205.

---

[69] Commission, *Reviewing the Working Time Directive*, above n. 31, 5.

8. Worker protection and participation

This chapter will focus primarily on the various ways in which EU labour law seeks to create or preserve opportunities for workers, as a group, to have a say in what goes on at their workplace. As we shall see, collective involvement of the workforce in decision-making can bring benefits for both the employer and the workers. For the workers, participation can provide opportunities to redress grievances and improve satisfaction at work. For the employer, worker participation can be costly but can also improve loyalty and job performance, and lead to better-informed decision making. Although mechanisms for workforce participation can be quite general in nature, they come into particularly sharp focus when there are changes to the firm: changes of ownership or legal structure, mergers, insolvency and redundancies. In these situations, participation mechanisms provide workers with an opportunity to argue against job losses or changes to their terms and conditions of employment. As we shall see, the law sometimes offers substantive as well as procedural protection in these situations.

The chapter is divided into three parts. In the first part, we will examine three directives from the 1970s, on collective redundancies,[1] insolvency,[2] and changes in the ownership of the business (the 'transfer of the undertaking').[3] These directives were designed to address workers' concerns at a time of serious economic crisis in the EU and, arguably, to reduce their resistance to change. We will also consider some of the EU's other policy approaches to these problems, particularly the use of money from the structural funds to regenerate areas of high unemployment. In the second part, we will consider two more modern measures designed to

---

[1]   Originally Directive 75/129/EEC on the approximation of the laws of the Member States relating to collective redundancies, as amended. The current rules are to be found in Directive 98/59/EC.

[2]   Originally Directive 80/987/EEC, as amended. The current text is Directive 2008/94/EC of the European Parliament and of the Council on the protection of employees in the event of the insolvency of their employer.

[3]   Originally Directive 77/187/EEC, as amended. The current text is Council Directive 2001/23/EC on the approximation of the laws of the Member States relating to the safeguarding of employees' rights in the event of transfers of undertakings, businesses or parts of undertakings or businesses.

promote the development of mechanisms for regular consultation between employers and workers: the European Works Councils Directive,[4] which provides for pan-European consultation in very large firms, and the Information and Consultation Directive which applies to larger national firms.[5] And in the third part, we will consider some attempts by the EU to preserve national traditions of consultation (such as the German system of having employee representatives on company boards) against undercutting, through the relevant provisions of measures such as the European Company Statute[6] and the Directive on Cross-Border Mergers.[7]

COMMON THEMES

Each part of this chapter will highlight a slightly different subset of common themes within EU labour law. But before we get into the detail, it is worth noting two broader themes which will be relevant throughout the chapter: the preservation of the autonomy of the Member States, and the role of trade unions.

We saw in Chapter 1 that national autonomy is a big concern in EU labour law. Given the Member States' diverse traditions of labour law, it is generally thought to be unrealistic for the EU to seek to provide a uniform labour code applicable in all the Member States. When it comes to employee participation mechanisms, these concerns are particularly acute. One important difference is between 'dual' and 'single channel' systems. Some Member States have a 'dual channel' tradition of collective bargaining through trade unions on pay and other terms and conditions, coupled with a system of worker participation through works councils. The works council consists of elected representatives who meet with management on a regular basis to discuss issues of concern. Other Member States, like the UK, historically had a 'single channel' system in which worker involvement only took place through trade unions. Another important difference is between countries which allow worker representation on company

---

[4]   Originally Directive 94/45/EC, extended to the UK by Directive 97/74/EC. The current text is Directive 2009/38/EC of the European Parliament and of the Council on the establishment of a European Works Council or a procedure in Community-scale undertakings and Community-scale groups of undertakings for the purposes of informing and consulting employees (Recast).

[5]   Directive 2002/14/EC of the European Parliament and of the Council establishing a general framework for informing and consulting employees in the European Community.

[6]   Council Directive 2001/86/EC supplementing the Statute for a European company with regard to the involvement of employees.

[7]   Directive 2005/56/EC of the European Parliament and of the Council on cross-border mergers of limited liability companies.

boards, and countries which do not. In Germany, for example, companies may have a two-tier board structure with a management board responsible for the day-to-day running of the company which is accountable to a supervisory board including worker representatives.

Against this background, it is understandable that the EU has faced difficulties in legislating on these topics. This has manifested itself in various ways. The most obvious is that it has taken many years to reach agreement on some of the directives we shall consider, because of worries on the part of the Member States that national protections for workers will either be undermined or be significantly enhanced in new and unfamiliar ways. Another feature of these directives is the discretion they give to the Member States to mesh EU legislation with their own national traditions, for example, by specifying how worker representatives are to be elected and what protections they are to be afforded.

Another over-arching theme for this chapter is the role of trade unions. In some respects, this is the 'elephant in the room'. As we saw in Chapter 2, the EU has no power to legislate on freedom of association or the right to strike.[8] So there is no EU legislation on collective bargaining. However, it is difficult (particularly for single channel countries) to think about worker involvement without thinking about trade unions. This raises a number of questions. Are unions threatened by EU legislation on worker participation? Can unions make use of the opportunities created by the legislation to increase their role in some workplaces? We will not be able to answer these questions fully, but they are an important background to the chapter.

BUSINESS REORGANISATIONS

This section will examine the directives on collective redundancies, employer insolvency and transfers of undertakings (the Acquired Rights Directive or ARD). We will begin by identifying the most important themes running through this material: the shift in EU policy over time, and the role of the Court of Justice.

Themes

The three directives to be considered in this section were introduced in the 1970s. At that time, manufacturing was beginning to decline in the EU and

---

[8] Article 153(5) TFEU.

levels of unemployment in traditional industries were rising.[9] The directives can be regarded as having both economic and social aims.

In economic terms, we can identify two main justifications for these directives. One was to reduce workers' resistance to the process of transition from manufacturing towards other forms of work. The idea was that restructuring was necessary, so EU law should not seek to prevent it, but should instead encourage workers to accept it by providing them with some protection, such as wage payments from the public purse if their employer became insolvent. This would reduce the likelihood of industrial action which would be damaging to the EU economy. The other possible justification is the familiar 'race to the bottom' argument. When firms have several factories in different Member States, and want to close one or two of them, they will consider the relative costs of closure in each Member State. Presumably they will avoid closures in 'expensive' Member States where high levels of redundancy payments are required. Although this might appear to suggest a 'race to the top' in worker protection, the reality might be rather different. Firms might decide not to locate at all in Member States with good protection, because of worries about the costs of closure. This might prompt a demand for regulation at the EU level.

In social terms, EU intervention can be justified because it is a 'good thing' to protect workers when their employer restructures. After all, this may lead to lost wages, dismissal and other detrimental consequences, none of which is the fault of the individual worker concerned.

An interesting issue relating to these economic and social arguments is whether they have stood the test of time: do the arguments made in the 1970s still apply today? As we saw in Chapter 1, the EU's 'flexicurity' agenda involves encouraging workers to focus on their employability in the EU market generally, rather than on attaching themselves to a particular job with a particular firm. As we shall see, the Collective Redundancies Directive fits with these objectives in the sense that it does not provide workers with any strong form of job security, just with a right to be consulted before large-scale job losses take place. The ARD, however, is concerned with job security in the traditional sense – keeping workers in their jobs with the same terms and conditions even if the business changes hands – and it remains to be seen how this will fare in the proposed review of the *acquis* discussed in Chapter 2. Of course, the recent economic downturn caused by the financial crisis means that, at the time of writing, the parallels with the 1970s are particularly acute. In employment terms,

---

[9]   For historical background, see J. Kenner (2003), *EU Employment Law: From Rome to Amsterdam and Beyond* (Oxford: Hart), Chapter 2.

the EU's main response to the current recession has been to use the long-established structural funds to support regeneration of particular areas, and we will consider this policy below.

The other major theme for this section is the role of the Court of Justice in interpreting the legislation, particularly the ARD on transfers of undertakings.[10] As we saw in Chapter 2, a major role for the Court is to fill gaps in vague or ambiguous legislation and to adapt the legislation to changing circumstances. There have been two problems with the ARD. First, it contained no definition of its central concept, the transfer of an undertaking, when it was enacted, leaving this matter entirely to the Court to figure out. Second, during the 1980s in particular, governments began to make increasing use of the private sector to deliver public services. This wave of privatisation and contracting out could not have been envisaged when the ARD was enacted, so the Court was required to determine whether and how the ARD applied to these novel situations. We will examine how the Court has coped with these challenges in what follows.

Collective Redundancies

The Collective Redundancies Directive aims to ensure that a process of consultation with worker representatives takes place before the employer implements large-scale redundancies.[11] Before analysing the Directive's provisions in greater detail, it may be helpful to note some of its important limitations. First, the Directive is a procedural measure: it seeks to provide workers with a forum for the discussion of collective redundancies with the employer. Although consultation should include 'ways and means of avoiding' collective redundancies,[12] the Directive is not designed as a measure for the prevention of redundancies. Second, although the Directive gives the Member States a choice how to define 'collective redundancies' in respect of the number of workers affected, it is clearly focused on larger-scale job losses.[13] And third, the Directive does not afford rights to individuals who are being made redundant, although of course the consultation process might lead to improvements in their situation.

---

[10] For a detailed discussion of this issue, see S. O'Leary (2002), *Employment Law at the European Court of Justice* (Oxford: Hart), Chapter 6; G. Barrett, 'Deploying the Classic "Community Method" in the Social Policy Field: The Example of the Acquired Rights Directive' (2009) 15 ELJ 198.

[11] Directive 98/59/EC. For an analysis of recent case-law, see C. Kilpatrick, 'The European Court of Justice and Labour Law in 2009' (2010) 39 ILJ 287.

[12] Directive 98/59/EC, Art 2(2).

[13] Ibid, Art 1.

The concept of 'collective' redundancy

The Directive adopts a broad definition of redundancy: 'dismissals effected by an employer for one or more reasons not related to the individual workers concerned'.[14] The 'collective' element is at the discretion of the Member State, which may choose between:

(i) either, over a period of 30 days:
– at least 10 in establishments normally employing more than 20 and less than 100 workers,
– at least 10% of the number of workers in establishments normally employing at least 100 but less than 300 workers,
– at least 30 in establishments normally employing 300 workers or more,

(ii) or, over a period of 90 days, at least 20, whatever the number of workers normally employed in the establishments in question.[15]

There are two significant exclusions: cases in which the workers were employed on fixed-term contracts which have expired, and workers in the public sector.[16] The latter exclusion is significant because the ARD, to be discussed below, does not contain this exclusion and, as a result, that Directive has had a significant impact in the public sector.

The employer's duties

The Collective Redundancies Directive requires the Member States to place the employer under two main duties: to consult with workers' representatives (with a consequent obligation to provide them with information), and to notify the national authorities about the redundancies.

The duty to consult is set out in Article 2:

1. Where an employer is contemplating collective redundancies, he shall begin consultations with the workers' representatives in good time with a view to reaching an agreement.
2. These consultations shall, at least, cover ways and means of avoiding collective redundancies or reducing the number of workers affected, and of mitigating the consequences by recourse to accompanying social measures aimed, inter alia, at aid for redeploying or retraining workers made redundant.

Importantly, this offers a 'strong' definition of consultation since it indicates that the aim should be to reach an agreement.[17] However, there is

---

[14] Ibid, Art 1(1)(a). This has been interpreted broadly by the Court: Case C–55/02 *Commission v Portugal* [2004] ECR I–9387, but cf Case C–323/08 *Rodríguez Mayor v Dávila (decd)* [2009] ECR I–11621.

[15] Directive 98/59/EC, Art 1(1)(a).

[16] Ibid, Art 1(2).

[17] See Case C–383/92 *Commission v UK* [1994] ECR I–2479, [34]–[7].

no *obligation* to reach an agreement and it may be difficult in practice to demonstrate that the employer has approached the negotiations without any intention of agreeing. The second sub-paragraph indicates that the consultation is wide in scope, covering both minimisation of redundancies and support for workers who are made redundant. Article 2(3) provides a comprehensive list of information which must be supplied to the representatives during the consultation process.

The timing of the consultation has given rise to some difficulties in the case-law. If the process is to have any effect, it must take place before the employer's mind is made up. But does this extend to commercial decisions (for example, a decision on how many factories to keep open) which might impact on employment levels? These questions were addressed in *AEK*, in which it was held that:

> [t]he consultation procedure must be started by the employer once a strategic or commercial decision compelling him to contemplate or to plan for collective redundancies has been taken.[18]

However, it was not necessary to begin the consultation when merely contemplating the commercial decision that might give rise to the redundancies.[19] This ruling seems problematic. On one hand, if the commercial decision makes the redundancies inevitable, the consultation process will be of limited benefit in preventing redundancies if it only starts once the commercial decision has been made. On the other hand, it may be harsh to expect employers to engage in redundancy consultation when they are taking a decision that initially may not appear to them to be workforce-related.

The identification of workers' representatives is a matter for national law.[20] However, as the UK experience indicates, this does not afford an unfettered discretion. The UK's approach to employee representation was traditionally the 'single channel' model, in which representation was only provided through trade unions. As a result, the UK initially implemented the Directive by stating that employers were obliged to consult trade union representatives about redundancies. This meant that no consultation on collective redundancies – or any other topic – took place in workplaces with no recognised trade union. The Court found that this was an inadequate implementation of the Directive and the UK government was forced to develop a mechanism for identifying workplace representatives

---

18 Case C–44/08 *AEK v Fujitsu Siemens Computers* [2009] ECR I–8163, [48].
19 Ibid, [46]. See also Case C–583/10 *USA v Nolan* currently before the Court.
20 Directive 98/59/EC, Art 1(1)(b).

in non-unionised workplaces.[21] This necessitated a fundamental shift away from the 'single channel' approach.[22]

Early experience with the Directive revealed that employers sometimes argued that they were not responsible for large-scale redundancy decisions or were unable to supply information to workers' representatives because they were controlled by a parent company which took the decisions or held the information.[23] This led to an amendment in 1992 to insert Article 2(4), which makes it clear that the presence of a controlling undertaking cannot be used as a defence by the employer.[24]

Under Article 3, the employer is to be placed under a duty to notify the relevant national public authority of the collective redundancies. Under Article 4, the Member State may provide that the redundancies should not take effect for 30 days from the date of the notification, though there are possibilities for varying this period. This suggests that the framers of the Directive regarded collective redundancies as giving rise to social problems which were the concern of national governments and should not just be regarded as a matter for the employer and the affected workers.

Remedies

In general terms, it is for the Member States to decide what remedies should be provided in the event that an employer breaches the obligation to consult on collective redundancies. But this is subject to the general EU law requirements that the remedies should be effective and equivalent to those available for similar actions in national law, so the Court is sometimes called upon to review remedies for their conformity to these requirements.

One issue with regard to collective redundancies is who should have the right to bring a claim about the employer's alleged non-compliance: the representatives, the affected workers, or some combination of the two? This arose in *Mono Car*, a case concerning Belgian law.[25] The law allowed workers' representatives to challenge any aspect of the employer's compliance, but workers themselves only had limited possibilities of challenge. The Court held that the consultation rights provided by the Directive

---

[21]   *Commission v UK*, above n. 17, [19]–[27].

[22]   See P. Davies, 'A Challenge to Single Channel' (1994) 23 ILJ 272; and P. Davies and C. Kilpatrick, 'UK Worker Representation After Single Channel' (2004) 33 ILJ 121.

[23]   The point was argued (unsuccessfully) in, for example, Case C–449/93 *Rockfon v Specialarbejderforbundet i Danmark* [1995] ECR I–4291.

[24]   Council Directive 92/56/EEC of 24 June 1992 amending Directive 75/129/EEC on the approximation of the laws of the Member States relating to collective redundancies, Art 1.

[25]   Case C–12/08 *Mono Car Styling v Odemis* [2009] ECR I–6653.

were 'collective in nature',[26] so the provision of an unlimited challenge to workers' representatives counted as an effective remedy. Individual possibilities of challenge were an extra layer of protection and could therefore be restricted.[27]

Another interesting question is whether the Member States are obliged to provide that redundancies cannot take place unless the consultation process has been carried out. In *Junk*, the Court stated that:

> [t]he effectiveness of [the obligation to negotiate] would be compromised if an employer was entitled to terminate contracts of employment during the course of the procedure or even at the beginning thereof. It would be significantly more difficult for workers' representatives to achieve the withdrawal of a decision that has been taken than to secure the abandonment of a decision that is being contemplated.[28]

And in *AEK*, the Court held that the subsidiary in that case was obliged to complete the consultation procedure before acting on the parent company's instruction to make the workers redundant.[29] These statements could be read as requiring the Member States to provide remedies which force employers to complete the procedure,[30] for example by making the redundancies invalid if there is no consultation or by giving representatives the opportunity to obtain injunctive relief. However, it might still be open to a Member State to argue that an obligation to compensate affected employees for a failure to consult acts as a deterrent and is therefore an effective remedy.

Insolvency

The Insolvency Directive requires each Member State to set up a 'guarantee institution' to pay employees' outstanding wages if their employer becomes insolvent.[31] Like the directives on redundancies and transfers, its aim is to mitigate the consequences for employees of these inevitable developments. It differs from the other two directives considered in this part because it does not require states to place any duties on employers, and because it is about worker protection rather than consultation.

---

[26] Ibid, [42].
[27] Directive 98/59/EC, Art 5, makes clear that the Directive is only intended to set minimum standards on which the Member States may improve.
[28] Case C–188/03 *Junk v Kühnel* [2005] ECR I–885, [44].
[29] Above n. 18, [70].
[30] See Kilpatrick, above n. 11, 297.
[31] Directive 2008/94/EC.

The Italian government's failure to implement the Insolvency Directive led to one of the best-known decisions in EU law, *Francovich*, in which the ECJ established the principle of state liability in damages for non-implementation of a directive.[32]

The Directive defines insolvency as follows:

> For the purposes of this Directive, an employer shall be deemed to be in a state of insolvency where a request has been made for the opening of collective proceedings based on insolvency of the employer, as provided for under the laws, regulations and administrative provisions of a Member State, and involving the partial or total divestment of the employer's assets and the appointment of a liquidator or a person performing a similar task, and the authority which is competent pursuant to the said provisions has:
> (a)   either decided to open the proceedings; or
> (b)   established that the employer's undertaking or business has been definitively closed down and that the available assets are insufficient to warrant the opening of the proceedings.[33]

Under Article 13, the Member States are obliged to notify the Commission of the forms of insolvency proceedings in their national law which fall within this definition.

Other definitional matters – notably 'employer', 'employee' and 'pay' – are for the Member States themselves to define.[34] However, they may not exclude part-time, fixed-term or temporary workers from the scope of the Directive, nor may they require employees to have worked for a particular qualifying period before being able to bring a claim for unpaid wages.[35]

The Member States are also entitled to limit the liability of their guarantee institutions in various ways. First, the Member States may impose a limit on the unpaid wages the employees may claim, though this must normally be no less than three months' wages.[36] The Member States may opt to use a reference period to even out any fluctuations in wages over time. This must be at least six months where wage claims are limited to three months. But if the Member State adopts a reference period of eighteen months or more, it may limit the employees' claims to eight weeks' wages. Second, the Member States may set 'ceilings on the payments made by the guarantee institution', provided that such ceilings 'must not fall below a level which is socially compatible with the social objective of [the]

---

[32]   C–6/90 and C–9/90 *Francovich and Bonifaci v Italian Republic* [1991] ECR I–5357.
[33]   Directive 2008/94/EC, Art 2(1).
[34]   Ibid, Art 2(2), though Art 3 stipulates that severance pay is included where national law so provides.
[35]   Ibid, Art 2(3).
[36]   Ibid, Art 4(2).

Directive'.[37] The method of calculating any such 'ceiling' must be notified by the Member State to the Commission. Third, the Member States are entitled to take measures to prevent abuse, for example, where the employer colludes with the employees in order to transfer liability to the guarantee institution.[38]

For many individuals, one of the most worrying consequences of employer insolvency is the possibility that the employer's pension fund may also become insolvent because the employer can no longer contribute to it. This is particularly problematic for former employees who are already receiving a pension or for older employees coming up to retirement, because they will not have the opportunity to build up contributions in another scheme. Article 8 of the Directive therefore requires the Member States to introduce protection for occupational pension schemes run by firms outside the national social security regime. In the *Robins* case, the UK government was found to have failed to implement the Directive properly when it provided limited benefits to individuals in this situation.[39] Although the Court held that a Member State was not obliged to fund pension schemes in full, it was not acceptable for individuals to receive less than half their expected benefits.

Finally, the Directive makes provision for transnational situations, in which an insolvent firm operates in more than one Member State. In these cases, the obligation to pay the employees' outstanding wage claims falls upon the guarantee institution in the state in which those employees 'work or habitually work'.[40] This represented something of a departure from the Court's rulings on the topic,[41] which had focused on the firm's place or places of establishment. In *Everson*, the Court held that where the employer had an establishment in more than one Member State, the employees should claim in the state in which they were employed.[42] However, in *Mosbæk*, where the employer was established in the UK but the employee worked in Denmark, in effect as a posted worker, the Court held that she should claim in the UK, where the insolvency proceedings had commenced.[43] The Directive would probably reverse the result in the *Mosbæk* situation unless it could be demonstrated on the facts that the posting to Denmark had been temporary only, so that the employee's

---

[37] Ibid, Art 4(3), and see Case C–19/01 *INPS v Barsotti* [2004] ECR I–2005.

[38] Ibid, Art 12.

[39] Case C–278/05 *Robins v Secretary of State for Work and Pensions* [2007] ECR I–1053.

[40] Directive 2008/94/EC, Art 9.

[41] As acknowledged by the Court in Case C–310/07 *Sweden v Holmqvist* [2008] ECR I–7871, [25].

[42] Case C–198/98 *Everson v Secretary of State for Trade and Industry* [1999] ECR I–8903.

[43] Case C–117/96 *Mosbæk v Lønmodtagernes Garantifond* [1997] ECR I–5017.

normal place of work was in the UK. On one hand, the *Mosbæk* decision can be defended on the grounds that the employer is unlikely to have made any contributions to the insolvency fund (if required) in a state to which it posts workers. On the other hand, it may be more difficult for the workers to bring claims in a state other than that of their normal place of work.

Transfers

The third directive to be considered in this part is the Acquired Rights Directive.[44] This Directive was first passed in 1977, revised in 1998, and consolidated in its current form in 2001. It is designed to protect workers' rights when a business changes ownership, by ensuring that the employees can transfer to the new owner if they want to, that their terms and conditions of employment (including collective representation arrangements) are preserved, that the transfer itself cannot be used as a reason for dismissal, and that the employees are consulted during the run-up to the transfer. Importantly, the Directive does not seek to prevent or deter changes in business ownership (though views differ on whether or not its efforts to protect employees might have that effect). Although redundancies and insolvency are more obvious employment consequences of an economic downturn, business reorganisations are also important: for example, firms may seize the opportunity to buy up failing competitors, or to divest themselves of their less profitable divisions. There is a very great deal of case-law on this topic, so this chapter can only give an overview.

Partial harmonisation
A first point to make clear about the Directive is that it is a measure of *partial* harmonisation and was introduced in the context of wide variations in existing practices as between the Member States. In the UK, a change in the legal identity of the employer would automatically lead to the termination of the contract of employment, whereas in some of the other Member States there was already settled law protecting employees in the event of a transfer.

Because it is a partial harmonisation measure, the Directive allows the Member States to introduce more favourable provisions. It also leaves a number of key aspects to be defined at the national level. These include the concepts of 'employee' and 'employee representatives', and the remedies to be provided for breach of the Directive. Of course, these matters are not left entirely uncontrolled by the Court of Justice, because of the

---

[44] Directive 2001/23/EC.

requirements for proper implementation and the provision of effective and equivalent remedies, but nevertheless, they leave important discretions to the Member States.[45]

Which changes in business ownership are covered by the Directive?
This is the thorniest issue in the Directive.[46] Ultimately, the question whether there has been a transfer of an undertaking is a question requiring the application of law to the facts of the case, and is therefore a task for the national court. However, the Court has become engaged in the task of providing detailed guidance for the national courts, and the development of this guidance has generated considerable litigation.

Who is the transferor? The two parties to the transfer are known as the transferor and the transferee. According to the Directive, the transferor is the natural or legal person who 'ceases to be the employer' of the employees because of the transfer, and the transferee is the natural or legal person who 'becomes [their] employer'.[47] At first sight, this might suggest that it is necessary for there to be a contract of employment between the transferor and the employees. However, the Directive uses the phrase 'contract of employment or employment relationship'.[48] In the recent *Albron* case, uncertainty arose because the affected employees were employed by one company in a group (the 'contractual employer'), worked for another company in the group on a day-to-day basis (the 'non-contractual employer'), and were then transferred by the non-contractual employer to an unrelated entity.[49] The Court held that it was possible to treat the 'non-contractual employer' as the transferor to ensure the effective application of the Directive.

Transfer The definition of a transfer is set out in Article 1(1)(a):

> This Directive shall apply to any transfer of an undertaking, business, or part of an undertaking or business to another employer as a result of a legal transfer or merger.

Although the concept of a 'legal transfer or merger' has been defined relatively broadly by the Court, we should note a significant exclusion before

---

[45] Case C–382/92 *Commission v UK* [1994] ECR I–2435.
[46] For a detailed discussion of the case-law, see G. Barrett, 'Light Acquired on Acquired Rights: Examining Developments in Employment Rights on Transfers of Undertakings' (2005) 42 CMLR 1053.
[47] Directive 2001/23, Art 2(1).
[48] For example, in Art 2(2). Both concepts are for national law to define.
[49] Case C–242/09 *Albron Catering BV v FNV Bondgenoten* [2010] nyr.

examining that case-law. In some Member States, including the UK, businesses generally 'change hands' through the purchase of shares. A natural or legal person becomes the new owner of the business by acquiring a majority shareholding. This is not captured by the concept of a 'transfer ... to another employer' because the legal identity of the employer remains the same throughout,[50] with the result that not all changes in business ownership attract the application of the Directive.[51] However, transfers between companies in the same group are covered by the Directive, at least where the companies have separate employment relationships with their employees.[52]

The most obvious form of transfer covered by the Directive is a straightforward contract through which the new owner (the transferee) agrees to purchase a business from the old owner (the transferor). However, the Court has extended the concept by holding that there need not be any direct relationship between the transferor and the transferee. To use a simple example, imagine a case in which a large manufacturing firm A contracts out the operation of its canteen to specialist catering firm B. This transaction is likely to constitute a transfer for the purposes of the Directive.[53] But a transfer also takes place when A terminates B's contract and contracts the catering operation out to one of its competitors, C, even though there is no direct legal relationship between B and C.[54] It is also the case that a decision by A to abandon contracting out by bringing the catering operation back in-house is covered by the Directive.[55]

The Directive is limited in its application to the public sector, in the sense that transfers of public activities between public bodies are not covered.[56] This is set out expressly in Article 1(1)(c):

---

[50]   This conclusion might conceivably be challenged by a broad interpretation of *Albron*, ibid, but this seems unlikely because it would make a much bigger hole in the corporate veil (the doctrine that courts do not look behind the legal structures of companies) than *Albron* itself.

[51]   The Takeover Bids Directive (Directive 2004/25/EC) does contain a requirement for the offeror and offeree companies to inform employee representatives about a takeover bid, including 'the likely repercussions on employment' (Art 6), but there is no real requirement for consultation (see Art 9(5)) and certainly no attempt to preserve job security.

[52]   Case C–234/98 *Allen v Amalgamated Construction Co Ltd* [1999] ECR I–8643. It is arguable that *Albron* (above n. 49) may extend this principle to situations in which the group companies have separate but non-contractual relationships with their employees, even though the employees all have the same contractual employer.

[53]   For example, Case C–392/92 *Schmidt v Spar- und Leihkasse der früheren Ämter Bordesholm* [1994] ECR I–1311.

[54]   For example, Case C–13/95 *Süzen v Zehnacker Gebäudereinigung GmbH Krankenhausservice* [1997] ECR I–1259.

[55]   For example, C–127/96 *Hernández Vidal SA v Pérez* [1998] ECR I–8179.

[56]   See Case C–298/94 *Henke v Gemeinde Schierke and Verwaltungsgemeinschaft Brocken* [1996] ECR I–4989.

> An administrative reorganisation of public administrative authorities, or the transfer of administrative functions between public administrative authorities, is not a transfer within the meaning of this Directive.

However, the same provision also makes clear that the Directive applies to 'public and private undertakings engaged in economic activities whether or not they are operating for gain'. So transfers between public bodies are caught where the transferred entity is not engaged in the exercise of public powers and may be in competition with private firms, such as a cleaning service for state-run schools.[57] Moreover, transactions between public bodies and private or voluntary bodies are covered. So the contracting-out, contracting-in and change-of-contractor situations in the example above would also be subject to the Directive where A was a public body rather than a private firm. Importantly, though, the Court has also held that legislative or administrative acts of public bodies – not just contracts – may also be caught by the Directive. So, for example, where a public body privatises a service,[58] or awards a grant to charity C instead of charity B,[59] a transfer may also have taken place.

The effect of all of this is quite significant in economic terms. Where a contract is put out to tender, whether by a private firm or a public body, the bidders cannot simply assume that they will be able to use their own workforce or hire the existing staff on reduced terms and conditions, because the Directive might apply to protect the workers' jobs and pay. In other words, labour costs are 'taken out of competition', forcing firms to find other ways of outbidding each other. The Directive has proved particularly significant in the public sector because of the increasing trend of private involvement in public service provision over the 1980s and 1990s, a development not envisaged when the Directive was enacted. Of course, the use of the Directive in this way is controversial. On one hand, a broad interpretation of a 'transfer' helps to secure the Directive's worker-protective purpose: that a change in ownership of the business should not be to the workers' detriment. On the other hand, as the case-law illustrates, contracting out has been prevalent in labour-intensive sectors such as cleaning and catering where staff costs are a crucial factor for businesses. Having said all of that, the broad definition of a 'transfer' has been somewhat undermined by problems with the definition of an 'entity', and it is to this concept that we will now turn.

---

[57] See Case C–108/10 *Scattolon v Ministero dell'Universitàe della Ricerca* [2011] nyr.
[58] For example, Case C–4/01 *Martin v South Bank University* [2003] ECR I–12859.
[59] For example, Case C–29/91 *Dr Sophie Redmond Stichting v Bartol* [1992] ECR I–3189.

Entity The original Directive 77/187 did not attempt to define the concept of an 'undertaking' or 'business' for the purposes of determining whether or not a transfer had taken place. This created confusion in the national courts which, in turn, forced the Court to develop some definitions through the case-law.[60] This then led to an initiative at the political level to define 'undertaking' in the Directive. Whilst this proposal was being debated, the Court decided the *Süzen* case,[61] arguably narrowing the approach it had previously taken.[62] This definition was then crystallised into legislation in Directive 98/50 and it remains in force in the current Directive:

> [T]here is a transfer within the meaning of this Directive where there is a transfer of an economic entity which retains its identity, meaning an organised grouping of resources which has the objective of pursuing an economic activity, whether or not that activity is central or ancillary.[63]

The claimant in *Süzen* was a cleaner in a school who lost her job when the school terminated the contract with the firm employing her and awarded the cleaning contract to another firm. As we saw above, it is possible for a transfer to occur in this situation even though there is no direct relationship between the transferor and the transferee. However, the Court insisted that there must be a transfer of an identifiable 'entity'.

In order to determine whether or not an 'entity' has been transferred, the Court in *Süzen* and subsequent case-law drew a distinction between labour-intensive and asset-intensive businesses. Where the business is labour-intensive, the Court found that the key focus should be on the workforce and on whether or not they had been transferred to the new contractor. If that had been the case, then it would be possible to find that an 'entity' had been transferred. Conversely, where a business depended heavily on assets (a transport operation with lots of lorries, for example), the focus should be on whether or not the assets had been transferred.

This seemingly straightforward approach is, in fact, highly problematic. Imagine a situation in which the 'transferee' does not want a transfer to take place within the meaning of the Directive, for example because it wants to be able to offer the existing workers employment with worse terms and conditions. As a worker-protective measure, the Directive should operate in this situation to force the transferee to take on the workers and

---

[60] Case 24/85 *Spijkers v Gebroeders Benedik Abattoir* [1986] ECR 1119.
[61] Above n. 54.
[62] See Kenner, above n. 9, 345–8.
[63] Directive 2001/23/EC, Art 1(1)(b).

to preserve their existing terms and conditions of employment. However, if the business is asset-intensive, the 'transferee' can avoid creating a transfer situation by refusing to take on the transferor's assets. For example, in *Oy Liikenne*, a city terminated its contract with its existing bus operator and contracted the service out to a new operator.[64] The Court held that no transfer had taken place because bus services were asset-intensive, not labour-intensive, and the new operator had chosen to buy new buses instead of taking on the old ones. This might have occurred for many different reasons: perhaps the new operator could not agree a price with the old operator, or perhaps the buses were unreliable or too polluting. It seems bizarre that the rights of the workforce (many of whom had moved to the new employer but on worse terms and conditions) should depend on these factors. Similarly, if the business is labour-intensive, the 'transferee' can avoid creating a transfer situation by refusing to take on the transferor's workers. This was the case in *Süzen* itself, where the new holder of the cleaning contract had not hired the claimant. It does not make logical sense to say that the transferee is only obliged to take on the transferor's workforce where it has agreed to take on the transferor's workforce.[65] As Davies argues, the *Süzen* approach effectively makes compliance with the Directive 'voluntary'.[66]

Of course, a further consequence of this approach is that much turns on whether the activity is classified as asset- or labour-intensive. This problem is illustrated by *Abler*, a case involving the termination and re-tendering of a hospital catering contract.[67] The new contractor had taken over the hospital kitchen but had refused to take on any of the staff. It claimed that there was no transfer because catering is labour-intensive, but the Court disagreed, finding that catering is asset-intensive. Of course, there are bound to be grey areas in any classification, but the division of business activities into asset- and labour-intensive categories seems particularly difficult to predict.

Finally, it is important to note that, in labour-intensive businesses, the more recent case-law has shown that it is not necessarily enough for the workforce to be transferred in order to prove that there has been a transfer within the meaning of the Directive. The 'entity' in question must also 'retain its identity'. This poses significant problems where the transferee incorporates the transferred workers into its existing organisational

---

[64] Case C–172/99 *Oy Liikenne Ab v Liskojärvi* [2001] ECR I–745.
[65] P. Davies, 'Taken to the Cleaners? Contracting Out of Services Yet Again' (1997) 26 ILJ 193, 196.
[66] Ibid.
[67] Case C–340/01 *Abler v Sodexho* [2003] ECR I–14023.

structures. The Court has held that this does not preclude a transfer, but there must be a 'functional link between the various elements transferred' and they must be used by the transferee 'to pursue an identical or analogous economic activity'.[68] This suggests that, if the employees were integrated into the putative transferee's business and directed to perform a range of new tasks, it might be arguable that no transfer had taken place.

Comment   We can draw three broader themes from this discussion. First, as many commentators have noted, the ARD's scope of application may not be broad enough to secure its stated objective of protecting workers in the event that the business employing them changes hands. As we have seen, transfer by sale of shares is not covered, and even where there is a transfer within the meaning of the Directive, the definition of an 'entity' has generated significant possibilities for avoidance. Barnard suggests that the Court's older, pre-*Süzen* case-law, which focused on the 'activity' being transferred, was more labour-friendly.[69] However, the codification of the *Süzen* test in the Directive probably precludes a return to this approach unless the Directive itself is amended.

This leads to a second and related point. The simple focus on worker protection from the 1970s does not sit easily with the current focus of EU labour law on flexicurity. O'Leary suggests that the Court has sought to strike a balance between the interests of workers and the interests of businesses (and governments) in its case-law, and has to some extent taken responsibility for developing the Directive away from its 1970s roots.[70] Although in many ways the Court has expanded the protection afforded by the Directive (for example, to cover novel public sector contracting-out situations) it has also protected business interests through the *Süzen* line of case-law. This raises the endlessly difficult question in EU law about the relative responsibility of the Court and the political actors for making these kinds of choice.

Third, as O'Leary argues, the case-law illustrates the profound problems with the preliminary ruling procedure and the relationship between the Court of Justice and the national courts.[71] It is easy to forget when reading some of the case-law that the responsibility for determining whether or not there has been a transfer of an entity lies with the national courts and not

---

[68]   Case C–466/07 *Klarenberg v Ferrotron Technologies* [2009] ECR I–803, [48]. As we shall see below, this is not the same as the 'autonomy' requirement for the continuation of established structures of collective representation.

[69]   C. Barnard (2006), *EC Employment Law* (3rd edn, Oxford University Press), 636–44, and see *Schmidt*, above n. 53.

[70]   O'Leary, above n. 10, 285–9.

[71]   Ibid, 289–92.

the Court of Justice. Clearly, the national courts have found it difficult to answer this question and this has generated a high volume of references. However, the Court's provision of highly detailed guidance may have exacerbated the problem by making it harder to discern general principles in the case-law and therefore encouraging national courts to seek specific advice relating to the facts of the case before them. In turn, this contributes to the more general problem of the Court's excessive workload.

Insolvencies

We saw above that EU law takes steps to protect workers in the event of their employer becoming insolvent. But another potentially more attractive option in an insolvency may be for all or part of the business to be sold to another firm, raising the possibility that at least some of the workers may be able to keep their jobs. A key question is whether or not it is a good idea to apply the Directive in these situations. On one hand, to do so would force the transferee to take on the affected workers, making it more likely that their jobs would be maintained (though there is always the possibility of making the workers redundant, to be discussed below). On the other hand, the prospect of having to take on the workers may deter potential transferees from buying insolvent businesses, thereby removing the workers' escape route altogether.

The original Directive 77/187 did not say anything about insolvencies, and the Court of Justice concluded in the *Abels* case that it was not applicable.[72] Barnard suggests that this reflects a reluctance on the part of the Court to use the Directive to disrupt the normal order of priorities that the national legal systems apply in insolvencies.[73] The current version of the Directive reflects the *Abels* approach: the Member States may choose to apply the Directive where the transferor is insolvent but they need not do so.[74] Even where a Member State does choose to apply the Directive, there are various possibilities for limiting workers' rights.

In some legal systems, there are 'pre-insolvency' proceedings designed to give the failing firm a break from its creditors and an opportunity to restructure. In these situations, the Directive does apply. As Barnard points out, this may be the wrong way round, in the sense that the deterrent effect of ARD obligations applies at the point at which the failing firm is most likely to be sold.[75] However, empirical evidence would be needed to determine how the incentives play out in practice.

---

[72] Case 135/83 *Abels* [1985] ECR 469.
[73] Barnard, above n. 69, 648.
[74] Directive 2001/23/EC, Art 5.
[75] Barnard, above n. 69, 649.

Protection against dismissal

Having considered the Directive's scope of application, we are now in a position to consider the protections it affords. Put simply, the main objective of the Directive is to ensure that the transferred workers are able to continue in their jobs after the transfer, on the same terms and conditions as they enjoyed prior to the transfer. This objective is pursued by protecting the workers against dismissal because of the transfer, and by requiring the transferee to take over the transferor's obligations under the employees' contracts of employment. This section will explore the former mechanism and the next section will explore the latter.

Dismissal is addressed in Article 4(1) of the Directive:

> The transfer of the undertaking, business or part of the undertaking or business shall not in itself constitute grounds for dismissal by the transferor or the transferee.

Article 4(2) further makes clear that employees must be protected in 'constructive dismissal' situations in which their terms and conditions of employment are changed to their detriment and they opt to resign as a result.

However, Article 4(1) is subject to a significant qualification in respect of what are often known as 'ETOR' dismissals:

> This provision shall not stand in the way of dismissals that may take place for economic, technical or organisational reasons entailing changes in the workforce.

In *Bork*, the Court said:

> In order to determine whether the employees were dismissed solely as a result of the transfer, contrary to Article 4(1), it is necessary to take into consideration the objective circumstances in which the dismissal took place and, in particular, in a case such as this, the fact that it took effect on a date close to that of the transfer and that the employees in question were taken on again by the transferee.[76]

Beyond this, there is very little guidance in the case-law on how to distinguish so-called ETOR dismissals from dismissals as a result of the transfer. This is a worry because a broad interpretation of ETOR could make it relatively easy for the transferor or the transferee to dismiss all or part of

---

[76] Case C–101/87 *P Bork International v Foreningen af Arbejdsledere i Danmark* [1988] ECR 3057, [18].

the workforce around the time of the transfer without incurring any liability related to the Directive.

Our discussion so far has proceeded on the assumption that the employees affected by the transfer will want to continue employment with the transferee, because this will enable them to keep their jobs. But this may not always be the case. For example, since pension rights are not protected (see below), an employee nearing retirement might want to stay with the transferor. The Court has held that employees cannot be forced to transfer without their consent.[77] This is consistent with general principles of freedom of contract. However, this does not necessarily have the effect of preserving their jobs with the transferor, because the Court went on to say that it was for each Member State to determine the consequences of a refusal to transfer. In English law, for example, a refusal to transfer leads to the automatic termination of the employee's contract with the transferor.[78]

Terms and conditions of employment
The second limb of protection offered by the Directive is preservation of the terms and conditions of employment enjoyed by the transferred employees prior to the transfer. In other words, the transferee must not only take on the workers but also maintain their existing benefits. The central provision is Article 3(1):

> The transferor's rights and obligations arising from a contract of employment or from an employment relationship existing on the date of a transfer shall, by reason of such transfer, be transferred to the transferee.

There is a significant exception in Article 3(4), allowing the Member States to exclude benefits arising under company pension schemes.

Article 3(1) raises a difficult issue in relation to changes in the employees' terms and conditions of employment. If those terms and conditions could simply be changed by the transferee as soon as the transfer took place, the worker-protective objective of the Directive would be defeated. However, it would be harsh from the transferee's perspective if the transferred workers' terms and conditions were preserved in aspic for all time. These issues were addressed in the *Daddy's Dance Hall* case.[79] Because the Directive is a partial harmonisation measure, it:

---

[77] Case C–132/91 *Katsikas v Konstantinidis* [1992] ECR I–6577, [31]–[6].
[78] Transfer of Undertakings (Protection of Employment) Regulations 2006/246, r. 4(7) and (8).
[79] Case 324/86 *Foreningen af Arbejdsledere i Danmark v Daddy's Dance Hall* [1988] ECR 739.

can be relied on only to ensure that the employee is protected in his relations with the transferee to the same extent as he was in his relations with the
transferor under the legal rules of the Member State concerned.[80]

This means that the transferee is free to alter the transferred employees' terms and conditions insofar as this is permitted by national law.
However, the transfer itself 'may never constitute the reason for that
amendment',[81] even if the employees consent to the change and even if
the change means that they are no worse off, overall, than before. Thus,
the Directive prevents the employer from simply bringing the transferred
employees' terms and conditions into line with those of existing employees at the time of the transfer.[82] It remains unclear how long the employer
would have to wait – or what the employer would have to prove – in
order to achieve this result without being found to have made the change
because of the transfer. The public sector appears to benefit from an
exception to this rule. In *Delahaye*, the claimant worked for a private
firm and was 'transferred in' to the public sector.[83] In many EU Member
States, the rules for public employment are quite different to those for
private employment, making it impossible for the transferred workers'
contracts to be maintained in precisely the same form. However, it is clear
that the Court did expect the state to mitigate the adverse consequences
for the employee, and if this was impossible, to allow her to claim constructive dismissal.

In some legal systems, Article 3(1) would be enough to preserve collectively agreed terms and conditions for the transferred employees.
However, Article 3(3) addresses collective agreements explicitly:

> Following the transfer, the transferee shall continue to observe the terms and
> conditions agreed in any collective agreement on the same terms applicable to
> the transferor under that agreement, until the date of termination or expiry
> of the collective agreement or the entry into force or application of another
> collective agreement.
>   Member States may limit the period for observing such terms and conditions
> with the proviso that it shall not be less than one year.

This is particularly useful in those Member States in which there is no
automatic incorporation of collectively agreed terms and conditions into
individual contracts of employment. However, again, a balance needs to

---

[80]   Ibid, [16].
[81]   Ibid, [17].
[82]   *Martin*, above n. 58.
[83]   Case C–425/02 *Delahaye v Ministre de la Fonction publique* [2004] ECR I–10823.

be struck between the preservation of the employees' rights, and flexibility for the transferee. This is illustrated by the *Werhof* case, in which the collective agreement in force at the time of the transfer was renegotiated at a later date.[84] The transferee was bound to observe the original collective agreement by virtue of Article 3(3), but was not a party to the renegotiation. The question before the Court was therefore whether the transferee was bound by the new collective agreement. The Court held that the transferee was not so bound, for two main reasons. First, the purpose of the Directive was to 'safeguard the rights and obligations of employees in force on the day of the transfer', not to protect 'hypothetical advantages flowing from future changes to collective agreements'.[85] Second, if the transferee were bound by the collective agreement, its freedom of association – in the sense of its right not to join an employers' association for the purposes of collective bargaining – would be infringed.[86] In this way, the Court sought to strike a balance between the employees' rights and the transferee's freedom to organise its own business affairs.

One of the consequences of the worker protections contained in Article 3 is that they alter the dynamics of the commercial contract between the transferor and the transferee. The transferee is forced to take on some quite substantial risks, including potential claims arising out of the transferor's conduct towards its employees prior to the transfer. Although these are matters for the parties' commercial negotiations, Article 3 addresses them to some extent. First, it gives the Member States the option of requiring the transferor to disclose all its employment liabilities to the transferee, though a failure to provide full disclosure may not be used by the transferee as a defence against claims by the employees.[87] Second, the Member States may choose to make the transferor jointly and severally liable with the transferee for claims arising prior to the date of the transfer, instead of allowing all those liabilities to fall on the transferee.[88]

A final point to note about the treatment of the transferred employees is that the transferee may be obliged to respect the arrangements for the collective representation of those employees in force at the time of the transfer. This is significant because it may help to limit the use of business restructuring as a way of escaping collective representation obligations,[89]

---

[84] Case C–499/04 *Werhof v Freeway Traffic Systems* [2006] ECR I–2397.
[85] Ibid, [29].
[86] Ibid, [35].
[87] Directive 2001/23/EC, Art 3(2).
[88] Ibid, Art 3(1).
[89] We will discuss this problem in more detail below.

and because it provides collective protection for the transferred employees at a time when they may be feeling particularly vulnerable. The position is governed by Article 6(1), which provides in part:

> If the undertaking, business or part of an undertaking or business preserves its autonomy, the status and function of the representatives or of the representation of the employees affected by the transfer shall be preserved on the same terms and subject to the same conditions as existed before the date of the transfer by virtue of law, regulation, administrative provision or agreement, provided that the conditions necessary for the constitution of the employees' representation are fulfilled.

There are two limitations on this provision. First, it only applies where the transferred entity has retained its 'autonomy'. We have already come across the idea that the transferred entity must retain its 'identity' as one of the requirements for a transfer to have taken place. But the decision in *UGT-FSP* states that 'autonomy' is a distinct concept.[90] Once it has been established that a transfer has taken place, there must be a further enquiry as to whether the transferred entity has retained its autonomy in the transferee's organisational structure. This will be the case if:

> the powers granted to those in charge of that entity, within the organisational structures of the transferor, namely the power to organise, relatively freely and independently, the work within that entity in the pursuit of its specific economic activity and, more particularly, the powers to give orders and instructions, to allocate tasks to employees of the entity concerned and to determine the use of assets available to the entity, all without direct intervention from other organisational structures of the employer, remain, within the organisational structures of the transferee, essentially unchanged.[91]

In effect, then, the employees are only able to demand the continuation of their representation arrangements when the transferred entity is run as a separate concern within the transferee's business. This has a certain logic to it but – given the troublesome concepts involved – might be rather difficult to apply in practice. Second, the continuation of representation envisaged by Article 6 may be defeated where national law requires different representation arrangements to be put in place.[92] This reflects the role of the Directive as a measure of partial harmonisation only.

---

[90] Case C–151/09 *UGT-FSP v Ayuntamiento de La Línea de la Concepción* [2010] nyr, [33]–[5].

[91] Ibid, [56].

[92] Directive 2001/23/EC, Art 6(1).

Information and consultation

A third limb of protection for the affected employees consists of rights to information and consultation. Importantly, the obligations to inform and consult apply to both the transferor and the transferee. Although the transferor's employees probably face the most substantial disruption as a result of the transfer, an influx of new colleagues is likely to have some consequences for the transferee's employees too, and this is acknowledged in the Directive. The duties to inform and to consult are separate, so we will consider each in turn.[93]

The obligation to inform is set out in Article 7(1), as follows:

> The transferor and transferee shall be required to inform the representatives of their respective employees affected by the transfer of the following:
> – the date or proposed date of the transfer,
> – the reasons for the transfer,
> – the legal, economic and social implications of the transfer for the employees,
> – any measures envisaged in relation to the employees.

The information must be given 'in good time' prior to the transfer.

The duty to consult is triggered where the employees will experience changes as a result of the transfer. This duty is set out in Article 7(2):

> Where the transferor or the transferee envisages measures in relation to his employees, he shall consult the representatives of his employees in good time on such measures with a view to reaching an agreement.

It seems likely that this duty will always be triggered in respect of the employees who are going to be transferred to the new employer, since this in itself must constitute a 'measure'. Consultation is defined in this Article in a relatively strong way, requiring the parties to consult 'with a view to reaching an agreement', though of course this does not require an agreement to be reached.

In the early years of the Directive, firms sometimes tried to argue that the decision to transfer all or part of the business was taken by a parent company, making it impossible for them to fulfil any obligations to inform and consult the employees. In effect, they argued that they were as much in the dark about the transfer as the workers were. This was addressed through an amendment to the Directive which is now found in Article 7(4). This provides that the duties to inform and consult still apply even

---

[93] According to Art 7(3), Member States with compulsory arbitration systems may implement a reduced version of the obligations in Art 7(1) and (2).

where the decision is taken by a controlling undertaking, and that a failure on the part of the controlling undertaking to supply the employer with information cannot be used as a defence.

Because the Directive is a partial harmonisation measure, the mechanisms for appointment of employee representatives are for the Member States to determine. For example, Article 7(5) allows the Member States to limit the obligations of information and consultation to cases in which the thresholds for representation laid down in national law are satisfied. However, as we saw above in relation to redundancy consultation, the Member States do not have unlimited discretion in this matter. In the UK, where collective representation was traditionally confined to workplaces with a recognised union, the government was obliged to create new representation mechanisms for non-unionised workplaces in order to implement the Directive effectively.[94] The Directive also contains a default provision requiring the provision of information to the employees on an individual level 'where there are no representatives . . . through no fault of their own'.[95]

Employment Policy and the Structural Funds

As we saw in Chapter 2, the Europe 2020 strategy has as one of its main targets getting 75 per cent of the working age population into work by 2020. This is a challenging target given that the employment rate in 2010 was 69 per cent and (at the time of writing) European economies are experiencing little or no growth.[96] Nevertheless, it is important to consider this target and some of the Commission's plans for pursuing it, since they give us the broader policy context against which to assess the legal protections for workers in the event that their employer needs to restructure.

Not surprisingly, the Commission's strategy places considerable emphasis on flexicurity as the appropriate policy option. In the particular context of restructuring, the Commission notes that some job losses are inevitable, but suggests two policies designed to improve job security.[97] One is to reduce differences between typical and atypical workers, by adopting indefinite contracts with gradually increasing levels of protection. The other is to encourage 'internal flexibility' within firms, in which measures such as reductions in working time are used instead of redundancies as a

---

[94]   Above n. 22.
[95]   Directive 2001/23/EC, Art 7(6).
[96]   European Commission, *An Agenda for New Skills and Jobs: A European Contribution Towards Full Employment* (COM (2010) 682 final), 2.
[97]   Ibid, 5.

way of weathering the downturn. Interestingly, the Commission does not make the obvious connection between this latter point and the Collective Redundancies Directive.[98] During redundancy consultations, worker representatives may put forward alternatives like shorter working weeks, thereby helping to avoid redundancies. However, as we saw in Chapter 2, the Commission is also proposing a review of existing EU labour law, and it remains to be seen how the traditional worker-protective measures we have considered in this section – particularly where they go beyond obligations to consult – will fare during that process.[99]

Another dimension to the EU's response to unemployment is to use its financial resources to support the achievement of the Europe 2020 targets. The EU has various funds to deploy but for reasons of space we will focus on the European Social Fund (ESF) and the European Globalisation Adjustment Fund (EGF).

Set up in 1957, the ESF is a venerable institution that funds projects in the Member States to promote employment. Its budget for 2007–13 is €75 billion.[100] Funding is allocated to different regions within the Member States according to their relative wealth. The current objectives of the ESF are laid down in Regulation 1081/2006/EC. For present purposes, the most important element is Article 3(1)(a), which lists as a priority 'increasing adaptability of workers, enterprises and entrepreneurs with a view to improving the anticipation and positive management of economic change'. The Regulation goes on to list various strategies for achieving this, including the promotion of 'lifelong learning' and training for workers facing restructuring.[101] Projects in South Wales give a flavour of the kinds of activity supported by the ESF in relation to workers.[102] In this area, there is a high level of unemployment because of the demise of industries such as coal and steel. ESF-funded projects help the long-term unemployed to undertake work placements with a view to identifying suitable alternative careers, and to undergo training to develop new skills.

Another more specific fund is the EGF.[103] This has a budget of €500 million per year to assist workers whose jobs are lost because of globalisation. This might occur, for example, when a factory closes because the

---

[98]   Above n. 1.
[99]   Above n. 96, 14–15.
[100]   See, generally, http://ec.europa.eu/esf/home.jsp?langId=en.
[101]   See also Commission, *Cohesion Policy: Investing in the Real Economy* (COM (2008) 876/3), [2.1].
[102]   For detail, see http://wefo.wales.gov.uk/?lang=en.
[103]   Regulation (EC) No 1927/2006 of the European Parliament and of the Council of 20 December 2006 on establishing the European Globalisation Adjustment Fund, and see generally http://ec.europa.eu/social/main.jsp?catId=326&langId=en.

employer has outsourced the jobs to a non-EU country with lower labour costs. The EGF funds short-term assistance to the redundant workers. This might take the form of help with looking for a new job or retraining. Unlike the ESF, the EGF does not provide any support for businesses: it is focused solely on the affected workers. At the time of writing, the EGF had been extended on a temporary basis to cover workers affected by the economic crisis as well as by globalisation.[104]

It is easy to be sceptical about these initiatives. The EGF in particular has an obvious political motivation. Workers who lose their jobs as a result of globalisation are no more deserving of special help than workers who are made redundant for other reasons. Nevertheless, they do reflect an important acknowledgement of the fact that the 'high skill' economy promoted by the Commission will not come about without significant investment.[105] Although employers may take some responsibility for training workers, the training they provide is likely to relate specifically to the skills needed by the firm, and may not help with more general skills gaps. And if workers are facing redundancy or have been made redundant, there is no point in looking to employers to provide training. In these respects, the ESF and the EGF can be a useful supplement and encouragement to the Member States' activities in this area.

GENERAL MECHANISMS FOR WORKER PARTICIPATION

This part of this chapter will focus on the various means by which EU law seeks to encourage the participation of workers in the decision-making processes of the employing enterprise. In the previous part, we saw that EU law gives rise to a duty to consult the workforce as part of the management of significant events in the life of the firm, such as transfers of ownership or collective redundancies. In this part, we will examine two measures designed to generate more regular or routine employee involvement: the European Works Councils (EWC) Directive[106] and the Information and Consultation of Employees (I&C) Directive.[107]

---

[104]   Regulation 546/2009.
[105]   For discussion, see M. de Vos, 'Flexicurity and the European Globalisation Adjustment Fund: Propaganda or Panacea?', in M. de Vos (ed) (2009), *European Union Internal Market and Labour Law: Friends or Foes?* (Antwerp: Intersentia).
[106]   Directive 2009/38/EC.
[107]   Directive 2002/14/EC.

Themes

An important theme in this part is the concept of 'reflexivity', which we first met in Chapter 2.[108] Reflexive law theories are concerned with recognising the limits of what law can achieve through traditional 'command and control': telling people what to do and punishing them if they fail to do it. Instead, we should try to steer people in the right direction by, for example, giving them incentives to behave in particular ways or giving them forums in which to come up with their own solutions to problems. In Chapter 2, we saw that this approach could be used to justify the social dialogue as a means of developing norms to regulate labour (whether subsequently enacted as law or not).

These reflexive law ideas are particularly relevant to EWCs and information and consultation arrangements because it is very difficult for the law to force firms to develop good consultation arrangements with the workforce. The law cannot compel people to get along, or to discuss issues openly, or to take account of each other's opinions. But what it can do is to provide them with forums for discussion, in the hope that they will make good use of them. Moreover, as we shall see, there are reflexive elements in the detailed design of the legislation. For example, in the EWC Directive the employer can only be required to negotiate with the workforce about information and consultation if a proportion of workers request this.[109] From a worker-protective perspective, this can be seen as a weakness of the legislation, in that it places an obstacle in the way of setting up an EWC. Those who are enthusiastic about such arrangements may find it difficult to persuade their colleagues to get involved, particularly where they have not seen the benefits or where they fear a negative reaction from the employer. But, from a reflexive perspective, it can be argued that there is no point trying to impose an EWC on an indifferent workforce.

A second theme of particular relevance to the EWC provisions is the issue of market integration and competition between workers in different Member States. This was an issue that came to the fore in Chapter 3. In theory at least, EWCs are an interesting response to this problem. They provide a forum in which workers from different Member States can come together to discuss matters of common concern with the employer. So if there is a need for cost cutting, for example, instead of there being an unfettered competition between factories in the different Member States to stay open, the EWC might be able to negotiate a more satisfactory

---

[108] See, generally, G. Teubner, 'Substantive and Reflexive Elements in Modern Law' (1983) 17 *Law and Society Review* 239, and the discussion in Chapter 2.

[109] Directive 2009/38/EC, Art 5.

solution, such as efficiency savings in all the firm's factories. Of course, the law cannot require the parties to behave in this way, but the EWC Directive is an interesting attempt at least to provide the workforce with a transnational forum for discussion. In a parallel development, unions are beginning to think beyond national borders and to negotiate transnational company agreements (TCAs) with firms. We will examine this development as well.

The I&C Directive brings out a third theme. This is the familiar idea of setting minimum standards in EU labour law in order to avoid undercutting and a potential race to the bottom, but with a twist: promoting coherence in EU and national labour law as a whole. As we saw above, some Member States have a long tradition of I&C mechanisms whereas others do not. This led to a degree of pressure from Member States with such traditions for the EU to intervene. But this was supplemented by the worry that the provisions on redundancies and transfers considered in the first part of this chapter do not work effectively in Member States with no general provisions on consultation.[110] They do not mesh with existing institutions because those Member States do not have any. So the I&C Directive was also an attempt to solve this problem and to improve the coherence of EU law on worker participation.

The EWC Directive

The original EWC Directive was the first product of the Agreement on Social Policy adopted at Maastricht.[111] The UK refused to accept the proposed social policy provisions in the Treaty, so the other 11 Member States decided to proceed on their own. In accordance with the Agreement, the Commission's proposal for the directive was first put to the social partners for consideration in the (then new) social dialogue. When the employer side refused to agree, the Commission put a revised proposal before the Member States for agreement as a directive through the normal legislative route. The EWC Directive was the result. According to some commentators, this swift legislative response helped to secure some of the early successes of the social dialogue: by making clear that the Member States

---

[110] Commission, *Communication on Worker Information and Consultation* (COM (95) 547 final), [10].

[111] Directive 94/45/EC. See, generally, J.R. Bellace, 'The European Works Council Directive: Transnational Information and Consultation in the European Union' (1996–7) 18 *Comparative Labor Law Journal* 325; G.J.J. Heerma van Voss, 'Directive on European Works Councils in Community-Scale Undertakings. The Introduction of Double Subsidiarity in European Labour Law' (1995) 2 *Maastricht Journal of European Comparative Law* 339; C. McGlynn, 'European Works Councils: Towards Industrial Democracy?' (1995) 24 ILJ 78.

would act if the social partners could not agree, it gave the social partners themselves more reason to compromise.[112] After a change of government in the UK in 1997, the social policy provisions were incorporated into the Treaty of Amsterdam and the EWC Directive was 'extended' to the UK.[113] The Directive was revised in 2009.[114]

Setting up the EWC or information and consultation procedure

The EWC Directive only applies to larger firms operating on a cross-border level. This is apparent from Article 2(1):

> For the purposes of this Directive:
> (a) 'Community-scale undertaking' means any undertaking with at least 1000 employees within the Member States and at least 150 employees in each of at least two Member States;
> (b) 'group of undertakings' means a controlling undertaking and its controlled undertakings;
> (c) 'Community-scale group of undertakings' means a group of undertakings with the following characteristics:
> – at least 1000 employees within the Member States,
> – at least two group undertakings in different Member States, and
> – at least one group undertaking with at least 150 employees in one Member State and at least one other group undertaking with at least 150 employees in another Member State.

It may be difficult for employees to determine whether or not their employer falls within the scope of the Directive. This is addressed by a duty in Article 4(4) of the Directive on all parts of the undertaking to provide the necessary information, codifying the Court of Justice's earlier case-law on the matter.[115]

Importantly, it is not mandatory for a firm falling within the scope of the Directive to set up an EWC. The position is governed by Article 5(1), which provides that:

> the central management shall initiate negotiations for the establishment of a European Works Council or an information and consultation procedure on

---

[112] See Chapter 2, and Kenner, above n. 9, 248–9.
[113] Directive 97/74/EC.
[114] Directive 2009/38/EC. For a critique, see A. Alaimo, 'The New Directive on European Works Councils: Innovations and Omissions' (2010) 26 *International Journal of Comparative Labour Law and Industrial Relations* 217; S. Laulom, 'The Flawed Revision of the European Works Council Directive' (2010) 39 ILJ 202.
[115] See, for example, Case C–349/01 *Betriebsrat der Firma ADS Anker v ADS Anker* [2004] ECR I–6803.

its own initiative or at the written request of at least 100 employees or their representatives in at least two undertakings or establishments in at least two different Member States.

This explains why, according to the Commission, only 36 per cent of eligible firms (admittedly covering around 60 per cent of eligible employees) had an EWC in 2007.[116] Of course, a provision of this kind limits the effectiveness of the Directive because it places an obstacle in the way of employee action, particularly where there is limited or no contact between establishments in different Member States making it hard to co-ordinate requests. But, as we noted above, it can be justified on reflexive grounds.[117]

Once the process has been initiated, the central management must take responsibility for the setting up of a Special Negotiating Body (SNB). The role of the SNB is to determine:

> with the central management, by written agreement, the scope, composition, functions, and term of office of the European Works Council(s) or the arrangements for implementing a procedure for the information and consultation of employees.[118]

The SNB must consist of worker representatives drawn in suitable proportions from the different Member States in which the firm is established.[119] The arrangements for their election or appointment are for the relevant Member State to determine, a point we shall return to below.[120] The central management is required to hold a meeting with the SNB,[121] but not to reach an agreement with it. There are default EWC arrangements (referred to in the Directive as 'subsidiary requirements')[122] which come into effect within six months if management refuses to open negotiations or within three years if the negotiations do not result in an agreement.[123]

Again, the presence of the 'subsidiary requirements' can be seen as a reflexive element in the regime. Although the 'subsidiary requirements' do not in theory lay down minimum standards for the EWC, they might have that effect in practice. There is no particular incentive for the SNB to agree to less favourable arrangements than the 'subsidiary requirements' because these will eventually come into force by default. However, this

---

[116] Commission, *Impact Assessment* (SEC (2008) 2166), 4.
[117] The same can be said of the exception for firms which already have pan-European consultation arrangements in place: Directive 2009/38/EC, Art 14.
[118] Ibid, Art 5(3).
[119] Ibid, Art 5(2).
[120] Ibid.
[121] Ibid, Art 5(4).
[122] Ibid, Annex 1.
[123] Ibid, Art 7.

positive view of the 'subsidiary requirements' is complicated by the fact that the SNB has the power to discontinue the negotiations altogether (which triggers a two-year waiting period before another employee request can be made)[124] or to agree to the setting up of an 'information and consultation' procedure instead of an EWC.[125] The latter may be just as effective as an EWC but there is much less detail in the Directive about how it must be set up, leaving the position worryingly uncertain. Although these possibilities continue the reflexive theme, by allowing the worker representatives a considerable degree of autonomy, the workforce might be left significantly worse off as a result. One potentially important innovation in the Directive is that the SNB may be given access to expert advice (including help from European trade union representatives)[126] at the employer's expense.[127] This may help to ensure that SNB members are fully informed about the options open to them.

The role and functioning of the EWC
Since the operation of an EWC is very much a matter for the parties themselves to determine, there is a limit to what we can learn about EWCs by looking at the legal provisions. However, with that caveat in mind, it is worth looking in some detail at the Directive as the framework within which the parties must operate. The provisions can be grouped, loosely, into those focusing on procedure and those focusing on the substance of negotiations.

Procedural matters Article 6(2) of the Directive lists the matters to be addressed in the EWC agreement reached by management and the SNB. These matters include the coverage of the EWC within the undertaking or group of undertakings, the composition of the EWC, the frequency of its meetings, the resources available to it and the duration of the agreement. This gives the parties autonomy to determine the content of the agreement whilst at the same time encouraging them to focus on the most important issues.

The original Directive did not make any provision for the situation in which the corporate structure changed. This was a significant omission because it could result in the abandonment of existing EWC arrangements, forcing the workers to begin all over again in initiating the negotiating process. Article 6(2)(g) of the current Directive provides that the EWC agreement should include provisions governing how and when it can be

---

124 Ibid, Art 5(5).
125 Ibid, Art 6(3).
126 Ibid, Art 5(4).
127 Ibid, Art 5(6).

renegotiated, including in the event of corporate restructuring. If no such provision is made, or if there is a conflict between provisions of more than one EWC agreement, Article 13 comes into play. This provides that negotiations for a new EWC should be initiated in the normal way – either by management or by a request from the workforce – but, importantly, while the negotiations are ongoing, the existing EWC or EWCs should continue to operate. Where more than one EWC is in place, management may have a significant incentive to negotiate a new arrangement in order to simplify the consultation process and save money.

Worker representatives are always potentially vulnerable to detrimental treatment from the employer. This is addressed in Article 10 of the Directive which requires that SNB and EWC members be given 'similar' protection to other worker representatives in national law. Article 10(3) states that representatives should be given paid time off to perform their duties. Article 10(4), which was a new provision in the recast Directive, creates an entitlement to (paid) training for representatives. As we saw above, the EWC process is likely to work best when the representatives are aware of their legal rights and obligations, so this may be another way of improving their knowledge.

Substantive requirements   In this section, we will consider the substance of what EWCs are supposed to do. Again, this is done with the caveat that the practical operation of EWCs is very much a matter for the firm and the worker representatives to determine, so we are simply focusing on the surrounding legal frameworks.[128]

The Directive provides detailed definitions of the concepts 'information' and 'consultation'. These offer some idea of what is envisaged:

    (f) 'information' means transmission of data by the employer to the employees' representatives in order to enable them to acquaint themselves with the subject matter and to examine it; information shall be given at such time, in such fashion and with such content as are appropriate to enable employees' representatives to undertake an in-depth assessment of the possible impact and, where appropriate, prepare for consultations with the competent organ of the Community-scale undertaking or Community-scale group of undertakings;

    (g) 'consultation' means the establishment of dialogue and exchange of views between employees' representatives and central management or any more appropriate level of management, at such time, in such fashion and with

---

[128]   For some empirical evidence, see J. Rojot, A. Le Flanchec and C. Voynnet-Fourboul, 'European Collective Bargaining, New Prospects or Much Ado about Little?' (2001) 17 *International Journal of Comparative Labour Law and Industrial Relations* 345.

such content as enables employees' representatives to express an opinion on the basis of the information provided about the proposed measures to which the consultation is related, without prejudice to the responsibilities of the management, and within a reasonable time, which may be taken into account within the Community-scale undertaking or Community-scale group of undertakings . . . [129]

There are some significant features of these definitions for the Member States to take into account when implementing them in national law. First, they place considerable emphasis on the timeliness of the information. A potential problem with information and consultation regimes is that – either deliberately or through inefficiency – management may provide the workforce with information either after decisions have been made or at such short notice that they cannot reasonably absorb the information and give their views. Second, the definitions also make reference to the content of the information. Although this is vague, it could be used as the basis for a variety of stipulations about the information: for example, that it should be translated for members of the EWC from different countries, or that complex financial information should be presented in a comprehensible format. These features of the definitions are reinforced by the general obligation in Article 9 for the parties to work in a 'spirit of co-operation'.

However, the definition of consultation also makes clear that the ultimate responsibility for decision making lies with management. The role of the EWC is to engage in 'dialogue' with management and to express an 'opinion' which 'may be taken into account' but there is no obligation to reach an agreement. This is not a mechanism for joint regulation of the workplace. For some, this is disappointing: it does not go far enough to create Europe-wide bargaining at the level of the firm. But this would be difficult given the restrictions on the EU's competence, discussed above. Transnational collective bargaining implies transnational collective action, but without EU competence over the right to strike it seems likely that the collective enforcement of such bargaining will depend, for the foreseeable future, on national law. Moreover, it may be better to allow novel institutions such as EWCs some time to 'bed in' before becoming too ambitious about them. In accordance with reflexive principles, they may develop into more powerful bodies in an organic way.

A new development in the recast Directive is that EWCs are confined to the consideration of 'transnational questions'. These are defined in Article 1(4) as follows:

---

[129]   Directive 2009/38/EC, Art 2(1).

Matters shall be considered to be transnational where they concern the Community-scale undertaking or Community-scale group of undertakings as a whole, or at least two undertakings or establishments of the undertaking or group situated in two different Member States.

The Commission justified this move as part of other changes to the Directive (to be discussed in the next section) which are designed to bring about better linkages between the European-level consultation in EWCs and national-level consultation, whether through EU-inspired measures or national ones.[130] Whilst this makes a certain amount of sense, there is a potential problem of defining what constitutes a transnational issue with the accompanying risk that EWCs might become bogged down in juris-dictional disputes. To give an obvious example, assume that the firm has factories in three different Member States and wants to close one of them. Ideally, we might expect the firm to consult the EWC on the choice of which factory to close, and then to use national consultation mechanisms to deal with the consequences of the decision, such as collective redundancies. However, if the firm simply announces the closure of its UK factory, for example, there does not appear to be much scope for the EWC to become involved.

The relationship with national law
One concern about the EWC Directive in its original form was that its provisions did not necessarily fit very well with existing national mechanisms for employee participation. This situation was exacerbated to some extent by the EU's own expansion in this area through the subsequent enactment of the I&C Directive.[131] This set of issues is addressed through Article 12 in the recast EWC Directive, which states that the EWC arrangements should be 'linked to' national arrangements. This should occur through EWC agreements themselves, but with a responsibility on the Member State to make provision where the EWC agreement is silent on the matter. In particular, Article 12(3) provides for parallel consultation as the default:

Where no such arrangements have been defined by agreement, the Member States shall ensure that the processes of informing and consulting are conducted in the European Works Council as well as in the national employee representation bodies in cases where decisions likely to lead to substantial changes in work organisation or contractual relations are envisaged.

---

[130] Commission, *Proposal for a European Parliament and Council Directive on the establishment of a European Works Council or a procedure in Community-scale undertakings and Community-scale groups of undertakings for the purposes of informing and consulting employees (Recast)* (COM (2008) 419 final), 8.

[131] Directive 2002/14/EC.

On one level, this is a good approach. It addresses the obvious problem that a firm might refuse to consult at the national level because it is consulting with the EWC, and vice versa. But once we move beyond this basic problem it is not clear that consultation along purely parallel lines is the best solution. For example, it might be desirable for the EWC consultation to take place after the national-level consultation, so that the EWC can weigh up the competing views of different national representative bodies when formulating its own representations to management. But the Directive does not require any co-ordination and (given issues surrounding confidentiality)[132] it is not even clear to what extent EWCs can engage in dialogue with national bodies. There is a risk that the Directive might facilitate a 'divide and conquer' strategy in which different groups of workers are played off against each other instead of being encouraged to identify common positions.

Transnational Company Agreements

Before we leave the subject of Europe-wide consultation, it is worth giving brief consideration to a related but somewhat separate development – the emergence of transnational company agreements (TCAs).[133] This term refers to agreements between employers and workers' representatives which deal with matters of more than just national concern.

TCAs are not just a European phenomenon: they can be found in other parts of the world too. Many TCAs are negotiated by unions in developed countries to address the working conditions of workers in developing countries, as part of an attempt to improve worker protection throughout supply chains.[134] But our particular focus will be on what the Commission terms 'European' TCAs: agreements designed to address issues of common concern across pan-European firms.[135] According to the Commission's research, these agreements address a variety of different issues, with a particular focus on providing procedures for dealing with company restructuring and its impact on employees.[136]

EWCs are signatories to most of the TCAs identified by the

---

[132] On which see Directive 2009/38/EC, Art 8.

[133] See, generally, Commission, *The Role of Transnational Company Agreements in the Context of Increasing International Integration* (COM (2008) 419 final), and S. Sciarra, 'Notions of Solidarity in Times of Economic Uncertainty' (2010) 39 ILJ 223.

[134] Commission, *Mapping of Transnational Texts Negotiated at Corporate Level* (2008), 4–5.

[135] Ibid.

[136] Ibid, 15–21.

Commission.[137] However, these TCAs cannot simply be regarded as the 'output' of EWCs. This is because, in many cases, international trade union federations or national trade unions (usually from the Member State in which the company has its headquarters) are also signatories to the agreement. This suggests that the trade union movement has been able to work with, or make use of, EWCs.

From a legal perspective, a significant difficulty with TCAs is determining their legal status.[138] Because they are transnational in nature, it may be difficult to tell which national law, if any, would be applicable in the event of a dispute, though some agreements do contain a choice of law clause. And since the concept of a 'collective agreement' has a very specific meaning in many legal systems, TCAs may fail to qualify as collective agreements in some or all of the Member States to which they are relevant. Where national trade unions are involved in the negotiations, this sometimes appears to be a mechanism for ensuring that the TCA can take effect as a collective agreement in the country in which the firm has its headquarters. More generally, it seems that the parties regard the agreements as 'binding' to some extent, regardless of their technical status in the different Member States.

From a reflexive perspective, TCAs are an interesting phenomenon. They show that the creation of EWCs can have a broader influence on the industrial relations landscape. The agreements go beyond the mere 'dialogue' envisaged in the EWC Directive, and they often involve trade unions. Worries about their legal status may not matter if the parties are happy to abide by them, as the UK experience of collective agreements shows. However, TCAs also bring into sharp focus the EU's inability to help because of the limits on its competence. As we saw in Chapter 2, the EU is unable to legislate on freedom of association or the right to strike.[139] For this reason, there is no prospect of the development of EU law to support transnational collective bargaining.[140]

The Directive on Informing and Consulting Employees

The Directive on Informing and Consulting Employees, sometimes referred to as the Framework Directive or the I&C Directive, has much

---

[137]   Ibid, 9–10.
[138]   Ibid, 21–3.
[139]   Article 153(5) TFEU.
[140]   Though cf E. Ales, 'Transnational Collective Bargaining in Europe: The Case for Legislative Action at EU Level' (2009) 148 *International Labour Review* 149, arguing for such a development and suggesting various Treaty bases.

broader ambitions than any of the other measures we have so far encountered.[141] Unlike the EWC Directive, it is not confined to pan-European firms. Instead, it applies to firms operating at the national level, though not to smaller or medium-sized enterprises. Nor does it focus on the creation of information and consultation rights in the event of a specific change of circumstances affecting the workforce, such as collective redundancies or mergers. Its aim is to foster the creation of mechanisms for information and consultation to be used as a matter of routine.

Like the other Directives we have considered in this chapter, the I&C Directive was bogged down in the legislative process for a very long time before finally being enacted and, even after its enactment, it remained controversial as evidenced by the failure of many Member States to transpose it by the applicable deadline.[142]

What is information and consultation?

The Directive identifies its purpose as being 'to establish a general framework setting out minimum requirements for the right to information and consultation of employees'.[143] Information is defined in Article 2(f) as 'transmission by the employer to the employees' representatives of data in order to enable them to acquaint themselves with the subject matter and to examine it', and consultation is defined in Article 2(g) as 'the exchange of views and establishment of dialogue between the employees' representatives and the employer'. It will be apparent that these definitions are less elaborate than those to be found in the EWC Directive, but some of the matters dealt with in the EWC Directive via the definitions are addressed elsewhere in the I&C Directive.

Setting up the information and consultation procedure

As we noted above, the I&C Directive is more ambitious in its scope than the EWC Directive, in that it applies to firms operating at a national level. However, it is confined to larger firms in a way which leaves significant discretion to the Member States:

> This Directive shall apply, according to the choice made by Member States, to:
> (a) undertakings employing at least 50 employees in any one Member State, or
> (b) establishments employing at least 20 employees in any one Member State.

---

[141]   Directive 2002/14/EC. For an overview from a UK perspective, see B. Bercusson, 'The European Social Model Comes to Britain' (2002) 31 ILJ 209.
[142]   Commission, *Communication on the Review of the Application of Directive 2002/14/ EC in the EU* (COM (2008) 146 final), 4.
[143]   Directive 2002/14/EC, Art 1(1).

> Member States shall determine the method for calculating the thresholds
> of employees employed.[144]

Although the definitions are rather murky, this seems to give the Member States the choice of placing obligations at the level of the enterprise or at the lower level of the 'unit of business'. Most Member States have opted for the former.[145]

The discretion to 'determine the method for calculating the thresholds' has been used by some Member States as a reason to exclude certain categories of employee from counting for information and consultation purposes.[146] But the Court of Justice has shown itself willing to apply a degree of scrutiny to such exclusions. For example, in a measure purporting to deal with the unemployment situation, the French government sought to exclude workers under the age of 26 from counting towards the thresholds.[147] The Court held that this amounted to a failure to implement the Directive because it deprived these workers of protection.

Another contrast with the EWC Directive is that the mechanism for setting up the information and consultation procedure is a matter for national law. This would not have been possible under the EWC Directive given the pan-European nature of the issues to be addressed. There are two potential limitations on the Member States' discretion to determine the arrangements for setting up information and consultation procedures. First, Article 4(1) of the Directive contains a non-regression obligation, stating that it is 'without prejudice to any provisions and/or practices in force more favourable to employees'.[148] Second, the arrangements must be 'in accordance with the principles set out in Article 1'. These include a requirement for 'effectiveness'. Moreover, both Article 1 and Article 4 refer to information and consultation as a 'right'. Ales, in a review of the implementation of the Directive around the EU, argues that the use of the term 'right' implies that the employer should be under a correlative duty to set up an information and consultation procedure.[149] If this is not the case, the Member State has not met its obligation to transpose. This raises interesting questions for countries such as the UK in which a 'trigger' mechanism operates: in other words, a requirement that a number of employees

---

[144]   Ibid, Art 3(1).
[145]   E. Ales (2007), *Directive 2002/14/EC Synthesis Report* (Cassino: Labour Asociados Consultores), 12.
[146]   Ibid, 13–15.
[147]   Case C–385/05 *CGT v Premier ministre* [2007] ECR I–611.
[148]   Though, as we saw in Chapter 2, the practical effect of such clauses may be limited. See also Directive 2002/14/EC, Art 9(4).
[149]   Ales, above n. 145, 9.

initiate the setting up of an information and consultation procedure.[150] On one hand, it is arguable that this is insufficient recognition of information and consultation as a right enjoyed by the employees. If some employees want to be informed, but they cannot obtain enough signatures to start the process, their rights are not being respected. On the other hand, it might be argued that information and consultation procedures are inherently collective and that the employer should not be required to set them up unless a reasonable proportion of the workforce is interested in participating in them. As we saw in our theoretical discussion above, information and consultation is more likely to work effectively where the parties are willing participants.

The role and functioning of the information and consultation procedure
The I&C Directive sets out a number of basic requirements for the information and consultation procedure, whilst leaving its exact form to the discretion of the Member States.[151] Again, this contrasts with the EWC Directive which is designed to result in the setting up of a particular type of consultation mechanism, the EWC, and which requires a greater degree of uniformity across the Member States.

Perhaps most importantly, the Directive specifies the topics on which information and consultation should take place. This aspect of the Directive is designed so that the level of employee involvement increases in proportion to the impact the matter is likely to have on the employment situation in the undertaking. Thus, at the first level, information (but not consultation) is required on 'the recent and probable development of the undertaking's or the establishment's activities and economic situation'.[152] At the second level, information and consultation is required on 'the situation, structure and probable development of employment within the undertaking or establishment and on any anticipatory measures envisaged, in particular where there is a threat to employment'.[153] And at the third level, consultation 'with a view to reaching an agreement'[154] (which clearly goes beyond the normal definition of 'dialogue')[155] is required 'on decisions likely to lead to substantial changes in work organisation or in contractual relations'.[156] These include redundancies and transfers

---

[150] Information and Consultation of Employees Regulations 2004/3426, r. 7.
[151] Directive 2002/14, Art 4(1).
[152] Ibid, Art 4(2)(a).
[153] Ibid, Art 4(2)(b).
[154] Ibid, Art 4(4)(e).
[155] Ibid, Art 2(g).
[156] Ibid, Art 4(2)(c).

covered elsewhere in EU law, so this aspect of the I&C Directive ensures that the law on these matters is coherent across the various EU measures.

Article 4(4) also includes a number of procedural requirements. These reflect a number of the requirements dealt with in the definitions of 'information' and 'consultation' under the EWC Directive. Thus, for example, 'information shall be given at such time, in such fashion and with such content as are appropriate to enable, in particular, employees' representatives to conduct an adequate study and, where necessary, prepare for consultation'. And consultation must take place 'at the relevant level of management' and must enable the employees' representatives to obtain a response to their opinion.

Whilst it is usually the case that Member States can entrust the implementation of employment directives to the social partners at national level, the I&C Directive goes further.[157] It provides that the social partners may be entrusted with determining the practical arrangements for information and consultation at the level of the enterprise or undertaking.[158] Moreover, (as with the EWC Directive) the Member States may allow the parties to rely on agreements already in force prior to the transposition of the Directive. Importantly, the Directive makes it clear that the Member States may allow the parties to reach agreements which do not comply with Article 4, if they so choose. This is a controversial provision. On one hand, it can be seen as a means of respecting the autonomy of the social partners and encouraging voluntary agreements (which might be more effective in practice than statutory requirements). On the other hand, it may result in a situation in which weak or ill-informed worker representatives agree to arrangements which do not meet the minimum conditions laid down in the Directive.

Remedies

When the Directive was under consideration, the Commission proposed that in certain serious cases, such as collective redundancies, the employer's action would have no effect unless previous consultation had taken place.[159] This is a particularly effective means of ensuring that consultation takes place because, on the whole, employers want to be able to get on with implementing their decisions. However, the UK government blocked the proposal and, in the end, the Directive as enacted simply requires 'adequate' sanctions which must be 'effective, proportionate and

---

[157] For a recent interpretation, see Case C–405/08 *Ingeniørforeningen i Danmark (on behalf of Holst) v Dansk Arbejdsgiverforening* [2010] ECR I–985.

[158] Directive 2002/14, Art 5.

[159] Bercusson, above n. 141, 239–40.

dissuasive'.[160] In practice this has resulted in considerable diversity among the Member States. According to Ales, some Member States do provide for employer decisions to be invalidated in some circumstances, but this is unusual.[161]

PRESERVING NATIONAL TRADITIONS

In this part of this chapter, we return to a familiar theme: the 'race to the bottom'. For countries with high levels of worker participation (such as worker representatives on company boards) opening up markets within the EU poses a potential threat to their protective regimes. The worry is that firms will use their market freedoms to move elsewhere in the EU in order to 'escape' national laws on participation. Of course, the most obvious option is for the firm simply to close down its operations in that Member State altogether and to move to a cheaper EU location. There is very little that a Member State can lawfully do to prevent this because firms enjoy freedom of establishment.[162] However, more complex problems arise when the firm continues to exist and to operate in the worker-protective Member State, but seeks to rearrange its corporate structure with a view to escaping that state's worker participation laws.[163]

This set of problems held up the development of EU company law for many years. Member States with strong worker participation rules refused to agree to harmonisation measures unless they included equivalent worker participation rules. But countries with lower levels of worker involvement refused to agree to the 'export' of other Member States' approaches. The rules as eventually enacted seek to produce a compromise between these two positions. Firms can be required to preserve existing worker participation regimes because of a series of measures designed to prevent 'escape', but there is no general requirement to observe the highest possible standards (so there is no general 'export' of such standards).[164] There are three main examples of this compromise: the worker participation provisions

---

[160] Directive 2002/14/EC, Art 8.

[161] Above n. 145, 32.

[162] Articles 49 and 54 TFEU. For an examination of recent case-law, see A. Johnston and P. Syrpis, 'Regulatory Competition in European Company Law after *Cartesio*' (2009) 34 EL Rev 378.

[163] For a detailed analysis of this phenomenon, see Johnston and Syrpis, ibid, and D. Komo and C. Villiers, 'Are Trends in European Company Law Threatening Industrial Democracy?' (2009) 34 EL Rev 175.

[164] The 'export' and 'escape' terminology is from P.L. Davies, 'Workers on the Board of the European Company' (2003) 32 ILJ 75, 87, quoting the European Parliament.

applicable to the European Company Statute, the European Co-Operative Society[165] and the Directive on Cross-Border Mergers.[166] For reasons of space, we will focus on the first of these. As we shall see, the empirical evidence on the effects of these measures is mixed.

The SE

In 2001, the EU adopted a Regulation on the European company (*Societas Europaea* or SE).[167] This offers a European alternative to the formation of a company under a particular national law, though the SE regime remains dependent on national law for various purposes (for example, a SE must be registered in one of the Member States). The SE form is entirely optional so firms can decide whether or not it is to their advantage to adopt it.[168] The Regulation creating the SE was accompanied by a Directive on worker participation which will be the focus of our discussion.[169] Whilst this Directive shares some common features with the EWC Directive, it needs to be viewed in the context of its own particular agenda: to ensure that the SE does not facilitate a race to the bottom in terms of worker participation.

The Anti-avoidance Agenda

The tone of the SE Directive is set by Article 11:

> Member States shall take appropriate measures in conformity with Community law with a view to preventing the misuse of an SE for the purpose of depriving employees of rights to employee involvement or withholding such rights.

The reference to 'conformity with Community law' presumably means that any such anti-avoidance measures must be proportionate and must not deter firms from becoming SEs.

---

[165] Council Regulation (EC) No 1435/2003 on the Statute for a European Cooperative Society (SCE); Council Directive 2003/72/EC supplementing the Statute for a European Cooperative Society with regard to the involvement of employees.
[166] Directive 2005/56/EC of the European Parliament and of the Council of 26 October 2005 on cross-border mergers of limited liability companies, Art 16. The Commission has also proposed legislation on a European Private Company aimed at smaller firms, containing worker participation provisions, but at the time of writing this had not been agreed.
[167] Regulation 2157/2001/EC on the Statute for a European company.
[168] On which see Davies, above n. 164, 76–8.
[169] Council Directive 2001/86/EC of 8 October 2001 supplementing the Statute for a European company with regard to the involvement of employees.

The onus is on management to initiate negotiations for the establishment of worker involvement once it has been decided to set up an SE:

> Where the management or administrative organs of the participating companies draw up a plan for the establishment of an SE, they shall as soon as possible after publishing the draft terms of merger or creating a holding company or after agreeing a plan to form a subsidiary or to transform into an SE, take the necessary steps, including providing information about the identity of the participating companies, concerned subsidiaries or establishments, and the number of their employees, to start negotiations with the representatives of the companies' employees on arrangements for the involvement of employees in the SE.[170]

Interestingly, this gives the workforce no say in the question whether or not to set up an SE, though of course avenues for this may be available through national mechanisms. Instead, the focus is on the creation of mechanisms for involvement within the SE. The negotiations take place through the SNB, which must represent the workforce in the different Member States in appropriate proportions, and must also include representatives of any companies that will cease to exist as separate entities when the SE is created.[171] It is a matter for the Member States to determine the exact methods for the election of representatives within their own territories.

Like the EWC Directive, the SE Directive seeks to regulate information and consultation, defined in roughly the same way.[172] But the SE Directive adds a third and crucial concept: participation.[173] This is defined as the right of worker representatives to elect or appoint, or recommend or oppose the appointment of, members of the firm's supervisory board. In theory at least, the SNB may negotiate with management for the establishment of participation arrangements, whether or not such arrangements were in place prior to the creation of the SE.

But what is more significant in practice is the attempt made in the SE Directive to ensure that, where participation arrangements are in place prior to the creation of the SE, participation remains a feature of the company's worker involvement regime. There are three main sets of provisions on this. First, and most generally, Article 4(4) of the Directive provides that where the SE is formed through 'transformation' there may not be any consequential reduction in the level of worker involvement. This is

---

[170]   Ibid, Art 3(1).
[171]   Ibid, Art 3(2).
[172]   Ibid, especially Arts 4 and 7.
[173]   Ibid, Art 2(k).

where an existing company simply turns itself into an SE without merging with another firm or otherwise changing its legal form. This would otherwise be the most obvious way of using the SE as a way of evading employee participation laws.

Second, where a reduction in participation arrangements is proposed, the members of the SNB can only agree to it by a two-thirds majority. A reduction in participation denotes 'a proportion of members of the organs of the SE . . . which is lower than the highest proportion existing within the participating companies'.[174] This provision applies where the SE is formed by merger and at least 25 per cent of the employees were covered by participation arrangements prior to the merger, or where the SE is formed by the creation of a holding company or subsidiary and at least 50 per cent of the employees were so covered. This requirement can be seen as helping to preserve participation arrangements in two ways. First, it makes it more difficult for the SNB simply to negotiate away existing participation rights, by requiring a high degree of consensus before this can be done. Second, it may indirectly discourage management from proposing such arrangements because of the greater difficulty of securing agreement to them.

Third, the default arrangements which apply where the SNB and management cannot reach agreement provide for participation to continue where it exists already.[175] Again, the provisions on this are complex and depend on the method of formation of the SE. The most straightforward provision is that, where the SE is established by transformation, participation rules that applied to the firm before it became an SE continue to apply. The default participation rules also apply where the SE is established by merger and at least 25 per cent of the employees prior to the merger were covered by participation, or where the SE is established by the creation of a holding company or a subsidiary and at least 50 per cent of the employees prior to the merger were covered by participation. In the latter two cases, the default rules provide for board-level participation 'equal to the highest proportion in force in the participating companies concerned before registration of the SE'. As Davies points out, this will not necessarily preserve the most *effective* form of national participation because it focuses solely on the *numbers* of worker representatives on the board.[176] However, these provisions are important because – as we saw in the EWC case above – employee representatives (provided that they are well-informed) have no reason to agree to less protective arrangements than those that will eventually take effect by default.

---

[174]   Ibid, Art 3(4).
[175]   Ibid, Art 7.
[176]   Davies, above n. 164, 85–7.

Relationship with Other Employee Involvement Mechanisms

As we saw above, another central concern about EU-level mechanisms for employee involvement is the need to mesh with other related mechanisms, whether of national or EU origin. The SE Directive addresses this matter in Article 13. First, the SE is not subject to the EWC Directive (where it would otherwise apply) unless the SNB decides not to open negotiations or to terminate negotiations under the SE Directive.[177] Second, national rules on participation (as defined above, to mean board-level involvement) do not apply to the SE.[178] Third, all other national rules on involvement – including participation on the boards of subsidiaries – should be preserved in accordance with Article 13(3):

> This Directive shall not prejudice:
> (a) the existing rights to involvement of employees provided for by national legislation and/or practice in the Member States as enjoyed by employees of the SE and its subsidiaries and establishments, other than participation in the bodies of the SE;
> (b) the provisions on participation in the bodies laid down by national legislation and/or practice applicable to the subsidiaries of the SE.

Importantly, the Member States may provide for existing mechanisms to continue even where a company will lose its separate legal identity as the result of the creation of the SE.[179]

Effectiveness

In terms of the effectiveness of these provisions, the evidence is not very promising. The Commission itself has noted that there is an obvious mechanism for avoidance.[180] This is to set up the SE with no employees at all, so that none of the anti-avoidance provisions are applicable, and then to transfer the workforce to the SE at a later date. The evidence is that 'normal' SEs with employees and activities are in the minority.[181] Of course, the resulting firm might be subject to other European legal provisions on information and consultation, but none of these gives a right

---

[177] Directive 2001/86/EC, Art 13(1).
[178] Ibid, Art 13(2).
[179] Ibid, Art 13(4).
[180] Commission, *Communication on the review of Council Directive 2001/86/EC of 8 October 2001 supplementing the Statute for a European company with regard to the involvement of employees* (COM (2008) 591 final), 7.
[181] See the ETUI's SE database at http://www.etui.org/Services/European-Company-SE-Database (last visited 21 September 2011).

to board-level participation. The resulting firm would also be subject to national rules on employee involvement, but it seems unlikely that the firm would be set up in a country with elaborate requirements in this regard. More generally, as we saw above, there is no obligation on firms to use the SE form so they may be able to find other ways of escaping co-determination. Although it might be hoped that some firms will see benefits in this form of employee participation and will therefore want to keep it,[182] it seems unlikely that the SE regime will stand in the way of a firm which is determined to escape.

FURTHER READING

The material in this chapter has been organised around the theme of 'worker participation', since this is common to both the older and the newer directives we have been considering. However, it would also be possible to draw out 'job security' as a theme of the older directives, particularly the Collective Redundancies Directive and the Acquired Rights Directive. This does not fit well with the Commission's current emphasis on flexicurity, and you may find it helpful to revisit European Commission, *Towards Common Principles of Flexicurity: More and Better Jobs Through Flexibility and Security* (COM (2007) 359 final) when thinking about these directives. Another way to conceptualise the material is to think about it in terms of the emergence of a European form of collective bargaining, and to group it with the material on the social dialogue and on union involvement in the implementation of directives which we considered in Chapter 2. For an example of this type of analysis, see B. Bercusson, 'The Collective Labour Law of the European Union' (1995) 1 ELJ 157.

Another link between the older and the newer material in this chapter is the recurring theme of economic crisis: this was an important part of the policy context when the older directives were enacted, and at the time of writing it has resurfaced. For historical background, see J. Kenner (2003), *EU Employment Law: From Rome to Amsterdam and Beyond* (Oxford: Hart), Chapter 2, and for a contemporary defence of worker participation in times of economic crisis, see N. Bruun, 'Employees' Participation Rights and Business Restructuring' (2011) 2 *European Labour Law Journal* 27.

---

[182] W. Njoya, 'Employee Ownership in The European Company: Reflexive Law, Reincorporation and Escaping Codetermination' (2011) 11 *Journal of Corporate Law Studies* 267.

The role of the Court of Justice in interpreting vague legislation has been an important theme of this chapter, and to explore this further (with particular reference to the Acquired Rights Directive) you could look at S. O'Leary (2002), *Employment Law at the European Court of Justice* (Oxford: Hart), Chapter 6, and more recently G. Barrett, 'Deploying the Classic "Community Method" in the Social Policy Field: The Example of the Acquired Rights Directive' (2009) 15 ELJ 198.

9.   Postscript

EU labour law is constantly changing and, however immersed you might be in the subject, there is always the potential for a surprise. It is no exaggeration to say that the much-debated *Viking* and *Laval* cases transformed the subject's landscape. So with the caveat that predicting the future is a dangerous game, I want to conclude this book by revisiting some of the themes from Chapters 1 and 2 and considering the prospects for the immediate future.

We saw in Chapter 1 that the justifications for EU labour law have shifted over time. At present, there is a particular focus on the competitiveness of the EU in a globalised world economy. This concern has been enhanced by the economic crisis and worries about the stability of the euro. This focus manifests itself through Commission policy documents on flexicurity, talk of 'modernising the European Social Model', and the 'regulating for competitiveness' argument. This agenda – like similar 'third way' agendas at national level – is ambiguous in important ways about the role of labour law. On one hand, it is not explicitly hostile towards labour law. For example, the 'regulating for competitiveness' agenda is concerned with identifying and promoting the economic benefits of regulated labour markets. On the other hand, some aspects of labour law do not seem to fit very easily into the policy prescriptions. For example, under flexicurity the shift of focus from job security (keeping people in a job) to employment security (keeping people employed in some job or other) makes laws on unfair dismissal and redundancy seem old-fashioned.

Two practical consequences for labour law might follow from the flexicurity and modernisation agenda. The first is that we may not see very much new legislation in the field of labour law in the near future. The 1990s and 2000s have seen a steady flow of new worker-protective directives, but it is increasingly common for the Commission to talk about the *acquis* in the past tense, as if nothing more is likely to be added.[1] The second, and more radical, possibility is that if there is new legislation, it might be deregulatory in outlook. We have already seen some elements of

---

[1]   European Commission, *Renewed Social Agenda: Opportunities, Access and Solidarity in 21st Century Europe* (COM (2008) 412 final), 15.

this in the 'atypical' work directives where they require Member States to remove obstacles to the use of atypical work. And as we saw in Chapter 2, this has given rise to problems of interpretation in relation to the 'non-regression' clauses also contained in these directives.

If the immediate future of EU labour law does involve deregulation, a number of possible problems may arise. First, it has traditionally been assumed that the EU's intervention in areas like labour law has helped to give it a human face and to make it more popular with EU citizens. If this assumption is correct, deregulation may lead to a loss of support for the EU. Second, deregulation is unlikely to be popular with the trade union movement and may lead to difficulties surrounding the role of social dialogue as a means of developing labour standards. While this may provide an alternative to the traditional legislative method, we saw in Chapter 2 that it depends on implicit support from the Commission and the Member States, so to counterbalance deregulation by this route may not be possible. Third, there are implications for national autonomy. A thorough adoption of 'third way' policies would require changes in national laws which are not the subject of EU competences. As we have seen, the Europe 2020 strategy and the OMC involve setting targets for the Member States and encouraging them to adopt policies to meet those targets. This provides an opportunity for the EU to broaden its influence. But it may prove controversial, at least in those Member States where the electorate continues to support a more worker-protective understanding of labour law.

Another important theme identified in Chapter 1 was the 'constitutionalisation' of EU labour law, particularly (but not exclusively) through the legal effect given to the EU Charter of Fundamental Rights after Lisbon. For many labour lawyers, this is an exciting development because it has the potential to ground worker-protective measures in fundamental human rights. Of course, most obviously, this may strengthen workers' claims, but it also has the benefit of linking EU labour law to external sources, such as ILO norms or rights in the ECHR. This external dimension will be enhanced with the EU's own accession to the ECHR. However, an obvious counterweight to this set of arguments is the Court of Justice's approach to the right to strike in *Viking*, *Laval* and other cases. As we saw in Chapter 3, these are complex cases and the Court's approach was dictated, in part at least, by the surrounding legal regime: the fact that the EU Charter did not have legal force at that time, the weaknesses of Sweden's implementation of the Posted Workers Directive and so on. Nevertheless, the Court prioritised the free movement provisions of the Treaty over the right to strike, which does not suggest a very positive outlook for the constitutionalisation of labour law. The EU's accession to the ECHR may prompt a change of view on the right to strike itself, given the ECtHR's recent expansive jurisprudence on the subject. But the key question in relation to workers' rights is how to balance them against competing considerations, such as the rules of the EU internal market, or economic arguments put forward by employers. This is true whether the rights are protected in EU law just through the EU Charter, or through the ECHR as well, and in the latter case this may well become an area of significant tension between the Court and the ECtHR.

Barnard has written recently of a 'battle for the soul' of EU labour law.[2] I hope this book has given you a map of the battleground, and has helped you to form your own views on what the 'soul' of EU labour law should be.

---

2   C. Barnard, 'EU "Social" Policy: from Employment Law to Labour Market Reform', in P.P. Craig and G. de Búrca (eds) (2011), *The Evolution of EU Law* (2nd edn, Oxford University Press), 676.

Index